Louis P. Gratacap

# Philosophy of Ritual

apologia pro ritu. Second Edition

Louis P. Gratacap

**Philosophy of Ritual**
*apologia pro ritu. Second Edition*

ISBN/EAN: 9783337300258

Printed in Europe, USA, Canada, Australia, Japan

Cover: Foto ©Thomas Meinert / pixelio.de

More available books at **www.hansebooks.com**

## WHAT WAS SAID OF THE FIRST EDITION.

"No theological library can be complete without some such work."—*Church Press*.

"This volume will win for itself a place of honor in the literature of the Church."—*Churchman*.

"We commend it to such of our readers as take interest in the grave questions at issue."—*N. Y. Times*.

"The work cannot but be helpful to every thinking mind."—*The Rev. J. H. Hopkins, S. T. D.*

"One of the best and most instructive of this century."—*Rev. N. W. Camp, D.D.*

*In Press*, by the same Author :

THE ANALYTICS OF A BELIEF IN A FUTURE LIFE.

# PHILOSOPHY OF RITUAL

## APOLOGIA PRO RITU

BY

L. P. GRATACAP, A.M.

*SECOND EDITION.*

NEW YORK

JAMES POTT & CO., PUBLISHERS

14 AND 16 ASTOR PLACE

1888

Press of J. J. Little & Co.
Astor Place, New York.

# PREFACE.

THE numerous defenses, palliative reminders, and decorous appeals which have been made by the friends and professors of ritualism, do not seem to have dispelled the ill-concealed suspicion that it is either sentimentality or Romanism disguised. And, indeed, had they quieted apprehension, they would not have established the *rationale* of rites, nor settled their use upon strictly scientific and philosophic grounds, and so would leave no tests of their reasonableness except historic ones, which, although excellent within limits, are apt to be viewed with contempt, and somehow considered a proper reason for the rejection of the very uses such tests would confirm. In truth, much that has been said about ritualism has barely scratched the surface, and has been said in a feebly apologetic tone, which neither pleased nor convinced its critics. We are told that St. Paul wished all to be done "decently and in order," and this almost trivial enjoinder was made to excuse the chasuble and maniple of the priest, the eucharistic lights, the ablutions, the genuflexions, the seven lamps, and the incense—a variety of extensions of meaning which the most athletic exegesis could scarcely extort from the text. Obviously, such a remark as this of St. Paul's would apply about as well to the simple and orderly proceeding of a meeting-

house as to the sublime and touching symbolism of
the cathedral service. Again, the poetry of symbolism itself was dwelt upon, and effectively. The usage
of the past and the sacred continuity of holy practices
were justly emphasized ; but to many this was retrogression, and as long as the creed suffered no diminu-
tion, *as they thought*, it was to them wiser to avoid an
offense, and to shun the risk of strengthening superstitious observances.

The want felt in this matter does not really arise
from any lack of publication of excellent reasons for
ritualistic methods, but rather from their disconnected
or very technical presentation, as well partly from the
secondary, extrinsic value of some reasons adduced. It
is the writer's wish to gather into a consecutive series
of arguments the considerations and thoughts which
sustain ritualism, and to attempt to discover the underlying principles and inherent concordances in nature
which justify and enforce it. And here it is, perhaps,
best to say one word of personal explanation. The
author is not a professed ritualist, damaging as that
confession may appear to some, for the value of his
work, but he has been led to examine the grounds
upon which the surprising rise of ritualism rests, and to
attempt to find principles or a law of human nature
which co-ordinate it with the inevitable order of things,
and make it perennial and perpetual. The term ritualism has not been used here in a very literal sense, and
has been defined in the opening chapter. Gathering
together the diverse expressions of ceremonial temper
in the Church under one name, this definition permits

the writer to avoid unnecessary discriminations, while it affords an opportunity to survey the entire field, and place rites in the abstract upon their proper basis, without entering into any minute discussion, for which he has not sufficient knowledge, as to whether special rites are necessary or prejudicial. In this connection he has not, however, hesitated to offer some observations upon a rule which can, or might, be regarded in the testing of the claims of rites to use in the Church, feeling confident that a rule must be framed which would guard against a surplusage of indifferent observances or positive error.

We anticipate censure and rebuke from many friends whose personal character and mental acquirements, strong and noble, have been nurtured under influences which are hostile to the views adopted in this essay. Surely it is not wrong to invite them to read what we have written, not with leniency, but with fairness, knowing that naught was put down with malice, and hoping that, should their judgment be adverse, we shall not be compelled to forfeit either their friendship or regard.

# ARGUMENT.

## PART I.

### *Ritualism Universal.*

Ritualism defined; its three Elements, Art, Symbolism, and Commemoration; their illustration in the Irvingites, Greek, and Roman Churches. These Elements shown to be present in the Great Religions and in Aboriginal Worship. The determining Causes of Ritualism defined and illustrated in the Religions of the World. The same Causes potential in Christianity.

## PART II.

### *The Reasonableness of Ritualism.*

Art in Ritualism; Art's Relations to Religion fundamental; its Value in Worship; its Comfort. Symbolism; its Nurture of Mysticism. Commemoration; its Mnemonic and Practical Uses.

# CONTENTS.

# PART I.
# RITUALISM UNIVERSAL.

# CHAPTER I.

THE increasing enrichment of the services in the Episcopal Church has, for the last twenty years, attracted considerable attention. It has reached every part of Church life, and has brought to notice features of the service which the injurious desuetude of years had almost obliterated. It has had all the character, in this respect, of renovation and innovation. It has heightened and deepened the music, reformed the architecture and ornamented the interior of churches, it has renewed the observance of holy-days, it has put upon the priest his vestments, it has reinstated the solemnity of worship, it has filled the sanctuary with beauty, it has applied and rehabilitated the system of symbolism in Church service, by which the mind becomes imbued with the poetic sentiment of religious analogies and the sweetness of religious memories; it has, in short, startled into life the historic Church, which seemed nodding in a decrepitude of respectability and sloth, and forced it to resume those habiliments of majesty and beauty which protected and published its claims, and preserved its faith. It was, and is, a unique movement, full of responsibilities and full of blessings. It has been universally recognized, and it has been called Ritualism. It is evident that this term must have a greatly expanded sense of definition, as its technical meaning is inadequate to cover the extension of usages, doctrines, and methods of the Catholic revival.

Ritualism strictly means a use of rites, forms of words, with motions or signs. This aspect of Church service has certainly been made more prominent since the rise of ritualism, but it would very imperfectly describe the movement if we should limit its significance to this partial view, and, indeed, it would do violence to the evident and correct popular impression that ritualism means a great deal more.

Mr. A. J. B. Beresford Hope has pointed out the inaccuracy of this term, and says : *

" I must take a preliminary objection to the term in its various forms of Ritualism, Ritualist, and Ritualistic, as being both indefinite and incorrect. These expressions are all used in reference to ceremonialism of a specific description, more ornate, that is, than that which is found in the usual run of English churches, and more immediately referable than we have for a long time been accustomed to think possible to the pre-reformational Church of England. It is obvious that there is nothing in the words themselves to point to the specific meaning, for a ritual *per se* may be a modern as well as an ancient one, a plain as well as a gorgeous one. So much for the indefiniteness of the expression ; but it is also grammatically incorrect. A ' Ritual' means a book which contains 'rites,' that is, the form of words by which certain Church privileges are conveyed, or Church conditions created—the rite of Baptism, for instance, or the rite of Confirmation, or the rite of Marriage. ' Ritualism ' accordingly means the science of such rites, so recapitulated in a ritual. It deals, in short, with the words, and not, as in its modern conventional sense, with the way of acting out those words. The phrase which the inventors of ' Ritualism' ought to have adopted, if they had intended to be grammatical without caring so much for being definite, was ' ceremonialism,' and they should have styled themselves ' ceremonialists.' "

---

* *Worship in the Church of England*, p. 5.

Ritualism, regarded with this wide extension of meaning, and not confining its application to religious observances only, may be defined as a system of observances which addresses the imagination, memory, and feelings through the senses, by a connective order or ceremonial of acts, or by structure, as buildings, etc., all intended to commemorate or reproduce events, to arouse or express proper feelings, or to illustrate an idea or belief in reference to special ends. It involves three principles—that of Art and Decoration, that of Symbolism, that of Commemoration, derived from the sense of historical continuity, and these are woven together and manifested conjointly, and forms of ritualism may be separated as one or two of these assume predominance, or the three are harmoniously mingled, or so counterbalanced as to reach the highest degree of perfect expression. While the above definition covers fairly enough any possible imaginary development or phase of ceremonial, and is intended to include the serious exercises as well of barbarians and pagans as Christians, usually religious, civic, or elegiac, it must be remembered that the motive which produces ritualism anywhere, the actual mainspring of its existence, is man's irresistible craving for expression in form, an impulse justified by every possible appeal to nature—indeed, we might say, involved *au fond* in the constitution of sentient being.

Perhaps the best way to prove the justness and value of this definition would be to examine some good and acknowledged examples of ritualism in the Christian Faith. We wished to show also that in purely civic organizations, based on a ceremonial government, the same characteristics could be seen, but we have abandoned the purpose, as the evidence is less striking and illustrative.*

Before proceeding with this examination, we must explain a little more fully our meaning of Art. We intend to imply something beyond those departments of culture and execution to which the word is usually confined. We do not restrict its meaning to architecture, music, and painting. We mean also by art the wide range of movement, vestments, dramatic presentation, solemnity of manner, postures, obeisances, lights, decoration, precedence of rank, etiquette of bearing, etc., which in ceremonies stimulate attention, arrest the eye, and instruct the mind.† We wish to establish our definition by an inspection of the Irvingites, the Greek and Roman Churches, which shall separately illustrate its value.

The Irvingites originated with Edward Irving, the distinguished Scotch preacher, who excited, in the first

---

* Especially we had intended to show that Masonry's redundant forms exemplified the application of these three ideas, but the study of Masonry so painfully impresses the student with a sense of its absurdity that it would have only impaired the earnestness of our inquiry to have analyzed its tiresome and affected rites.

† We seem justified in this position by the views of Hegel, as given in his *Æsthetics* (translated and edited by the Rev. John Steinfort Kedney), for he says, "it [art] addresses the sensibility and the imagination, and not the reflective faculty," and further, that it "is, subjectively considered, the endeavor to make real and apprehensible for human consciousness, in the combined relations of sense, understanding, and imagination, and in existing material, furnished by the physical world for sight or sound, or as symbol, an ideal of beauty or sublimity."

quarter of our century, so much interest, and who, first at Hatton Garden, and afterward in Regent Square, London, preached with astonishing power and eloquence to immense congregations, who were attracted as much by the commanding personality of the preacher, as by the powerful eccentricity of the preaching. "He was not satisfied with the ordinary idea of the gradual conversion of the world by missionary efforts, so that it should slide into the Church by a natural inclination. Such a slow and tedious process could not commend itself to his eager and impetuous expectations, and his notion of the overmastering power of Almighty God in working out His purposes. He began, therefore, to enter into the new ideas of the present dispensation drawing to its close, and of the near approach of 'a glorious and overwhelming revolution' which should transform this present state through the advent of our Lord and His reign upon earth." * United with Hartley, Frere, Henry Drummond, and others, he prepared the ground for a school, or church, of prophecy, which looked for the near approach of the second coming of Christ, and applied its ingenious or obscure speculations to the prophecies of the Bible. Irving designated the movement as "the school of the prophets." The spirit of prophecy itself soon changed this company of interpreters into a group of seers, and from reading they soon fell to delivering prophecies. The Rev. J. Holdane Stewart assisted the movement, and a reaction among pious and ardent

---

* *History and Doctrine of Irvingism,* Vol. I., p. 26. E. Miller.

spirits against the religious sloth of the day prepared
the way for extravagant and abnormal manifestations.
To Mary Campbell was given the gift of tongues,
then to Margaret Macdonald, and her brothers, James
and George. Other inspired or afflicted people appeared,
and a Church was formed, which was intended to su-
persede and replace all others. It became catholic in
its tendencies, and ritualistic in its services. Ministers
were consecrated; Drummond was made Angel of the
Church at Albury. There was an angel for every Church,
and six elders or presbyters. Irving was consecrated.
Prophets and apostles figured in the new hierarchy, and
imposing claims, infallible assertions, fanatical obstinacy,
imparted to this new Church an oddness that made it
momentarily attractive to religious enthusiasts. Zealous, expectant men they were, to whom the sensation
of a new dispensation, a revival of religious intensity
and animation, under the stimulus of an impending
judgment, was fascinating.

The apostles early began a study of existing faiths,
in order to fix upon some order of ceremonies.

" Before they left home, they learnt from their Biblical investi-
gations the high place which should be occupied in Christian worship by the sacrament of the Holy Eucharist. They studied deeply,
as has been told, the details of the ceremonial law of Moses, as
given in the Pentateuch. . . . Accordingly, from the remarkable prominence given to sacrifices under the Jewish law, the apostles learnt the leading position which belongs of right to the
Holy Eucharist in Christian worship." " They were led back into
the consideration of early liturgies. There they found that the remains of the first ages of the Church, whilst she was yet one and
undivided, witnessed with no unfaltering voice to the conclusion to
which they had been already directed. Liturgies, as is well known,

are simply offices for the Holy Eucharist. No other services have come down to us from the earliest times of the Church. Ecclesiastical history shows that forms of common prayer grew up later, and that they always presupposed a previous offering of the Eucharistic rite, or else led up immediately to the celebration of that sacrament." *

The drift of sentiment was overpoweringly toward ritualistic method, and the adoption of such schemes and systems of worship as would express this ritualistic tendency developed at once, in the Church, Art, Symbolism, and Commemoration, though from their artificial and provisional origin these expressions were not symmetrically or even well expressed. Art appeared in the use of expressive structure in their churches, which conformed to such architectural types as would indicate the related uses of different parts; altars were set up, vestments were adopted, and they were of an ornamental kind; externals of worship were multiplied; and the singular and effective rite of sealing was devised, which corresponded to the Confirmation of Catholics. All this was in the direction of Art, as we have defined it in this discussion, assisting the worship by an external sign, device, motion, or color. Further elaboration in the service followed, and "the principle of the fourfold ministry" was developed and illustrated. Thus "the Elder was ordered to say the Prayer of Dedication, the Supplications were assigned to the Pastor, the Prayers Commemorative to the Evangelist, the Prayers Intercessory to the Elder, and the Thanksgiving to the Prophet." Later, the use of lights and incense and holy water, and

* *History and Doctrine of Irvingism,* Vol. I., pp. 196, 198.
  1*

the benediction of holy oil, was introduced, offices of confession and absolution, with all of which was involved an interesting symbolism. All these separate contributions to the art element of the worship of this body were united and expanded in the beautiful Temple of Gordon Square, London.

The complement of clergy in a church with 3,000 communicants is large, and its use imposing in the ornate functions of the service.

It consists of—

| | |
|---|---|
| One Angel, who has an Angel's help, | 2 |
| Six Elders, each with an Elder's help, | 12 |
| Six Prophets, each with a Prophet's help, | 12 |
| Six Evangelists, each with an Evangelist's help, | 12 |
| Six Pastors, each with a Pastor's help, | 12 |
| Seven Deacons, each with a Deacon's help, | 14 |

The Church possesses a composite system of services and a liturgy of great dimensions. The church recently erected in New York, by this society, possesses some architectural pretensions, and its arrangement within expresses to the eye the idea of worship and consecration. A semicircular recess forms the sanctuary, at the extreme wall of which stands a white altar surmounted by a cross, two uprights, for lights, stand on either side, and seven lamps hang before it, while a small lamp suspended above it contains an ever-burning flame. Three wide platforms, each with a narrow step placed successively below each other, connect the sanctuary with the nave of the church. In the celebration of the Eucharist the celebrant, in white alb and chasuble broadly marked with a gold cross, enters, attended by·

two assistants vested in white tunics, or dalmatics, traversed with gold yokes. The three kneel at one of the outer platforms, prayer and praise ascend from the ministrants and congregation, and the three ministers, rising, approach nearer the altar and again pray. This over, they enter, as it were, the sanctuary, and, kneeling before the altar itself, again offer petitions and thanksgiving. The feeling of a gradual approach, a slow and beautiful crescendo of modulated worship, leading up in act and feeling to the sublime rite of Holy Communion, is impressive, and thoroughly illustrates the art idea in worship. The elements are now handed to the celebrant by an attendant deacon, while an acolyte, approaching from the choir, with swinging censer, fills the sanctuary with fragrance, enveloping the bending and silent group within in rising clouds. The Epistle and Gospel of the day are then read by the assistants, each in turn coming forward to the lowest platform after receiving the Testament from the priest at the altar. Then singing, in soft and gentle cadences, prepares the worshiper for the climacteric in the solemn consecration, after which the celebrant, taking the censer, incenses the altar; a litany is said, during which also incense ascends, as the visible type of the uprising thoughts and hopes and prayers. The elements are first partaken of by the assistants, who, in turn, distribute them to the communicants kneeling at the threshold of the sanctuary.

It is evident that the art principle, in the comprehensive sense we use it, and also in its narrow conventional use, is distinctively manifested in the service and usages of the Catholic Apostolic Church (Irvingites).

The Symbolism of the Irvingites is pervasive and elaborate.

" Symbolism and mysticism are almost the air which they spiritually breathe ; their system is full of it.   To such an extent do they deal in symbolical intricacies, ingenious contrivances, nets of complication, subtleties, balancings, mystifications, concealments, as to make practically a border between themselves and the rest of mankind, which it is in the highest degree unlikely that the latter will ever cross." *

Again, Mr. Miller instructively defines and indicates the use of Symbolism in this sect.

" They employ types and symbols, not merely as the application or the corollaries of doctrines otherwise established, but as the grounds upon which those doctrines are adopted and recommended for adoption.  Such, for example, is the reference to the four streams of Paradise, the four colors in which the cherubim were embroidered on the Tabernacle, the four ingredients of incense, and the four living creatures in the Apocalypse, for typifying the Four Ministries.  Similar to these were the interpretation of the bullock offered for a sin-offering as symbolizing the priesthood, and the goat as showing forth the whole Church ; of the two lights at the altar as standing for apostles and prophets ; and of the ' ministry ' of the Angel every morning, addressed principally to the elders, and the 'United Ministry of Adoration' every evening by the seven elders, as being foreshadowed by the trimming of the seven-branched candlestick in the morning by Aaron, and the lighting of it before the Lord every evening by the priests." †

No further evidence is required to show that this ritualistic religion, plainly, in its outward forms makes use of the principle of symbolism.

---

* *History and Doctrine of Irvingism*, Vol. II., p. 95.
† *Ibid.* p. 17.

In Commemoration we find ample illustrations of the use of commemorative services.

"There are proper services for all holy-days, including 'the Anniversary of the Separation of the Apostles' and 'Prayers for the Three Seasons.' These 'three seasons' precede Christmas, Easter, and Pentecost, being respectively (1) 'from the 16th to 23d December;' (2) 'from the Wednesday preceding to the Wednesday in Passion Week;' (3) 'and from the day after the Ascension to the Friday following, both inclusive.'"

The so-called Catholic Apostolic Church is certainly a very insignificant and useless body, its doctrines absurdly paltry so far as they distinguish this Church from other bodies of faith in Christianity, its practice a masquerade of artificial forms, and its influence inappreciable; but it is voluntarily ritualistic in its tendency and methods, being not unlike a diminutive Masonic order without technically secret vows. In this respect it serves our purpose as an example of a ritualistic Church, all of whose elements are referable to the three heads of Art, Symbolism, and Commemoration.

We now turn to an examination in the same manner of the Greek Church, an example of a Catholic body which is thoroughly ritualistic. In Art we find that its gorgeous and impressive temples, its mingled arrays and exhibits of color, precious objects, elaboration of movement, etc., are all expressions of this principle. The great Church of St. Isaac, at St. Petersburg, described in detail by Théophile Gautier, is an epitome of the art principle as applied in the church's architectural features, and forms a fitting envelope or shell for the artistic richness of its services. M. Gautier* has taken the greatest pains to allow no feature of this wonderful edifice to escape his reader's notice, and his description, too long to be even partially reproduced here, can leave in the reader's mind no doubt as to the art tendencies of the form of worship to which it is consecrated. In the Eastern Church, the Byzantine form of architecture is adhered to. The churches are cruciform, with the sanctuary at the eastern end, and frequently the roof rises in spacious domes, one central, at the intersection of the arms of the cross, and other lesser ones surrounding it, the whole imparting an expression of lightness and beauty otherwise quite incommunicable.

Two vestibules at the principal entrance admit penitents and catechumens, and, the great nave traversed, the visitor reaches the choir, behind which rises the *ikonostasis,* or altar screen, which, when its doors are shut, completely hides from view the altar.

" Access to the sanctuary is obtained by means of three doors. Those in the middle are called the royal or holy doors, through which none but a bishop, priest, or deacon may pass. These doors are also furnished with a veil or curtain, which is drawn across them at certain portions of the service. The south door is called *deacon's door,* and the north the *paranomarion,* through which ordinary servants of the Church may pass when they have duty to perform in the sanctuary." †

In the sanctuary is the holy table, on which stands a Tabernacle, in which the elements of the Holy Eucharist are reserved for the communion of the sick; on it is

* *Voyage en Russie.*
† *The Offices of the Oriental Church.* Introduction. Bjerring and Anketell.

also placed a cross and the book of the Gospels, while not infrequently a rich canopy, held up by four pillars, overshadows the sacred place. A table of preparation, or *prothesis*, is placed in the north-east corner of the sanctuary, where the elements are laid before removal to the holy table, while on the south side is the *diakonikon*, where the vessels, robes, and books are preserved. An *ambon*, or small platform, is raised before the holy doors, where the Gospel is read to the people and sermons preached, the choir of readers and singers being ranged on either side in the chancel, so disposed as to sing antiphonally.

In the inner porch of the church the font is placed, as indicative of the sacrament of Holy Baptism as the door of entrance into the Church of Christ.

The Church of St. Isaac, at St. Petersburg, is one of the most admirable examples of ecclesiastical construction, and is the embodiment, as it is the acme, of the artistic genius of the Greek Church. We will quote Gautier's enthusiastic words :

"At the first glance the effect is most satisfying. Whatever might be too severe, too serious, in a word, too classic, in the outline, is felicitously relieved by the richness and the color of materials the most beautiful that ever human devotion employed in the construction of a temple—gold, marble, bronze, granite. Without falling into any parti-colored effect, St. Isaac's borrows from these splendid materials a harmonious variety of tints, whose genuineness makes them the more enchanting ; there is no paint there, nothing fictitious ; nothing in all this magnificence utters a falsehood to God. The massive granite bears up the eternal bronze, indestructible marble clothes the walls, and pure gold shines from crosses, dome, and bell-towers, giving the building the Oriental and Byzantine stamp of the Greek Church."

The plan of the church is a cross, with arms of equal
length, surmounted by a great dome, and bearing four
bell-towers.  The foundation is granite, from which
wide steps le&d up to the four porticoes; the roof rises
upon colossal columns, and noble windows, ornate cor-
nices, elaborate pediments, and numerous statues, crowd-
ing, with picturesque groups in effective combinations,
the higher elevations of the fabric, combine to form a
marvel of architectural beauty, wherein the mingling
influences of sculpture and design unite with the most
consummate harmony.

" Thus, on the cornice surrounding the cupola, on the acroteria,
and along the edge of the roof, we have, without counting the figures in high relief of the pediments, the bas-reliefs above the portals, and the saints and angels who stand in niches of the doors—
fifty-two statues, thrice the natural size, forming for St. Isaac's an
eternal people of bronze in attitudes of great variety, and yet everywhere obedient, like an architectural chorus, to the cadences of a
linear rhythm."

On penetrating within this stupendous temple the
eye, in a different way, is startled with unexpected
splendors.

"As you enter, you are overpowered with amazement ; the colossal grandeur of the architecture, the profusion of the rarest marbles,
the brilliancy of the gilding, the color in the frescoes, the polished
pavement, like a mirror in which all objects are reflected, unite in
an effect absolutely dazzling, especially if your attention is directed,
as it must be, toward the side where stands the iconostase—iconostase, a marvelous edifice, a temple within a temple, a façade of
gold, malachite, and lapis lazuli, with doors of solid silver ; but
which is, after all, only the veil of the sanctuary.  Thither the eye
turns invincibly, whether the open doors reveal, in dazzling transparency, the colossal Christ painted on glass, or whether, closed,

they only show the crimson curtain, whose color seems dyed in the Divine blood."

Statues, paintings, columns and panels of marble, innumerable types and symbols, the glorious dome, flooded with light in which are bathed a blazing group of golden angels, arrest and bewilder the beholder, who only gradually awakens from his astonishment into the intelligent realization that this wilderness of display has been made subject to the inexorable laws of perfect art.

The iconostase, the screen of the sanctuary, seems to mark the climax of this architectural wonder, at least in sumptuousness and brilliancy.

"The architect has carried his iconostase to the height of the attics, so that it forms part of the architectural order, and suits well the colossal proportions of the building, of which it fills the whole breadth, from one wall to the other. It is, as I have said, the façade of a temple within a temple.

"Three steps of red porphyry form the base. A balustrade of white marble, with gilded balusters ornamented with precious marbles, traces the line of demarkation between the priest and the worshipers. The finest marble of the Italian quarries serves as the original material of which the wall of the iconostase is composed, and this wall, though elsewhere it would be itself superb, is nearly concealed from sight by the splendid ornaments which cover it.

"Eight columns of malachite, of the Corinthian order, fluted, with bases and capitals of gilded bronze, and two pilasters, compose the façade, and support the attic. The tone of the malachite, with its metallic luster, its green, coppery shades, strange and charming to the eye, its polish perfect like that of a gem, surprises by its beauty and magnificence.

"When the sacred door which occupies the center of this immense façade of gold and silver, lapis lazuli, malachite, jasper, porphyry, and agate, a giant jewel-box of all the wealth that human magnificence, deterred by no expense, can gather, closes mysteriously its leaves of silver-gilt, chiseled, sunk, wrought in waving patterns, and not less than thirty-five feet in height by fourteen in breadth, you can perceive, amid the glitter, pictures, in frames of wrought leafage, the most marvelous that ever surrounded work of pencil, representing the Four Evangelists in half-lengths, and, in full length, the Angel Gabriel and the Virgin Mary.

" But when, during the service, the sacred door opens its broad leaves, a colossal Christ, forming the window opposite, at the back of the sanctuary, appears in gold and purple, raising his right hand in benediction, in an attitude where modern skill is united to the stately Byzantine tradition. There is nothing more beautiful and more splendid than this figure, revealed in strong light as in a sky upon which opens the arched doorway of the iconostase. The mysterious darkness which reigns in the church, at certain hours, augments still further the brilliancy and the transparency of this superb window, which was painted at Munich."

Within this extraordinary and beautiful partition lies the Holy of Holies, wherein the rites of consecration are performed. It is a hall lighted by a colossal figure, on a painted window, of Christ, as though emblematic of that spiritual illumination which through Him has lighted all the world. Paintings of saints and celestial beings occupy its walls, and in its center stands the simple altar of white marble.

It is sufficiently shown that in the Greek edifice of worship, of which St. Isaac's is a consummate embodiment, the principle of art is recognized, and we shall find no less plentiful evidence of its influence in the Greek ritual of service, along with the play of a composite symbolism, and, less obviously, the use of commemorative emblems.

The service of the Divine Liturgy of St. John Chrysostom is used, with few exceptions, throughout Russia, and is the chief and central act of worship, embodying the celebrating of the Offering of the Holy Eucharist.

It consists * of the Offertory, the Liturgy·of the Catechumens, the Liturgy of the Faithful, which, combined,
form a prolonged service, beginning at eight or nine
in the morning, and lasting two or three hours, performed by priest, deacon, and readers. The service is
full of action; the processions and entrances, the appearance of the priest from, and his retreat to, the
sacred inclosure about the altar, all stimulate and
arrest attention, and, when intelligently followed, present a rich and eloquent memorial of Christ's Passion.

Before the opening of the service the bells of the
church ring, and as they fling out upon the air the
solemn summons to the faithful to approach the presence of God, the sexton in the church lights the
candles and lamps before the *iconas*, or images of the
Saviour, His mother, and other saints. When the congregation assembles in faithful and devout supplication,
the priest enters the church, bows toward the *iconas*,
passes into the altar, receives his stole, and, with the
deacon, utters some prayers before the royal gates,
kisses the *icons* in the altar-screen, bows, and again
entering the altar, assumes the remaining vestments,
which are signed by the priest. The deacon wears an
alb, scarf, and cuffs; the priest the alb and cuffs of the
deacon, and the stole, belt, and chasuble of his office,
all made of rich material, generally of brocade, and
bright in color, while for Christmas and Easter the
white silver cloth, with gold, forms a beautiful gar-

* We have used in the preparation of these descriptive notes the work
of H. C. Romanoff on the Liturgy of St. John Chrysostom, and the *Customs of the Oriental Church*, by Bjerring and Anketell.

ment, replaced in Lent by black cotton velvet canonicals trimmed with silver lace.

The investiture complete, the hands of the clergy are washed in pure water, and the Offertory, or preparation of the bread or wine, begins. It is done within the altar, and the congregation do not see the ceremony, and hear but slightly what is occurring. During this preliminary action the reader, in an alb, reads the Hours below the *ambon*.

The preparation of the elements being completed—a somewhat elaborate act, full of an erudite symbolism—the deacon waves incense, and a star, bathed in the fragrant smoke, is placed over the paten or dish holding the bread, while the coverings of all the holy vessels are thoroughly perfumed or incensed. These coverings, three in number, are of damask velvet or cloth of gold, embroidered and ornamented in various manners in rich gold and silver thread, with flowers and angels. The Offertory concludes with the Hymn to the Holy Ghost, said privately by the priest and deacon before the throne, and the second part of the Liturgy begins, indicated by the drawing aside of the veil behind the royal gates.

Then begins the Liturgy of the Catechumens, of which Romanoff says:

"In the earlier periods of the Church, catechumens, that is, persons who were preparing for baptism, repentant sinners, and even idolaters, were permitted to be present during the first and second parts of the Divine Liturgy, but they were obliged to leave the church when the consecration of the elements and Communion were about to take place. The place that they were allowed to attend after the Offertory, and which to this day is called the 'Liturgy of the Catechumens,' is a continuation of mystical types of the life and works of our Lord up to the time of His Passion."

The deacon, having received the blessing of the priest, appears from the altar at the left hand or deacon's door, and stands on the *ambon.* He bows toward the royal gates, and, holding his scarf aloft in his right hand, the other being thrown over his left shoulder, he begins the first litany.

This finished, the priest comes forth from the altar, followed by the deacon who carries the Gospels, and preceded by a reader who carries a burning candle, typical of John the Baptist and the prophets who preached of Christ's coming. This is the Lesser Entrance. They return, after prayer, through the royal gates, when chants. and responses and the Thrice -Holy Song are gone through with. The Epistle is read, and the Gospel, during which incense is waved both to the altar and toward the congregation, signifying the propagation of the Gospel. The Gospel reading is solemn and impressive, under the light of candles, which over, the book is reclasped, carried back to the altar, delivered to the hands of the priest, when the royal gates are closed, and the deacon, reappearing from the left hand deacon's door, stands at the *ambon*, and begins the augmented or redoubled litany.

With the conclusion of the prayer for the catechumens, the Liturgy of the Faithful begins. This commemorates the last days of our Blessed Lord on earth. A litany and prayers prepare for the approach of the heart and mind in faith to that supreme act of worship,

of offering up the Eucharistic Sacrifice. The deacon
then goes to the altar, the royal gates are opened, the
Cherubim Hymn is sung, during which the priest and
deacon enter from the altar, carrying the elements, which
forms the Great Entrance. The vessels of the altar, the
paten, chalice, star, censer, the cross, the spoon for receiving with, the spear, are borne by different priests,
while a reader precedes, carrying the high candlestick
with a burning candle. Prayers are intoned, and slowly,
impressively, they return to the altar. Functions are
there performed, symbolic, and commemorative of
Christ's burial, while the incense rises upward in clouds
of fragrance. Prayers and numerous minute observances follow, when prayers with responses are repeated.
The veil behind 'the royal gates is withdrawn as the
singular exclamation " doors, doors," sounds through
the church. The office increases in intensity, the
solemn movement onward of the devotional current
seems to deepen, and the chanting of the Nicene Creed
fixes the attention upon the acts of faith before the
words of institution are uttered, while a bell tolls, announcing to the world outside the Blessed Sacrament.
The deacon makes the sign of the cross with the star,
over the bread, while in alternate loud and silent ejacu-
lations the priest consecrates the elements. At the
conclusion the deacon takes the cup and paten, and in
his crossed hands gently elevates them, while the choir
sings an anthem. Prayer follows, and then blessing of
the elements with the sign of the cross, at which
moment the transubstantiation is supposed to take
place, when priest and deacon prostrate themselves.

Prayers follow, and litany, and then the deacon, standing before the royal gates, girds his scarf about him so as to form a cross on his back and breast; he enters the altar to partake of the sacrament, while the choir sing. The royal gates are opened, which typifies the opening of the sepulcher, and priest and deacon, with the elements, advance to the *ambon* and administer the sacrament. Then the Ascension of our Lord is symbolized, the congregation sealed with the sign of the Cross, and the choir sings a jubilate. A litany of thanksgiving is intoned; the priest then comes from the altar, intones a very beautiful prayer, the deacon standing with bowed head and outheld scarf before the *icon* on the outside of the royal gates. The elements are carefully consumed, the choir sings, and the clergy disrobe, saying: " Lord, now lettest Thou Thy servant depart in peace."

This service is almost a dramatization in its feeling, though it is not that, of course, in any literal way; it is replete with *Art*, and touches the senses so acutely as to leave the soul in an ecstasy of noble and pure thoughts.

In Symbolization the Greek Church is prolific; indeed, it reaches a point of exuberant obscurity, and has precipitated a conflict of opinions in reference to its meaning in some instances. We choose at random some illustrations of this prevalent tendency, only noting that the service we have reviewed is itself a monumental type.

Says a Church authority, quoted by Romanoff :

" The wax which we offer and burn, being the purest of materials, signifies the purity and sincerity of our offering; as a material which is capable of impression, it typifies the seal or sign of the

Cross, made on us at Baptism and Unction ; as a soft and yielding material, it represents our obedience and willingness to repent ; wax, collected as it is from the most fragrant flowers, signifies the grace of the Holy Spirit."

Again, the bread used in the Eucharist is made of salted wheaten flour and yeast, of which it is said, "the flour and yeast signify our souls, the water baptism, and the salt wisdom and the teaching of the Word." The sacramental loaves are made double, typical of the twofold nature of Christ, and they are stamped with a round seal bearing a cross, significant of the tribute found by St. Peter in the fish's mouth, the cross being the ransom price of our salvation. The cutting of the sacramental loaf is full of curious allusions to our Lord and His sufferings and mission, as well as to the prophets, apostles, bishops, and martyrs. In the preparatory service before the Litany of the Faithful, we are told :

" The worship of the Wise Men is here brought to remembrance. The perfumed star reminds us that they came from the East, to the stable at Bethlehem, by the guiding of a star, which appeared even before the birth of the Saviour. The fragrant coverings and the waving of incense before the paten and cup indicate the gifts of the Wise Men to the Divine Infant, honoring Him as King and Lord."

In the final preparation of the Eucharist a great variety of symbolical meanings are incorporated in the service.

" As this part of the Liturgy is intended to remind us of the burial of Christ, and His sojourn in the tomb, the veil is drawn over the royal gates, in order to typify the closing of the sepulcher, and the rolling of the stone to the door thereof. Then, reverently holding the Body of Christ, the priest, in remembrance of the Lamb of God, Who was sacrificed for the sins of the world, divides it (*i. e.,* the bread) into four parts, which he arranges crosswise on the paten, and then takes the uppermost morsel, makes the sign of the Cross with it over the cup and puts it into the wine, saying, ' The fullness of the Holy Spirit.' After this he blesses some warm water, and the deacon pours it—also crosswise—into the cup. By this union of the body and blood of Christ, and the addition of sensible warmth to them, is figured the returning to life of His most pure body at His Divine Resurrection."

The Symbolism penetrates all elements of the service ; indeed, as is philosophically just, it underlies, in many cases, the sensible art features of worship. Thus, the holy vessels, banners, lanterns, etc., which add so much of objective importance to ritualism in the Greek Church, as in other Catholic communions, are highly charged with symbolic implications. The star of two semicircles covers the paten, and typifies the star in the East, which guided the Magi ; the spear-formed knife, with cross on its handle, which is used to cut the " sacrificial loaf," is typical of the spear which pierced the Redeemer's side ; the seven-branched candlestick placed before the cross behind the holy table denotes the sevenfold gifts of God ; the great lights hold four candles, of which the central one indicates the Unity of the Trinity, and the three others the three persons of the Godhead ; the dyker, or two-armed candle, denotes the two natures in one person of Christ. It is needless to mention further instances of the omnipresent symbolic genius of the worship ; it extends through every part, and it involves a great display of vestments, altar coverings, and articles which give pomp and picturesqueness to the service.

The last principle developed in ritualistic practice,

that of Commemoration, is woven in with the two other
strands that compose the golden cord of ceremonialism,
and has been already illustrated in many rites and signs
and usages.

We learn from Bjerring and Anketell that :

" The principal feasts of the Russian Church are observed in remembrance of great events in the life of the Lord Jesus Christ and
of the Virgin Mary.   The second class are in honor of the apostles
and most celebrated saints ; while the third commemorates lesser
saints and martyrs.   The Church also observes with religious ceremonies the birth and name days of the imperial family, etc., etc.,
but the queen of all festivals is the feast of Easter.   For forty days
previous the Church observes the fast of Lent.   This devotion ter-
minates in the services of the Holy Week, when the *whole of the
Gospels is read aloud in the church.*

" On Good Friday the services are solemn and impressive, reminding the worshiper of the atoning death of his Redeemer.   The
next day is called the Great Sabbath, because it commemorates that
last great Sabbath when the Lord Jesus Christ lay in the tomb.
On that day the Liturgy of St. Basil is used at noon, and the Gospel speaks of the coming Resurrection of Christ.   In the meantime,
all the people, at home as well as in the church, are preparing to
celebrate the great feast.   Every one, even to the poorest, decorates
his house and dresses himself in his best clothing.   The churches
are crowded with worshipers, and the evening is spent in reading
the Acts of the Apostles.   At the stroke of twelve all the bells in
the empire ring forth a joyous peal, preceded, in St. Petersburg, by
the firing of a salute of artillery.   Lights flash forth from the houses
in all the streets ; the stately domes of the magnificent churches
are a blaze of light.   Meanwhile, within the churches the scene is
even more magnificent and beautiful.   The mourning over a dead
and buried Christ is suddenly changed into lively joy, which hails
the risen Redeemer.

" The holy doors before the sanctuary suddenly open, and a procession of clergy, dressed in their festive robes, enters the church
to the glad music of Easter songs.   They carry in their hands the
crucifix, and bear on their breasts the holy Gospel and a picture

of Christ's Resurrection. All the worshipers in the church have brought with them wax candles. These are in a moment lighted, and, amidst this illumination, the procession, with the Church banners borne before, passes out of the church and around it from west to east. Arrived at the main doors it finds them shut, and halts for a moment. Those who are within hear the words of the Easter anthem : 'Now is Christ risen from the dead, and become the first fruits of them that slept.' At the sound of these words the church doors are again opened, the procession enters the church, and the Litany of St. Chrysostom begins."

At Christmas the clergy visit the houses of the laity, with the crucifix, repeating the story of the birth of Christ, and on the Epiphany, which in the East commemorates the baptism of Christ, they visit the houses and sprinkle them with consecrated water. In Baptism, in Matrimony, and, in fact, in all the various sacraments of the Church, the ritualistic *facies* is absolutely preserved, and it consists in the interwoven application of these principles which we have indicated.

In the Roman Church we have an example of a ritualistic body which is at our doors, and which presents an illustration of ritualism which has had, perhaps, a beneficent influence in assisting the revival of Catholic doctrine and use in the Church, as it has certainly preserved those methods of worship which it is the aim and wish of High Churchmen, in a salutary measure, to restore to our worship.

In the Roman Church we discover the three elements of ceremonialism—Art, Symbolism, and Commemoration. In regard to the first, it is scarcely necessary to urge any specific proof of its existence. The wonderful cathedrals of Europe, the splendid churches of this com-

munion in our own land, their architectural arrangement, by which the eye is carried forward from the entrance, through nave and choir, to the sanctuary and
altar, are well known and commonly admired. The
wealth of decoration bestowed on the more sacred and
impressive portions of the edifice are matters of general
knowledge. The narratives of travelers and writers are
unanimous in their testimony to this. Writing of Ven-
ice, Mrs. Jameson, in the *Diary of an Ennuyée*, says:

"To-day we visited several churches—rich on the outside, with
all the luxury of architecture—with inside gorgeous with painting,
sculpture, and many-colored marbles. The prodigality with which
the most splendid and costly materials are lavished here is perfectly amazing; pillars of lapis lazuli, columns of Egyptian porphyry, and pavements of mosaic; altars of alabaster, ascended by
steps incrusted with agate and jasper—but to particularize would
be in vain."

The same authoress, writing of St. Peter's, at Rome,
says:

"The interior of St. Peter's is all airy magnificence and gigantic
splendor; light and sunshine pouring in on every side; gilding
and gay colors, marbles and pictures, dazzling the eye above, below,
around."

Bayard Taylor writes of the Church of St. Louis, at
Munich, as follows:

"How lightly the two square towers of gray marble lift their net-
work of sculpture! Over the arched portal stand marble statues
by Schwanthaler, and the roof of brilliant tiles, worked into mosaic,
resembles a rich Turkey carpet covering the whole. We must enter to get an idea of the splendor of the church. Instead of the
pointed arch which one would expect to find above his head, the
lofty pillars on each side bear an unbroken semicircular vault, which

is painted a brilliant blue, and spangled with silver stars. These pillars, and the little arches above, which spring from them, are illuminated with gold and brilliant colors, and each side chapel is a casket of richness and elegance. The windows are of silvered glass, through which the light glimmers softly on the splendor within. The end of the chancel behind the high altar is taken up with Cornelius's celebrated fresco painting of the ' Last Judgment ' —the largest painting in the world—and the circular dome in the center of the cross contains groups of martyrs, prophets, saints, and kings, painted in fresco on a ground of gold."

### Of the Duomo at Milan he writes :

" It is a mixture of the Gothic and Romanesque styles ; the body of the structure is entirely covered with statues and richly wrought sculpture, with needle-like spires of white marble rising up from every corner. But of the exquisite, airy look of the whole mass, although so solid and vast, it is impossible to convey an idea. It resembles some fabric of frost-work which winter traces on the window-panes.

"Ascending the marble steps which lead to the front, I lifted the folds of the heavy curtain and entered. What a glorious aisle ! The mighty pillars support a magnificent arched ceiling, painted to re-semble fretwork, and the little light that falls through the small windows above enters tinged with a dim, golden hue. A feeling of solemn awe comes over one as he steps with a hushed tread along the colored marble floor, and measures the massive columns until they blend with the gorgeous arches above."

### He writes, of the Royal Chapel at Munich :

" To enter it is like stepping into a casket of jewels. The sides are formed by a double range of arches, the windows being so far back as to be almost out of sight, so that the eye falls on nothing but coloring and gold. The lower row of arches is of alternate green and purple marble, beautifully polished ; but the upper, as well as the small chancel behind the high altar, is entirely covered with fresco paintings on a ground of gold. The richness and splen-dor of the whole church is absolutely incredible."

Nathaniel Hawthorne, writing of the Cathedral of San Lorenzo, at Rome, says: *

" I used to try to imagine how the English cathedrals must have looked in their primeval glory, before the Reformation, and before the whitewash of Cromwell's time had overlaid their marble pillars ; but I never imagined anything at all approaching what my eyes now beheld ; this sheen of polished and variegated marble covering every inch of its walls ; this glow of brilliant frescoes all over the roof, and up within the domes ; these beautiful pictures by great masters, painted for the places which they now occupied, and making an actual portion of the edifice ; this wealth of silver, gold, and gems, that adorned the shrines of the saints, before which wax candles burned, and were kept burning, I suppose, from year's end to year's end ; in short, there is no imagining, no remembering, a hundredth part of the rich details. And even the cathedral (though I give it up as indescribable) was nothing at all in comparison with a church to which the *commissionaire* afterwards led us ; a church that had been built four or five hundred years ago, by a pirate, in expiation of his sins, and out of the profits of his rapine. This last edifice, in its interior, absolutely shone with burnished gold, and glowed with pictures ; its walls were a quarry of precious stones, so valuable were the marbles out of which they were wrought ; its columns and pillars were of inconceivable costliness ; its pavement was a mosaic of wonderful beauty, and there were four twisted pillars made out of stalactites."

And of the Cathedral of Siena he writes: †

" Every sort of ornament that could be thought of seems to have been crammed into the cathedral in one place or another : gilding, frescoes, pictures ; a roof of blue, spangled with golden stars ; a magnificent wheel window of old painted glass over the entrance, and another at the opposite end of the cathedral ; statues, some of marble, others of gilded bronze ; pulpits of carved marble; a gilded organ; a cornice of marble busts of the popes, extending

---

* *Passages from the French and Italian Note Book,* Vol. I., p. 48.
† *Ibid.* Vol. II., p. 176.

round the entire church; a pavement, covered all over with a strange kind of mosaic work in various marbles, wrought into marble pictures of sacred subjects; immense clustered pillars supporting the round arches that divide the side aisles; a clerestory of windows within pointed arches. It seemed as if the spectator were reading an antique volume written in black-letter of a small character, but conveying a high and solemn meaning."

Of the beautiful Cathedral of Cologne Mrs. Trollope says: *

"It is difficult to speak of the Münster Church of Cologne, without employing words which would to many appear greatly misplaced when applied to a building not more than half completed. Were I to say, for instance, that the most exalted imagination could conceive nothing more perfect in Teutonic architecture, it might, perhaps, be asked, if I considered deal planks as the perfection of Gothic roofing; and if I confessed that the impression made upon my mind was more like the effect of magic than reality, I might hear that a tower half reared, and surmounted by a hideous crane, could be obtained without the aid of necromancy.

"Nevertheless, in both cases, I should speak the truth. I can never forget, nor perhaps ever again hope to enjoy, the exceeding delight I experienced from hearing high mass performed in the choir of this matchless church. The graceful windows, each one a separate wonder, rearing their bold and light proportions to the towering roof, let in such streams of gorgeous colored light, that the whole edifice glowed with it."

It would be wearisome to continue quoting the tributes of praise and enthusiastic admiration which the Roman houses of worship have evoked, but we may aptly complete this evidence as to the presence of Art in that Church, by quoting a description of Mr. Story's of the celebration of Mass at St. Peter's, Rome,† where-

---

* *Belgium and Western Germany.*
† *Roba di Roma.*

in is seen the artistic idea in the larger sense we employ
it in this book, as embracing not only the works of music, sculpture, and painting, but the numerous forms
of dramatic presentation and spectacular arrangement,
the poetry of movement and color. Mr. Story's pen-
picture is this:

> "At the elevation of the Host, the guards who line the nave
> drop to their knees, their side-arms ringing on the pavement, the
> vast crowd bends, and a swell of trumpets sounds through the
> dome. Nothing can be more impressive than this moment in St.
> Peter's. Then the choir from its gilt cage resumes its chant, the
> high falsetti of the soprani soaring over the rest, and interrupted
> now and then by the clear, musical voice of the Pope, until at last
> he is borne aloft in his papal chair on the shoulders of his attend-
> ants, crowned with the triple crown, between the high, white, wav-
> ering fans, all the cardinals, monsignori, canonici, officials, priests,
> and guards going before him in splendid procession."

In the service of the Roman Church the art principle
is fully embodied, in the sense we have defined it;
music, color, dress, and varied functions of obvious
beauty and much diversity are involved in it, and make
it a spectacle of great interest and splendor. This art
principle is again subordinately applied in the ornamentation of the accessories of the ritual; thus the holy
vessels are often sumptuously decorated, and are made
themselves commemorative of Christian doctrine, hopes,
and realities.

At the risk of appearing prolix, we will review the
order of the Mass, which is the central act or sacrament
of Roman worship, as it is the Holy Communion,
which is, or should be, the central fact of all Catholic
worship. If we follow this service through we shall

discover that not only does it exemplify the art idea
very perfectly, but that it is crowded with symbolism
and commemorative features; it abounds from first to
last with mystical import, and rehearses the solemn
drama of Christ's sacrifice. It is the composite result
of the play of these intermingling principles, and we
shall find that they alone suffice to give us a clue to
the classification and analysis of its parts; it is an example of their mutual interdependence, convergence, and
union.

As the priest prepares for the Sacrifice of the Mass,
and before putting on the vestments of his office, he
washes his hands, as significant of that purity of heart
necessary for the exercise of his office, and as a physical
lavation to secure absolute cleanness. He then " dresses
the chalice." On this beautiful vessel, upon which
often the highest skill of artisan industry and artistic
device have been expended, is placed a clean *purificator*,
over which is again laid the paten, with a large Host
resting on it, and over this the pall; the chalice veil is
cast over all, and the burse, with its contained corporal,
is put on top.

The priest now vests, putting on the *amice* or
shoulder-cloth, which is intended to signify armor, as
reminding the celebrant of his obligations to fight the
good fight of faith; the *alb*, a white garment of pure
linen entirely covering the body, and denoting newness
of life; the *cincture* or girdle, which signifies continence
and self-restraint; the *maniple*, which, hanging from his
arm, as a hindrance to his motions, reminds the priest
of the trials and troubles of life; the *stole*, or long band,

2*

hung behind the neck and over the shoulders, and which is only the selvage of a larger garment formerly used, and variously ornamented ; the *chasuble*, the final covering, which, covering the entire person, is emblematic of charity.* The commemorative suggestions of this

---

\* The following extract from the *Living Church*, of Chicago, 1886, gives a metrical form to these significations, more easily remembered.

THE VESTING OF THE PRIEST.—*The Irish Ecclesiastical Record* has the following rhyming translation of the prayers which the priest is directed to say while putting on the sacred vestments. Some of our clerical friends may be glad to cut this slip out and keep it before them when vesting for the Eucharist :

*Ad Amictum.*
The helmet of salvation place
  Upon my head, O Lord,
That I may crush the fierce assaults
  Of all the demon horde.

*Ad Albam.*
Lord, make me white, and cleanse my heart,
  That, in Thy blood made white,
O Lamb of God, I may enjoy
  Thy endless heaven's delight.

*Ad Cingulam.*
Gird me, O Lord, with purity,
  And quench lust's baleful fires,
That continence with me may dwell,
  High thoughts and chaste desires.

*Ad Manipulam.*
The maniple of grief and pain
  May I so learn to bear,
That I the recompense of toil
  Exultingly may share.

*. Ad Stolam.*
The stole of immortality,
  Which I had lost of yore,
In the first father's guilty fall,
  To me, O Lord, restore ;

elaborate vesture are, as quoted by the Rev. John O'Brien from Gavautus :

"The amice is the veil which covered the face of our Lord ; the alb, the vesture He was clothed in by Herod ; the cincture, the scourge ordered by Pilate ; the maniple, the rope by which He was led ; the stole, the rope which fastened Him to the pillar ; the chasuble, the purple garment worn before Pilate."

The priest, now bearing the chalice in his hands, proceeds to the altar with the very greatest solemnity of manner. He salutes the altar, ascends its steps, places the chalice upon the corporal cloth in the middle of the altar, and having opened the missal at the Epistle side of the altar, returns to its front bowing, and signing himself with the cross.

The Forty-second Psalm is recited, which is supposed to be most happily applicable here, concluding with the minor doxology. The confession is said, the priest bowing down in complete humility, the breast being struck three times, as reminding him of the essential parts of the Sacrament of Penance—contrition, confession, and satisfaction.

The priest now ascends the altar, the solemn acts of self-preparation being completed, and, praying, kisses

---

Though to Thy sacred mystery
Unworthy I draw nigh,
Yet may I earn the unending bliss
Of Thy bright home on high.

*Ad Casulam.*
Lord Who hast said : " My yoke is sweet,
My burden it is light "—
Make me so bear them that I may
Find favor in Thy sight.

the altar, saying: "We pray thee, O Lord, through the merits of thy saints, whose relics are here present, and of all the saints, that thou wouldst vouchsafe to forgive me all my sins." At Solemn High Mass the altar is here incensed.

The Introit begins, which consists in readings from the Psalms, or some pious composition sanctioned by the Church. The Introit has been defined as a key to the entire Mass, being joyful or sad as the occasion requires.

The Introit finished, the priest, coming to the middle of the altar, recites the Kyrie eleison, with the server, embracing nine separate petitions, which have been traditionally interpreted as referring to the mystical ascension of Christ through the nine choirs of angels. The Kyrie over, the Gloria in Excelsis follows, known as the major doxology, which is not used during Lent, or at requiem or burial services. The *Dominus vobiscum*, or the Lord be with you, having been said, the priest returns to the Epistle corner of the altar, and there extending his hands before him, reads the proper prayers. The collects over, the reading of the Epistle follows, and the priest lays his hands upon the missal-stand, indicative of his obligation not only to read but to do the Law.

After the Epistle the Gradual is sung, consisting of some verses from the Psalms, followed by Alleluias. The sequences, which vary in different seasons, follow; these are, in many instances, of great beauty, amongst which will be recognized by name the famous Stabat Mater and the wonderful Dies Iræ, which, when conjoined with expressive music, thrill and convulse the soul with their grand rhythm, their pathos and religious fervor, mingling at a solemn moment in the progress of the Mass, as the instant of the Divine Presence, to which they serve as prelude, approaches. The priest moves now slowly to the middle of the altar, and, bowing, prays for purity of heart and lip. The missal at this juncture is removed from the Epistle corner of the altar, and borne by the server to the Gospel side, which mystically represents the translation of the Word of God from the Jews to the Gentiles, as the subsequent return of the missal to the Epistle side prefigures to the eye the final acceptance of Christ by the Hebrews.

The reading of the Gospel then takes place, which at Solemn High Mass is accompanied by ceremonies of great solemnity and spectacular interest, and of considerable symbolic significance.

" At Solemn High Mass, where the Gospel is chanted in a loud tone of voice, the ceremonies are imposing and full of deep meaning ; as soon as the celebrant has passed from the middle of the altar, after the *'Munda cor meum,'* to the Gospel side, the deacon receives from the master of ceremonies the book of the Holy Evangels, which he carries to the altar with much reverence, and places in front of the tabernacle, in a horizontal position. He does not return immediately, but remains there to assist the celebrant at the blessing of the incense for the forthcoming procession. The incense having been put in the censer and blessed, the deacon descends one step and recites the prayer, *' Munda cor meum,'* at the conclusion of which he rises from his knees, and, having taken the book from the altar, kneels down with it before the celebrant, and asks the latter to bless him. Having received the blessing, he kisses the celebrant's hand, and then descends to the floor, where he awaits the signal for the procession to move to that part of the Gospel side of the sanctuary where the Holy Evangel is chanted.

A full corps of acolytes, with lighted candles, incense, etc., head the procession, and the deacon, walking immediately behind the subdeacon, moves in a slow and dignified manner, carrying the sacred codex elevated before his face. This is afterward given to the subdeacon, who holds it resting against his forehead during the entire time of chanting. Having given the usual salutation of ' *Dominus vobiscum*,' and announced the title of the Gospel, the deacon receives the thurible, or censer, and incenses the book in three different places—viz., in the center, at the right, and at the left. He then chants the text in a loud tone of voice, and, having finished, receives the censer again and incenses the celebrant at the altar, who stood facing the Gospel the whole time that the deacon was chanting it." *

The sermon succeeds, and, when finished, the Creed is said, the celebrant kneeling at the words, " and was made man." The Offertory, a musical feature sung during the collecting of the offerings of the people, is observed, and is generally of beauty and dignity. The chalice, which has stood on the corporal in the center of the altar, is now uncovered, and the oblation of the Host is made. Wine and water are now received from the server at the Epistle corner of the altar, the mixture being considered typical of the double nature of Christ, as also memorial of the blood and water which gushed from His side. The oblation of the chalice follows; then, having recited the prayer, " Come, O Sanctifier," the priest goes to the Epistle corner and there washes the tips of his fingers—not of all his fingers, but only of the thumb and index finger of each hand, as it is these, and these only, that are allowed to touch the Blessed Sacrament—and the priest, during the ablution,

* *History of the Mass and its Ceremonies*, p. 235, *et seq.* John O'Brien.

recites the Twenty-fifth Psalm, "I will wash my hands among the innocents." Besides the literal reason there is a mystical one, viz., that, in so great an office, the priest's conscience must be free from the slightest taint of sin (O'Brien).

Prayer follows, and the Secret, or silent petitions, are repeated by the priest; the prayers over, the Preface is said, and after more prayers the Canon of the Mass is repeated. A feature of the Mass at this point is to be noticed, viz., the picture, representing our Lord crucified and gazed at in sorrowful contemplation by the three Marys, which is inserted in the missal, for the purpose of fixing the mind of the celebrant upon his sacred office—a striking illustration of the use of sensible means to heighten the realization of the Mass's solemnity. The prayer, *Te igitur*, is recited, the priest bowed forward, and three crosses are made over the elements. Other prayers follow, in which the names of the living and of the dead are mentioned, forming a long list of illustrious saints and of obscure or worthy names. More prayers follow, and finally the Act of Consecration is reached, and the elements, as consecrated, are elevated for adoration. Prayers succeed, and the celebrant, for the first time after the Canon of the Mass was begun, breaks silence with the Lord's Prayer. The paten is wiped, the Host is placed upon it, and a sequence of the Lord's Prayer is used. The elements are mingled, or, at least, a particle of the Host is dropped into the chalice. The Agnus Dei succeeds, then, in order, the Pax, the Communion of the priest and that of the people, Post-communion, and Blessing, while in the end the priest, turning to the altar, reads the last Gospel, the first chapter of St. John's Gospel, "And the Word was made flesh, and dwelt among us," and then, saluting the altar, retires.

We have sketched in its barest outlines the order of the Mass, but we have not attempted to show to what extent it may be enriched by the employment of music and auxiliary functions. The whole religion of Romanism abounds with spectacle, and in its processions, its tableaux, exposures, elevations, fasts, and festivals, presents an accumulated wealth of ceremonialism which becomes finally colossal, and bewilders more than it stimulates the attention of the spectator. Any one who has been at Rome during the seasons of Christmas or Epiphany, Lent or Easter, will recall the variegated wonders of the Roman use, and if they have spent any time in their study, will have been fascinated, or perchance wearied, with the endless intricacies of symbolic interpretation and commemorative allusion involved in these picturesque services.

It is hardly necessary to pursue this subject further ; we have pointed out this interesting fact, that in three representative ceremonial religions, Art, in an unrestricted and composite sense, Symbolism, and Commemoration have been closely combined, and, being more or less united, have penetrated the entire service of each and formed the categorical elements of their structure. These religious practices are essentially ritualistic, and we are justified in drawing the conclusion that so-called ritualism, *alias* ceremonialism, whenever exhibited, involves these and only these same three elements.

# CHAPTER II.

## RITUALISM IN THE RELIGIONS OF THE WORLD.

WE have seen that our definition of ritualism covers three diverse manifestations of its spirit, and we may reasonably conclude that, as far as a definition can express the elusive limits of a general idea, art, symbolism, and commemorative exercises, or the recognition in ceremonies of an historical continuity, form its materials. In three contemporaneous exhibitions of ritualism we have observed the useful combination of these three, and we have also been insensibly tempted to admire their expressive appropriateness.

Having fixed the formative ideas of ritualism as we find it to-day, we will attempt to prove, as the opening essay of our thesis, that ritualism thus defined has shaped the externals of great religions of the world, or has very largely influenced them, and has been associated with, if not indicative of, their mature or final state. Thus ritualism is at least put upon an ethnic basis, and must primarily arrest the respectful attention of the philosopher, while it assumes to the scientific inquirer a possibly new value as representative of an enduring and inexpugnable passion.

Our study of the question will involve a slight examination of the religions of Egypt, India, China, Persia, Arabia, or Mohammedanism, and of Judea, or Judaism, with briefer references to less important religious movements.

The Egyptians were pre-eminently a race given to ceremonies and rituals of an elaborate and intricate character, and by the union of their religion with the state there was produced an involved religio-political cultus which pervaded the country, and elevated the offices of religion and the occupants of the throne to a fictitious eminence.

Wilkinson says :*

" No nation took greater delight in the pomp of ceremonies than the Egyptians, a partiality which the priests did not fail to encourage, as it tended to increase their own consequence, and to give them a great moral ascendancy over all classes. Grand processions constantly took place to commemorate some fanciful legendary event ; the public mind was entertained by the splendor of impressive and striking ceremonies, and a variety of exhibitions connected with religion were repeated, to amuse that lively and restless people."

It is difficult to select, from the numerous festivals and daily rites with which the secular and religious year was crowded, some or one to illustrate the play of the three formative ideas of ritualism without neglecting other significant examples. But it is not difficult to show that these ideas were influential in their ceremonial life. While it cannot be expected that we should describe the religion of Egypt in detail, we can acceptably quote Dr. Clarke's diagnosis of its genius, which is admirable and suggestive. He says:†

"Instead of spirit it accepts body; instead of unity, variety;

---

* *The Ancient Egyptians,* Vol. III., p. 354.
† *Ten Great Religions,* p. 226.

instead of substance, form. It is the physical reaction from Brahmanism. Instead of the worship of abstract Deity, it gives us the most concrete divinity wholly incarnated in space and time. Instead of abstract contemplation, it gives us ceremonial worship. Instead of the absorption of man into God, it gives us transmigration through all bodily forms. It so completely incarnates God as to make every type of animal existence divine, hence the worship of animals. It makes body so sacred that the human body must not be allowed to perish. As the Brahman, contemplating eternity, forgot time, and had no history, so, on the other hand, the Egyptian priest, to whom every moment of time is sacred, records everything and turns every event into history, and as it enshrines the past time historically on monuments, so it takes hold of the future time prophetically through oracles."

The Egyptians worshiped a congregation of gods, and one hundred animals of the world around them; they regarded these latter as dwelling-places of migrating souls, and elevated them to a station bordering upon divinity. Their religion abounded in minute articles of faith, recondite conceptions, and enigmatical speculation; they evolved an obscure philosophy which they saw reflected in nature, and which they illustrated by a precise and rigid symbolism. Science, Art, and Religion were in the hands of the priests, who controlled all learning, along with the rulers of the country, and an esoteric worship of excessive secrecy and exclusiveness was united to a popular theology, the whole linked together by rites and figures, ceremonies, phrases, offices, and pageants.

The artistic or spectacular features of the Egyptian worship were very abundant, both in their liturgies and architecture. The intricate services of the temples were made splendid by processions of robed priests and acolytes. We will select two examples, that of the Procession of Shrines and the ceremonies of their funeral rites, as representative of that element of ritualism we have broadly termed art.

In the Procession of Shrines, the latter were borne on the shoulders of the priests with much pomp, while there were frequently united with them in the exhibition the effigies of the king and his ancestors, and the statue of the principal deity whose worship was celebrated.

Twelve or sixteen priests performed the duty of bearers for each shrine.

"They were accompanied by another, of a superior grade, distinguished by a lock of hair pendent on one side of his head, and clad in a leopard-skin, the peculiar badge of his rank, who, walking near them, gave directions respecting the procession, its position in the temple, and whatever else was required during the ceremony."[*]

Upon reaching the temple every demonstration of respect announced the arrival of the shrine, and the king, if present, performed appropriate ceremonies in its honor.

"These consisted of sacrifices and prayers, and the shrine was decked with fresh-gathered flowers and rich garlands. An endless profusion of offerings was placed before it on several separate altars, and the king, frequently accompanied by his queen, who held a sistrum in one hand, and in the other a bouquet of flowers made up in the particular form required for these religious ceremonies, presented incense and libation."[†]

Further ceremonies and ceremonial adjuncts were

[*] *The Ancient Egyptians*, Vol. III., p. 355.
[†] *Ibid.*, p. 357.

associated in this service, in which decoration and an effective artistic arrangement were permitted a natural, if not an exaggerated, influence. If we examine the ceremonial of burial, we shall find that it was based upon an almost dramatic representation of the supposed experiences undergone by the soul in its passage to the life beyond the grave. These funeral rites varied with the degree of prominence assigned to the dead person, and were naturally most sumptuous and prolonged in the case of the king ; but a famous instance, known as the funeral procession of a royal scribe, delineated in the inscriptions at Thebes, will fully serve our purpose.

In the procession, after the solemn liturgies had been read in the temple, the servants came first, carrying tables covered with fruit, cakes, flowers, vases of ointment, wine, and other liquids, with geese and a calf for sacrifice, chairs and wooden tablets, napkins, etc. Then followed the mummies, or embalmed body of the deceased, with those of his ancestors, and images of the gods ; attendants succeeded, bearing various articles of use belonging to the scribe, also ornaments, possessions, and a multitude of trivial trinkets.

" To these succeeded the bearers of a sacred boat, and the mysterious eye of Shu or Horus, as god of stability, so common on funeral monuments. . . . Others carried the well-known small images of blue pottery, representing the deceased under the form of Osiris, and the bird, emblematic of the soul." *

Behind these came other attendants, bearing the material for offerings and libations, and yet others followed,

* *The Ancient Egyptians*, Vol. III., p. 444.

simulating woe with extravagant gestures and wailings.
The hearse, placed in a consecrated boat, succeeded,
drawn upon a sledge.   Arriving at the lake, across
whose sacred waters the mummy was to be floated to
the solemn abodes upon the opposite shores, a singular
and impressive trial took place, wherein, before forty-
two assessors or judges, the life of the deceased was
reviewed, and the eulogies of friends permitted to mingle with the accusations of enemies, in this curious pre-
judgment of the dead, typical of its ordeal before it
entered the regions of the blessed.

Diodorus, as quoted by Wilkinson, says: *

" Forty-two judges having been summoned and placed in a semi-
circle near the banks of the lake, a boat was brought up, provided
expressly for the occasion, under the direction of a boatman, called,
in the Egyptian language, *Charon.*"   " When the boat was ready
for the reception of the coffin, it was lawful for any person who
thought proper to bring forward his accusation against the deceased.   These forty-two assessors represented the forty-two crimes
a virtuous man sought to be free from when judged in a future
state, and prefigured accusing spirits.   If it could be proved that
he had led an evil life, the judges declared accordingly, and the
body was deprived of the accustomed sepulture ; but if the accuser
failed to establish what he advanced, he was subject to the heaviest
penalties.   When there was no accuser, or when the accusation
had been disproved, the relations ceased from their lamentations
and pronounced encomiums on the deceased."

Then the retinue of boats moved slowly across the
waters, a remarkable spectacle, as though the unseen
motion of the soul across the void beyond life was
typified in this august procession.   When the flotilla
had crossed the lake, the procession advanced to the

* *The Ancient Egyptians,* Vol. III., p. 453, *et seq.*

catacombs, the mummy taken from the sarcophagus was entombed, and the prolonged ceremonial was ended.

In the construction of their temples the Egyptians evinced the art influence of ritualistic notions; their solemn grandeur, their long approaches, the holy precincts about their altars, the distinctions of sanctity in different parts, all harmonize with those intentions of awakening reverence and a sense of the Divine Presence by which art, under ritualistic influences, is dominated.

If, again, we search the Egyptian ritual for symbolism, we shall find it intricate and pervasive; in fact, a religion so unusually intermixed with a complex natural philosophy must of necessity display an elaborate system of signs, and as all ritualistic observance springs primarily from an expression of ideas in forms, no more fertile field for symbolic growth could be devised than in Egypt. In the ceremonies of coronation the sacred sign of the *Tau* was presented to the king as a symbol of life and a prognostication of a long and glorious reign. A falchion delivered into his hand, upon expeditions abroad, indicated the defeat and conquest of all enemies. The scepter of purity was used in ceremonies, and placed in the hands of the gods as an emblem of virtue, without which life was vain. Upon the shrines and in the sacred boats or arks were delineated or placed the emblems of life and stability, and the sacred beetle of the sun, between two figures of the goddess Ma or Truth, and overshadowed by their wings, was also used to excite by its symbolic union ideas of reverence and holy aspiration. The priests approached their gods with gestures of respect, and knelt before them in

attitudes expressive of adoration.   In the anointing of
the king he received the emblems of majesty from the
gods, in token of his regal and godlike estate.   The
lotus-plant figured in their ceremonials and on their
sculptures.   It was typical of the sun, "which," as Pro-
clus says (Wilkinson), "it appeared to honor by the expansion and contraction of its leaves."   The ivy (?) was
the plant of Osiris, because it retained its leaves, and its
ever-green nature made it a token of perennial youth
and constancy.   In connection with vows, emblematic
offerings were made, among which figured a miniature
of Truth, the cynocephalus, which was the type of the
god of letters, and of the moon, the cow of Athor, the
Egyptian Venus, ointment, gold and silver, parts of
dress, etc.   The forty-two assessors of the dead signified the forty-two crimes which the virtuous hoped to
escape, and kept the minds of the spectators keenly
sensible of those faults whose personifications they beheld standing in the way of the soul's approach to Paradise, holding their watchful and envious guard over the
precincts of the happy.   The image or idol of Osiris
was clothed in white, for, as Plutarch says, "Osiris is
the First Principle, prior to all beings, and purely intelligent ; he must ever remain unmixed and undefiled."
The vestments of Isis were of every hue, as she was
concerned with the manifestations of material life, and
hence reflected in her multicolored garniture the diversity of nature.   The religious festivals were indicative
of special attributes of the deities in whose honor they
were held.   The Eleusinian Mysteries were associated
with every variety of recondite and fanciful imagery,

and an almost grotesque excess of symbolism; in fact, everywhere we encounter in the study of Egyptian worship a labyrinth of figurative uses. It is hardly necessary to press this point farther. The ritual of the Egyptians illustrated the principles of art and symbolism.

The third element of ritualistic observance is that of historical recording or pictorial presentation of events desirable to remember, in the estimation of the believers. This point needs scarcely any explicit treatment. The whole theory of the religious year in Egypt was to perpetuate their system of creeds by a stereotyped succession of feasts, fasts, and services, whereby every detail of its lengthy and obscure mythology and philosophy might be illustrated.

James Freeman Clarke says:*

" There were more festivals in Egypt than among any other ancient people, the Greeks not excepted. Every month and day was governed by a god. There were two feasts of the New Year, twelve of the first days of the months, one of the rising of the dogstar (Sirius, called Sothis), and others to the great gods, to seedtime and harvest, to the rise and fall of the Nile. The Feast of Lamps at Sais was in honor of Neith, and was kept throughout Egypt. The Feast of the Death of Osiris, the feast of his resurrection (when people called ' We have found him! Good luck!'), feasts of Isis (one of which lasted four days), the great Feast of Bubastis, greatest of all—these were festivals belonging to all Egypt."

In such festivals the things commemorated were figured by allegorical devices, as at the *fête* of Isis, when cakes, having a hippopotamus bound stamped upon

---

* *Ten Great Religions*, p. 216.

3

them, were used to recall her victory over Typho. Again, in the Osiris rites,* " it was customary to throw a cord in the midst of the assembly, and then chop it into pieces; the supposed purport of which was to record the desertion of Thoneris, the concubine of Typho, and her delivery from a serpent, which the soldiers killed with their swords as it pursued her in her flight to join the army of Horus." At the celebration of the death of Osiris, the priests of Isis carried branches of absinthium, and dogs headed the procession, to recall the recovery of his body. Again, the first fruits of the fields were offered at the festival of Isis in the harvest-time, which also referred to Osiris as the " beneficent property of the Nile." It is useless to linger longer in illustrating an almost obvious proposition. The ritual of the Egyptians, which was unmistakably a ritual of an elaborate and almost exorbitant character, displays markedly the signs we have indicated as inseparable from ritual in the abstract, viz., art, symbolism, and commemorative illustration.

Let us now turn to the ritual of a religion which presented in its philosophy and psychological development great contrasts to the multitudinous materializations of Egypt. We refer to Brahmanism and Buddhism. " In India," says Dr. Clarke,† " the whole tendency of thought is ideal, the whole religion a pure spiritualism. An ultra, one-sided idealism is the central tendency of the Hindoo mind. The god of Brahmanism is an intelligence, absorbed in the rest of profound contempla-

---

* *The Ancient Egyptians*, Vol. III., p. 376.
† *Ten Great Religions*, p. 83.

tion. The good man of this religion is he who withdraws from an evil world into abstract thought." But Brahmanism did not retain this mystical and contemplative cast ; it became degraded, or at least lowered, by the absorption of innumerable objects in its lists of adorable things, which, as the forms of a divine spirit which pervaded all creation, converted it into a pantheistic polytheism, supplying its devotees with innumerable concrete symbols which they finally worshiped. Or, as Professor Eggeling says, it was * "a worship of the grand and striking phenomena of nature, regarded in the light of personal, conscious beings, endowed with a power beyond the control of man, though not insensible to his praises and actions. It is a nature worship purer than that met with in any other polytheistic form of belief we are acquainted with—a mythology still comparatively little affected by those systematizing tendencies which, in a less simple and primitive state of thought, lead to the construction of a well-ordered pantheon and a regular organization of divine government."

A thin and attenuated religious system at its inception, it became a diversely varied hierarchical expression at its close. This change was inevitable, and in full accordance with the necessary evolution of ritualistic notions. We cannot stop here to anticipate our description of this evolution, nor to attempt to reconcile our belief in it with the well-attested fact of its apparently pernicious influence in India as elsewhere. Enough now to say that when Brahmanism reached a

---

* *Encyclopedia Britannica*, article on Brahmanism.

permanent state of equilibrium it had erected a somewhat intricate though not sumptuous ritual, in which art, symbolism, and pictorial illustration were more or less mingled.

Their art blossomed under the impulse of ritualistic tendencies, and wonderfully conceived temples, abounding in excessive decorative designs, were erected. We can only briefly refer to these architectural marvels. M. Grandidier, in his *Voyage dans les Provinces Méridionale de l'Inde*, describes many of the temples, pagodas, and gopurams—tall pyramidal towers, affording an entrance to the sacred enclosures where the altars, idols, shrines, and ponds are placed. The approaches to the temples are elaborately garnished with sculpture, carvings, etc., though the sanctuaries are plain and dreary, an anomaly itself explained by a poetic thought existing in the Indian mind, that the faithful did not dare to touch the holy residence of their divinity, and they elevated around it vast edifices, burdened with ornament and elaborate sculpture and imagery, as an impressive architectural prelude to the majesty of the unveiled god.

Amongst the numerous descriptions M. Grandidier has given of these extraordinary structures, he says, of the Temple of Madura:

" It is without doubt the most admirable and the most curious monument that the Hindoo genius has ever executed. I do not know in all my travels to have ever experienced an impression similar to that which I received whilst walking through the midst of the marvels of this *chef-d'œuvre* of the national architecture. As soon as one enters the sacred inclosure the eye is struck by the innumerable number of columns laden with *bizarre* and original sculpture, which start up in all directions. One passes from court to court, from gallery to gallery, from portico to portico, and everywhere discovers bas-reliefs and paintings. The obscurity of certain avenues of stone only adds to the effect produced by this multitude of monsters, which seem to emerge from the columns whence the Indian artist has summoned them to strike with terror the superstitious spirit of the devout. The general view is grandiose, and produces a profound impression upon the spirit of the visitor. It is not a special study of each statue that a temple of this character requires; it is necessary to content one's self with casting a glance over the whole; it is necessary to move rapidly in the midst of these chimeras, monsters of all sorts; of these beings *bizarre* in form, cruel in countenance, grotesque in pose; one would imagine himself under the power of a fantastic dream."

The temple of Srī-rangam is approached upon two sides, through an avenue of gopurams intricately ornamented with involved lines, and intermingled and crowded figures. Six inclosures surround the sanctuary of the god Vishnu, and residences are provided for Hindoos of a low caste, for Brahmans, and for Vishnu priests. The whole is a famous and extraordinary work, presenting a spectacle of singular novelty and unique beauty. M. Grandidier has borne eloquent testimony to the wonderful exuberance of the Hindoo imagination in the Brahma temples, where all the elements and objects of worship involved in the fable, poetry, and history of their faith are multitudinously mingled and recorded upon a prodigious scale.

Monier Williams mentions with admiration the Siva temple at Madura, and says, of the Siva temple at Trichinopoly : " No one could fail to be impressed with its beautiful colonnades, cloisters, and thousand-pillared Mandapa ;"* while of another he writes, " No

* *Religious Thought and Life in India*, Part I., p. 444.

sight is to be seen in any part of India that can at all
compare with the unique effect produced by its series of
seven quadrangular inclosures formed by seven squares
of massive walls, one within the other; every square
pierced by four lofty gateways, and each gateway surmounted by pyramidal towers, rivaling in altitude the
adjacent rock of Trichinopoly." * Fabulous sums have ·
been expended in its erection, and all classes of society have poured into its treasury contributions that
in the aggregate amount to millions of rupees. " The
idea is that each investing square of walls shall form
courts of increasing sanctity, which shall conduct the
worshiper by regular gradations to a central holy of
holies of unique shape and proportions. In fact, the
entire fabric of shrines, edifices, towers, and inclosures
is supposed to be a terrestrial counterpart of Vishnu's
heaven, to which his votaries are destined to be trans-
ported" (*idem*). The idol which is thus magnificently
enshrined is supposed to be immovable, but its porta-
ble substitute, which is taken out in religious processions, is sumptuously bedecked and incrusted with
precious stones of great worth, and has a marvelous
value.

The mind is appealed to in the ceremonies equally
through the senses, and decoration, motion, and a progressive order of liturgy compose them. That symbolism, and a pictorial or mnemonic representation of
events in their religion is united to these artistic tendencies is shown by these extracts from Eggeling : †

---

* *Religious Thought and Life in India*, Part I., p. 448.
† *Encyclopedia Britannica*, article on Brahmanism.

" The first three castes . . . are yet united by a common bond of sacramental rites (*sanskaras*) *traditionally connected from ancient times with certain incidents and stages in the life of the Aryan Hindoo*, as conception, birth, name-giving, the first taking out of the child to see the sun, the first feeding with boiled rice, the rites of tonsure and hair cutting, the youth's investiture with the sacrificial thread, and his return home on completing his studies, marriage, funeral," etc. Investiture with the sacred cord was an important event in the youth's life, it " being ·the preliminary act to the youth's initiation into the study of the Veda, the management of the consecrated fire, and the knowledge of the rites of purification, including the *savitu*, a solemn invocation to *savitu*, the sun, which has to be repeated every morning and evening, before the rise and after the setting of that luminary," and " is supposed to constitute the second or spiritual birth of the Arya. The *srauta* rites were expensive sacrificial rites connected with other ceremonies on the days of the new and full moon, the oblation at the commencement of the three seasons, the offerings of first fruits," etc. Very much more might be quoted, and evidence adduced to show that in its latest, and also comparatively earlier phases, Brahmanism had fully assumed the three marks of ritualistic life, art or decoration, symbolism, and commemorative services.

Monier Williams's book contains the more modern and most interesting contributions to this subject, and a few further illustrations will be pardoned on account of their intrinsic value in this connection. Describing

a festival, held in honor of Mīnākshī, called the oil festival, he says :

" A coarse image of the goddess, profusely decorated with jewels,
and having a high head-dress of hair, was carried in the center of
a long procession, on a canopied throne borne by eight Brahmans,
to a platform in the magnificent hall or mandapa of the Tirumell
Nāyak, opposite the temple. There the ceremony of undressing the
idol, removing its ornaments, anointing its head with oil, bathing,
re-decorating and re-dressing it was gone through amid shouting,
singing, beating of tom-toms, waving of lights and cowries, ringing
of bells, and deafening discord from forty or fifty so-called musical
instruments, each played by a man who did his best to overpower
the sound of all the others combined. At the head of the procession was borne an image of Ganesa. Then followed three elephants,
a long line of priests, musicians, attendants bearing cowries and
umbrellas, with a troop of dancing-girls bringing up the rear."

At the time of the annual festival at Srī-rangam, the
author says:

" This is the one day in the year on which the gate is opened,
and, on the occasion of my visit, the opening took place at four
o'clock in the morning. First the idol—bedecked and bejeweled
to the full— was borne through the narrow portal, followed by
eighteen images of Vaishnava saints and devotees ; then came innumerable priests chanting Vedic hymns, and repeating the thousand names of Vishnu ; then dancing-girls and bands of musicians
—the invariable attendants upon idol-shrines in the south of India.
Finally, a vast throng—probably fifty thousand persons—crowded
for hours through the contracted passage."

An attractive instance of symbolism is pointed out in
the famous temple of Srī-rangam at Trichinopoly :

" On the summit of the shrine were placed four pinnacles to de-
note the four Vedas, and around it were constructed seven walls
built in squares, one within the other, and forming seven quadrangular courts, figuring the seven divisions or degrees of bliss in
Vishnu's heaven."

In the intricate liturgical rites of the Brahmans, symbolism and commemorative exercises are profusely employed, but it is difficult with any detail to show this on account of the number and variety of their services, and it is often far from edifying on account of their repulsive and absurd character.

Perhaps a paragraph and some general examples from Monier Williams * will suffice :

" No country upon earth rejoices in a longer list of holidays, festivals, and seasons of rejoicing, qualified by fasts, vigils, and seasons of mortification, than India. Most of these fasts and festivals are fixed to take place on certain lunar days, each lunation, or period of rather more than twenty-seven solar days, being divided into thirty of these lunar days, fifteen of which, during the moon's increase, constitute the light half of the month, and the other fifteen the dark half. Some festivals, however, are regulated by the supposed motions of the sun."

Fasts are kept in honor of Vishnu. " The Saivas usually fast on the thirteenth or fourteenth day of the dark half of every month, on the day and night called ' Siva's night.' " Other festivals are *Sankrāut*, celebrating the sun's return north ; a spring festival, when, at Bengal, the goddess of arts is worshiped ; the *Hoti*, commemorative of the boyhood of Krishna ; Rama festivals, when his temples are illuminated and the Rāmāyana is read ; Dīvālī, or Feast of Lamps, in honor of Vishnu's wife ; the " nine nights," celebrating the victory of the wife of Siva over a buffalo-headed demon. Every day of the week has a sacred character, and the whole texture of the life of the more pious responds, sometimes in a beautiful, more generally in an incon-

* *Religious Thought and Life in India.*

3*

gruous and superstitious fashion, to the elemental promptings of ritualistic tendencies.

Buddhism has been, perhaps justly, termed the Protestantism of the East, inasmuch as the pure teachings of Gautama were a revolt against "a system of sacramental salvation in the hands of a sacred order," and was "a doctrine of individual salvation based on personal character." It was a religion in which self-subjection assumed a predominant position as the only possible prelude to the attainment of intellectual and emotional self-annihilation, or the adorable state of *Nirvana*, and would seem to be quite unconnected with ritualism as an essential accessory in its growth and propagation. As long as Buddha lived, his faith maintained the form of an exalted asceticism, practical benevolence, and mystical rhapsody, but at his death it rapidly appropriated the distinguishing features of ritualistic services. It followed an inevitable course of ceremonial change, until it presented the extraordinary spectacle of Lamaism in Thibet, which, as T. W. Rhys Davids says: * "with its shaven priests, its bells and rosaries, its images and holy water, its pope and bishops, its abbots and monks of many grades, its processions and feast days, its confessional and purgatory, and its worship of the double virgin, so strongly resembles Romanism that the first (Roman) Catholic missionaries thought it must be an imitation by the devil of the religion of Christ." †

---

* *Encyclopedia Britannica*, article on Buddhism.

† An able article in the October number, 1885, of *The Catholic World*, shows that the ecclesiastical organization of Lamaism was derived from the Nestorians.

In Ceylon, Buddhism presents a less corrupted aspect, but this description from Grandidier * fully exemplifies ritualistic ideas, though more pleasingly exhibited in a simplified and effective ceremonial :

" The Cingalese never enter their temples unless with offerings of flowers, rice, cloth, or some piece of money. The hands joined and raised to the level of the forehead, the faithful place their offering upon the altar at the feet of Buddha, invoking the *Sadlm*, the good and kind master, and after putting themselves under his protection confess the *Bana*, commending themselves to the clergy. The offerings offered, the people kneel, and the priest in the midst of his assistants, standing, recites in a clear voice the responsibilities of religion, which the assembly repeat after him sentence by sentence."

"At the new and full moon the Buddhists come to the temple, bringing their present, and they listen to the reading of the words of Buddha, or the expounding of his doctrines ; one part of the day should be consecrated to religious meditations. The monks have the head shaven and uncovered. They have three robes of a yellow color (consecrated to Ceylon), the *sanghati*, the *outtava sangha*, and the *antara masako;* these robes are simple pieces of cloth with which they encircle the body, leaving naked the shoulder and the right arm. . . . It is a vestment august and elegant."

In China, the worship of Kwan-yin is the prevalent form of Buddhism, and while it seems probable that a number of secondary influences, some Christian, have brought about its present liturgical character, it certainly presents a ritualistic elaboration rather remarkable.

" In arranging the temple, the image of Buddha is to be placed on an altar on the south side of the building. The figure of Kwan-yin must be put on an altar in the west of the building. This may be either one with ten arms or six or four or two [the

---

* *Voyage dans les Provinces Méridionales de l'Inde.*

arms represent the number of faces which, in the first place, were intended to represent the all-looking character of this being, but the phrase being perverted to a literal sense was symbolized by the actual number of arms and hands, which appear so gross and offensive in connection with this idolatry].   On the day appointed for the recitation of the service, in the morning early, the sacred precinct within which the worshipers are to say the words is to be defined.   This is done by the use of a marked line made with a knife and accompanied by the repetition of certain words.   Then pure water is sprinkled toward each quarter, *i.e.*, at each corner of the precinct, then clean incense dust is sprinkled on the floor, and afterwards a silken cord composed of threads of five colors is passed round the limits of the sanctuary, and the usual words repeated.

" This having been done, the adjuncts of worship are arranged— lamps, incense, flowers, banners, and offerings of food.   The incense is to be made of the finest sandal-wood dust of the purest kind.   Then mats for kneeling or stools for the same purpose are to be arranged.   The hours are thrice in the morning, and thrice in the evening (afternoon)." *

Personal cleanliness, avoidance of mixed conversation, an intent mind fixed on the " ten obligations," are previous requirements.   Great decorum in the service is insisted on.   A procession enters, and all heads are bowed while a general prayer is uttered.   The altar is invested three times, and, standing, the worshipers think upon their objects of worship.   A hymn of incense follows, then an invocation is repeated three times, then a chant with bowing, another, all kneeling and holding in their hands flowers and incense.   The congregation then light the incense, and scatter flowers, and repeat a sort of hymn of dedication; the priest then bows and the people meditate; then a chant, and

---

* *Buddhism in China*, p. 145, *et seq*.   Rev. S. Beal, 1884.

the service "proceeds in this way, with similar invocations to other objects of worship and similar reflections," with readings of the sacred words, which are "supposed to have a magical effect, and bring deliverance by their inherent virtue." Here we find a use of objects to arouse and fix the thoughts, or the art idea evolved, while symbolism and commemoration combine to enrich and dignify the ceremonies, the former markedly, the latter less apparently, except in the hours and days of worship which have probably some memorial significance.

Again, the rock temples, as the celebrated Caves of Ellora, were distinctive illustrations of an art principle embodied in Buddhistic worship. The triple features of ritualistic service are plainly seen in these descriptions, and it is not necessary to insist upon their specific forms. In all ritual, and in some perchance more than in others, these elements blend, and, while easily recognizable, are not so easily separated. We find, then, in the current form of Buddhism, its stable and present condition, art or decorative methods, symbolism, and commemorative service.

The doctrines of Confucius, the philosopher and sage of China, are certainly, in themselves, quite free from any ceremonial tendencies; indeed, they do not deal with man's destiny, the problems of sin, salvation, and immortality, or involve the functions of worship at all. They are a code of morals, proper sentiments, and expedient rules of conduct, based for the most part upon a reverence for the past, obedience to authority, and veneration for parents and ancestors, and a true desire to secure general happiness, and to establish virtue. After Confucius, whose mind seemed to have been of a practical and unimaginative cast, had died, a fusion of his moral code with the recondite, supernatural, and pietistic teachings of Lao-tse took place, though the Confucian precepts took precedence completely, and after modification by Choo-tsze dominated Chinese thought. The assumption of forms or ritual elements in this religion, unassisted by any inherent sacramental character in the religion, or any imaginative or spiritual insight amongst the Chinese themselves, was probably uncertain and slow, yet to-day they are apparent, and, in connection with funeral services, reach an extraordinary degree of pageantry. A multiplication of objects of worship and a certain play of symbolic imagery, combined with a liturgical law for the observance of rites, given by Confucius, has made the ritualistic idea very prominent, even in China.

Sacrifices are .made in the temples, when the emperor frequently officiates as a high-priest, and mandarins as his servers. The heavens, earth, sun, and moon are worshiped. In the worship of the heavens, at winter solstice, the high-priest is clad in silken robes of blue; in the worship of the earth, at summer solstice, his vestments are saffron-colored; he celebrates the adoration of the sun in crimson robes, and that of the moon in robes cream-white in color. Animals are offered in the sacrifices. The altars of heaven are round; those dedicated to the earth are square; fasts precede the sacrifices, and in worship prostrations are frequent. A semi-sacerdotal character pertains to the emperor, as unauthorized persons who use his ritual are punished.

A strange pantheon succeeds these elementary objects of worship, which must, from the varying characteristics of each object worshiped, lead to symbolic and pictorial design in their ceremonies. These persons and things are the Lord of Heaven, Confucius, patron of silk manufacture, patron of agriculture, patron of medicine, spirits of scholars and statesmen, gods of the earth and its produce, gods of heaven, earth, and the passing year, mountains, seas, hills, rivers, banners, and trophies.* The art instinct, with its varied utilization of symbol and embellishment, and historical portraiture, appears in their temples, where beautiful mosaics, bronzes, and tapestries compose and decorate the walls.

A description from Pumpelly will also convey an idea of the solemn and impressive beauty of the Temple of Heaven at Peking:†

" And now the great temple rises before us. There, high above the trees, is the azure triple roof, brilliant as a sapphire in the sunlight. The structure stands upon three terraced stages, each one ten feet high, respectively one hundred and twenty, ninety, and sixty feet in diameter. The form of these terraces is polygonal, and each one is surrounded by a balustrade ; on them stand many large and beautiful bronze vases for burning incense. The whole is built of pure white marble, highly sculptured, and covered with bas-reliefs representing the dragons and other animals of the early Chinese mythology. From each four points of the compass the terraces are ascended by broad inclined planes constructed with massive and

---

* *China, Historical and Descriptive.*  R. Sears.
† *Across America and Asia,* p. 275.

sculptured slabs of marble. Upon this really grand substructure
stands the temple, a large circular building painted vermilion, and
pierced with lofty windows. These openings are curtained with
rolling screens made of rods of blue glass, which shut out all view
of the interior. Over the main entrance is a tablet inscribed with
the name of Shangte, the Most High Ruler.

" A broad causeway leading southward and passing through an
arched gateway in a high red building, and under several elaborate
arches, connects the temple with the altar to heaven. This, like
the terraced substructure of the temple, is built of white marble,
and has also three terraced stages, the upper one of which, judging
from memory, is more than a hundred feet in diameter. It is covered with richly sculptured figures of mythical animals, while the
terraces are decorated with large incense vases of bronze, whose
dark color and graceful outlines stand in beautiful relief against the
white marble background. In the middle of the top platform three
altars or small tripod tables are ranged in a line from east to west,
while on one side a large iron basket seems intended for use in
offering burnt sacrifices. On the south side stands a sacred gateway, also of white marble. There can be but one Temple of
Heaven, and the emperor, the high-priest—Son of Heaven—alone
has the right to worship Shangte.

" I never entered this spot without being impressed with a feeling akin to awe, or, rather, with the sentiment which ever attaches
to the contemplation of those things which bear the stamp of great
antiquity, and are hidden behind the veil of mystery."

Quoting Dr. Williams,* we have this description of a
service wherein all the four elements of ritualistic ceremonial are blended, art, symbolism, and commemoration :

" The winter solstice is the great day of this state worship. The
emperor goes from his palace the evening before, drawn by an ele-
phant, in his state car, and escorted by about two thousand gran-
dees, princes, musicians, and attendants, down to the Temple of
Heaven. The *cortége* passes out by the southern road, reaching

---

* *The Middle Kingdom*, Vol. II., p. 196.

the Ching Yang Gate, opened only for his majesty's use, and through it goes on two miles to the *Trien Tan.* He first repairs to the *Chai Kung,* or Palace of Fasting, where he prepares himself by lonely meditation for his duty, ' for the idea is, that if there be not pious thoughts in his mind the spirits of the unseen will not come to the sacrifice.' To assist him he looks at a copper statue arrayed like Taoist priest, whose mouth is covered by three fingers, denoting silence, while the other hand bears a tablet inscribed with ' Fast three days.' When the worship commences, and all the officiating attendants are in their places, the animals are killed, and as the odor of their burning flesh ascends to convey the sacrifice to the gods, the emperor begins the rite, and is directed at every step by the master of ceremonies. The worship to heaven is at midnight, and the numerous poles around the great altar, and the fires in the furnaces, shedding their glare over the marble terraces and richly dressed assembly, render this solemnity most striking."

The worship of ancestors dominates the religious mind of China, and its ceremonial devices are expressive and interesting. We again appeal to Dr. Williams : *

"The hall of ancestors is found in the house of almost every member of the family, but always in that of the eldest son. In rich families it is a separate building ; in others a room set apart for the purpose, and in many a mere shelf or shrine. . . . In the first part of April, one hundred and six days after the winter solstice, during the term called *tsing-ming,* a general worship of ancestors is observed. In Kwangtung this is commonly called *pai shan,* or 'worshiping on the hills,' but the general term is *siu fânti,* or 'sweeping the tombs.' The whole population, men, women, and children, repair to their family tombs, carrying a tray containing the sacrifice, libations for offering, and candles, paper, and incense for burning, and there go through a variety of ceremonies and prayers. The grave is at this season repaired and swept, and at the close of the service three pieces of turf are placed at the back and front of the grave to retain long strips of red and white paper ; this indicates that the accustomed rites have been performed, and these fugitive testimonials remain fluttering in the wind long enough to announce it to all the friends as well as enemies of the family; for when a grave has been neglected three years it is sometimes dug over and the land resold."

In regard to the general presence of the ritualistic element of symbolism, Dr. Williams bears the following testimony : *

" The symbolism of the Chinese has not attracted the notice of foreign writers as much as it deserves. It meets us everywhere—on plates and crockery, on carpets, rugs, vases, wall pictures, shop signs, and visiting-cards."

Turning now to the forms of a most ancient and majestic faith, that of Persia, or Zoroasterism, we encounter again the recurrent marks of ritualistic service repeated in lines of strength and beauty. The religion of Darius and Xerxes, whose prophet was Zoroaster, and whose Bible is the Zend-Avesta, was a sublime doctrine of dualism, an enunciation, charged with poetry and philosophic insight, of the tremendous and eternal conflict between the powers of good and the principalities of evil—between Ormuzd and Ahriman. This faith exercises a strong fascination upon Christian minds, for its underlying precept harmonizes with their profound realization of the disaster of sin, its activity, and its corroding power. Neither was it, at least in its primitive form, a system of idolatry, though it encircled life with warring legions and taught an intricate mythology. At first the Persian religion was of a very simple character in the main, monotheistic, and absolutely free of any

---

* *The Middle Kingdom*, Vol. II., p. III.

idolatrous tendencies. Rawlinson says of it : * "In these early times it was doubtless that enjoined by the Zend-Avesta, comprising prayer and thanksgiving to Ormuzd and the good spirits of his creation, the recitation of Gathas or hymns, the performance of sacrifice, and participation in the Soma ceremony." This very early ceremony, which possessed such a powerful attraction for the Aryan races, is thus described by Rawlinson : † "The Soma or Homa ceremony consisted in the extraction of the juice of the Homa plant by the priests during the recitation of prayers, the formal presentation of the liquid extracted to the sacrificial fire, the consumption of a small portion of it by one of the officiating priests, and the division of the remainder among the worshipers. As the juice was drunk immediately after extraction and before fermentation had set in, it was not intoxicating. The ceremony seems to have been regarded in part as having a mystic force securing the favor of heaven, in part as exerting a beneficial influence upon the body of the worshiper." Worship seems to have been conducted in temples at this early period, and simple altars received the sacrificial offerings. Symbolism prevailed in a restricted though adequate degree, and was rapidly adopted when acquaintance with Assyria brought it more fully within the range of their choice and appreciation. ‡

---

* *Ancient Monarchies.*

† *Ibid.*

‡ Symbolism could not fail to reach fair proportions in a faith which professed such opinions as these : " Whatever is on earth is the resemblance and shadow of something that is in the sphere. While that resplendent thing remaineth in good condition it is well also with its

The three elements of ritualistic usage in religious observances are seen here, though not highly developed, and more strongly suggested, as we have little knowledge as to the exact practices of their worship. But the Persian worship passed from this earliest phase of monotheism, through a dualistic stage, verging upon polytheism, in which numerous powers, angels, and spirits, personifying principles, conditions, virtues, and vices, were worshiped. Then it came under the influence of Magism, as the Persians came in contact with the Scythic races. The Magi worshiped the objects of nature. Their fire-altars burned perpetually, and on the lonely summit of stony hills disclosed their quenchless flames to the unchanging skies. Water was reverenced by them, and lakes, fountains, and rivers received a sacred character, and were offered sacrifices uncontaminated by any defilement of blood or dirt. The earth claimed and received their adoration. "The Magian religion," says Rawlinson,* "was of a highly sacerdotal type. No worshiper could perform any religious act, except by the intervention of a priest, or Magus, who stood between him and the divinity as a mediator. The Magus prepared the victim, and slew it, chanted the mystic strain which gave the sacrifice all its force, poured on the ground the propitiatory libation of oil, milk, and honey, held the bundle of thin tamarack twigs

shadow. When that resplendent object removeth far from its shadow, life fadeth away. Again, that resplendent thing is the shadow of a light more resplendent than itself."—*Ker Porter*, extracted from the *Desatri*, a work of the old Pehlevi.

* *Ancient Monarchies.*

—the Zendic-barsom—the employment of which was essential to every sacrificial ceremony." "Clad in white robes," he continues, "and bearing upon their heads tall felt caps with long lappets at the sides, which concealed the jaw, and even the lips, each with his *barsom* in his hand, they marched in procession to their pyrœtheia, or fire-altars, and, standing around them, performed, for an hour at a time, their magical incantations."

When the Persians encountered this alien body of faith and practice, a conflict arose between rival systems, but the Magian practice impressed itself upon the Persian practice, and, aided by the invincible tendency of human nature in its imaginative and devotional moods, when awakened by impressive ceremonies, which the fierce and iconoclastic Persians could not repress, the Magian cult largely modified and enriched Persian ritual, though to the detriment of its purity of faith, as happened almost universally in early ages in such instances.

We hence discern, even in the primitive form of the Persian religion, the utilization of ceremony, although the three principles of ritualistic worship do not assume distinctive prominence in it; they are, however, rapidly introduced, and become active in its intermediate and later phases. Amongst modern Parsees, those of Bombay afford an instructive and suggestive illustration of religious methods. They worship the sun, as the symbol of the Supreme God, and their altar-fires are kept constantly kindled in their temples. The fire is carefully placed upon a silver netting, where it is fed with sandalwood. This fire is the fire of Behran, and claims an especial sanctity, lit, as they are supposed to be, from the burning oil-wells upon the borders of the Caspian Sea, which it is averred have never been extinguished. There are only three temples where these sacred flames are kindled. The other fire, that of Adaran, is more common, and is held in less veneration. The Parsees are not distinguished at Bombay very markedly from the Hindoos; they wear a white robe and white pantaloons, to which is added a fine shawl, in their ceremonies.

Their ceremonial year, which is a commemorative feature, comprises, amongst others, the following festivals: that of Nauroz, or the day of the New Year, when prayers are made in the temples, friends are visited, and the Sassanide king, Yazdijud, is remembered; a second festival is that of the tutelary angel of the month of Faronardine, celebrated on the nineteenth of that month; a third is the Ardibihisht, or festival of the angel holding the keys of Paradise; a fourth is the Khourdad-Sâl, the birthday of Zoroaster; a fifth, that of Nauroz-i-Jamshid, the Parsee carnival, celebrated at the equinox; the sixth is the festival of the dead, at the end of each year, when the faithful offer up their prayers before a pile of metallic vases filled with water, the water being regarded as a symbol of the pure souls in heaven.

The pictorial and touching beauty of the worship of the Parsees at Bombay, to-day, has been appreciatively described by Mrs. Leonowens, in her *Life and Travels in India*. A ceremony witnessed by Mrs. Leonowens, upon the anniversary of the birthday of Zoroaster, is thus mentioned:

"The building was quite small, circular in shape, with a sort of pentroof, small, iron-grated windows, and an iron-bound door, which was padlocked the moment the service was over.  Under the central arch of the temple was a low altar, on which burned a clear, bright fire ; the smoke had no means of escaping but through the windows, which made the place rather unpleasant to stay in for any length of time.  A number of priests, clad in simple white robes, and quite unadorned, fed the sacred fire with the different kinds of precious woods, and while some chanted, passing each his sacred thread through the fingers of his hands, others dropped perfumes and consecrated oil into the fire.  A great many silver trays, full of fruit, sweetmeats, and white robes, were placed on one side, offerings from the women to the fire-priests.  At the close of the service the entire congregation folded their hands across their breasts, and, having bowed their heads, retired, leaving the priests to heap precious fuel on the sacred fire, so as to preserve it from going out, for which purpose the temple is regularly visited during each day, and the fire is carefully preserved from year to year by certain priests who take turns to perform this most religious duty."

The sacred fire which burns upon the altars of the Parsee fire-temples, itself a subtile and fascinating symbol of purity, warmth, and life, is carefully prepared from a great number of various sorts of fire, as the dyer's, the potter's, the glass-blower's, blacksmith's, bricklayer's, gold and silversmith's, while numerous ingredients, odoriferous and combustible, are added.

"The collective fire, combined into one, and thus obtained, represents the essence of nature, the mystic wine of the poets, pervading the whole universe, even to the most distant stars.  This 'mystic wine' or 'life-water' is held to be the cause of all the growth, vigor, and splendor of the physical and mental qualities of animals, men, birds, beasts, and plants.  Before the collection and preparation of this fire, the priests who are to take part in the ceremony must undergo great purification for nine nights, nine being the most sacred number, as it is the period in which the human offspring is perfected."

Mrs. Leonowens shows the permeating symbolism of Zoroasterism penetrating every portion of their worship, and in this beautiful language describes the Parsee veneration for fire: " Zoroaster discovers God in the eternal, invisible fire. His wonder and joy over the first kindling of the flame arose from the spiritual symbolism that interpreted all nature to him. In it he recognizes the type of the immortal light, and the spiritual resurrection of the soul. Thrilling with religious fervor, he bows before the radiant light as the most subtile and all-dissolving element, and in feeling its mystery, acknowledges the mystery of God, its Supreme Creator."

Much more might be quoted from this lady's work which incidentally illustrates the art feeling, commemorative design—this perhaps less markedly—and symbolism of the modern form of the Persian faith, which are all blended in a delicate and persuasive phase of ritualism in its actual ministrations. A word-picture of the celebration of Zoroaster's birthday, somewhat contrasting with the description already quoted, will be welcomed.

" The men, women, and children, magnificently dressed in gold-wrought silks and flashing jewels, crowd the fire-temples with offerings of fruit and flowers. Long processions of priests, robed in pure white, take turns in officiating, and chant after chant ascends from the temples to the shining Ahura-Mazda, accompanied with invocations to the spirits of the righteous dead, and to the seven high angels around the throne. The beautiful half-veiled women, the lovely children, the noble-looking fathers of families, with their numberless sons standing at their right hand, and the priests magnifying and feeding the sacred flame from sunrise to sunset, form a sight as inspiring as it is novel."

The ceremonies attending burial are singular, but impressive and suggestive.

The elements of such a worship appeal to the senses, involving more or less the materials of art; they are symbolic and commemorative, or, in other words, they are ritualistic. In treating the religions of Assyria, Babylonia, Media, and Parthia, Rawlinson depicts the sometimes involved elaboration of art, symbolism, and the pictorial presentation of past events connected with the history of their religion. This was shown in their services and festivals, by no means always decorous, or even decent, but throughout impregnated with the spirit of ritualism.

Mohammedanism was based upon a most simple affirmation of faith, "There is but one God, and Mahomet is his prophet," and did not invite the use of an ornate ceremonial; its spirit was iconoclastic and unimaginative, and its devotions assumed a severe, if not jejune, formality. It did not suggest strongly those appeals to the senses which most deeply and naturally affect and stimulate the emotions. It had no pantheon, no sacrifice, no mystery, to evoke the reverential tributes of worshipers. It taught morals, had codes, and was fatalistic.

Yet art and symbolism and commemoration reached some development in it, and the undying beauty of its temples, though bare of portraiture or sculpture, awakened the spirit of prayer and devotion, and in color and arrangement spoke to the inextinguishable love of beauty. It is indeed characterized in its worship by striking and curious uses, even beautiful and

4

touching, which suggest, and practically typify, the ritualistic spirit, unhelped by a religion of ideas or a race of mystics.

Of the Koran, the Bible of the Mohammedan, Dr. Madden says, " Every alternate passage is a repetition of the former ; in every alternate page you have a recurrence of the injunction to exterminate unbelievers. The promise to the faithful, ' of a garden of delights with a river flowing through it,' sickens with its frequency, and the threat to the Christian ' of a couch of hell-fire, and a grievous couch it shall be,' is doled out till the reader is cloyed with the repetition." Such a work, which Volney contemptuously designated as *fade*, could scarcely prove a source of spiritual inspiration or devotional beauty.

Yet, of the six commandments in the Islam faith, three have a ritualistic tendency, viz., first, the observance of the Ramadan fast, the Mussulman's Lent ; second, the practice of the five prayers or ablutions ; third, the performance of the pilgrimage to Mecca ; and though those elements of ritualism indicated by art and symbolism are indifferently incorporated in their service, these rules emphasize the commemorative principle, which is perhaps the most important and distinctively valuable.

Amongst an oriental people, forms and features of worship more or less picturesque cannot be repressed, and in these we find amongst Mohammedans those spectacle effects which represent or stand for the art and symbolism more systematically involved in other systems of worship.   In the Mosque of St. Sophia, at

Constantinople, the rabbi goes up to read the Koran in the pulpit with a drawn scimiter in his hand, to indicate that St. Sophia is a mosque acquired by conquest; generally in the mosques the shoes of worshipers are removed, and the faithful pray kneeling on their carpets and turning toward Mecca, the birthplace of the Prophet; there are five canonical hours every day when prayer is to be uttered, and then the automatic Muezzins call from the minarets of the mosques to the faithful to draw near and pray—the scene afforded by this usage frequently awakening those devotional feelings which it is the office or purpose of ritualism legitimately to excite. Speaking of the muezzin, D'Amici says: "He stood a moment silent, then, covering his ears with his hands, and turning up his face to the sky, he chanted in a high, tremulous voice and very slowly, with a solemn and lamenting accent, the sacred words that were then resounding from every [*sic*] minaret in Africa, Asia, and Europe, 'God is great; There is but one God; Mahomet is the prophet of God; Come to prayer; Come and be saved; God is great; God is one alone; Come to prayer.'"

The worship is not without its beauty, and the rites of the dervishes are impressive and stimulating. Of the ordinary Friday worship, the cultivated and able author of *Twenty Years' Residence among the People of Turkey*, says:

"The view I thus obtained of the beautiful mosque of Sultan Ahmet was singularly impressive. The Ulemas (preachers), in their green and white turbans and graceful robes, absorbed in the performance of their religious duties; officers in bright uniforms, and civilians in red fez and black coat, side by side with wild-looking dervishes, and the common people, in the varied and picturesque costumes of the different nations, all knelt in rows upon the soft carpets, or went through the various postures of that religion before which all men are equal. Not a whisper disturbed the clear melodious voice of the old Hodja as he pronounced the Terravi prayers, which the congregation took up in chorus, now prostrating their faces on the ground, now slowly rising ; you could fancy it a green cornfield studded with poppies, billowing under the breeze. Above were the numberless lamps that shone in the stately dome."

Ramadan, the fast of Moslems, which lasts a lunar month, is observed by complete abstinence from food during the days, and eating at night, when wholesale rejoicings and banquetings ensue. In the *Letters of an American from Constantinople and its Environs*, the authoress says:

"During the Ramadan I made a visit to Constantinople, to see the illumination of the mosques, the magnificent representation of ships of war in the air, of equally splendid steamboats, of Arabic extracts from the Koran, and, in fact, of an illumination in different-colored lamps, the splendor of all which I had never conceived before, and have no power to describe. The minarets of every mosque in Constantinople made a blaze of splendor, and the decoration of the spaces between them was the fruit of the genius of all the Muftis and Ulemas of that vast city, based on the practice of many centuries.".

Such an occasion seems hardly calculated to deepen worship or strengthen faith, yet it bears unequivocal evidence of the deeply seated desire for ceremonial splendor or pictorial pomp (not in a bad sense), in connection with events which they deem it well to commemorate or distinguish. Again, pilgrimages to Mecca, which are especially enjoined by Mahomet, involve the leading idea of adoration and commemoration in an emphatic way, and nurture the religious feelings through outward action in a very intense and indisputable manner.

The author of *Twenty Years' Residence among the People of Turkey* says : "Pilgrimages, though less practiced now than formerly in Turkey, are still considered the holiest actions of a Mohammedan's life. The most perfect is the one embracing the pilgrimage to the four sacred spots of Islam—Damascus, Jerusalem, Mecca, and Medina—but the long journey that this would entail, the dangers and difficulties that surround it, are checks upon all but the most zealous of pilgrims, and only a few hardy and enterprising individuals perform the duty in full."

Amongst the sects of dervishes who are extremely popular, and exercise a really preponderating influence with the Turks, rites of a very peculiar and sense-arresting character prevail. The description of a public service amongst the Mevlevi dervishes, from the same work quoted above, is sufficiently declarative of this distinct tendency and its elaborate embodiment :

"Once or twice a week public service is performed at the Mevlevi Khané, to which spectators are admitted. The devotions begin by the recital of the usual *namaz*, after which the sheik proceeds to his *pistiki* or sheepskin mat, and, raising his hands, offers with great earnestness the prayer to the *Pir*, or spirit of the founder of the order, asking his·intercession with God on behalf of the order. He then steps off his *pistiki* and bows his head with deep humility toward it, as if it were now occupied by his Pir ; then, in slow and measured step, he walks three times round the Semar Khané, bowing to the right and left with crossed toes, as he passes his seat, his subordinates following and doing the same. This part of the ceremony (called the Sultan Veled Devri) over, the sheik stands on the *pistiki* with bowed head, while the brethren in the *mutrib* or orchestra chant a hymn in honor of the Prophet, followed by a sweet and harmonious performance on the flute.

"The Semar Zan, director of the performance, proceeds to the sheik, who stands on the edge of his *pistiki*, and after making a deep obeisance, walks to the center of the hall, and gives a signal to the other brethren, who let fall their *tennouris*, take off their *jubbés*, and proceed in single file with folded arms to the sheik, kiss his hand, receive in return a kiss on their hats, and there begin whirling round, using the left foot as a pivot, while they push themselves round with the right. Gradually the arms are raised upward, and then extended outward, the palm of the right hand being turned up, and the left bent toward the floor. With closed eyes, and heads reclining toward the right shoulder, they continue turning, muttering the inaudible *sikr*, saying, 'Allah, Allah,' to the sound of the orchestra, and the chant that accompanies it, ending with the exclamation 'O friend!' when the dancers suddenly cease to turn. The sheik, still standing, again receives the obeisance of the brethren, as they pass his *pistiki*, and the dance is renewed. When it is over they resume their seats on the floor, and are covered with their *jubbés*. The service ends with a prayer for the sultan."

If we turn to India we will find evidence of the beauty of Moslem worship. Their elaborate architectural displays in the superb mosques of the East, in which a delicate minuteness of execution in detail has combined with a truly imaginative splendor of conception, witness to their art instincts, and the relevant employment of their artistic powers to stimulate their religious habits.

It is true that the ritualistic expression, in anything like completeness, is distinctly wanting in Islamism; that where it is seen, its development is rather abnormal and its results grotesque ; and that it suffers from an unfavorable environment. Yet perhaps this state of things, this paucity and niggardliness of ceremonialism, when examined in the light of a review of the efficient causes of ritualism everywhere (Chap. III.), only serves to illustrate, and thereby strengthen, our position in reference to ritual's necessary presence in Catholic worship.

In Judaism we meet one of the most pronounced types, perhaps, of ritualistic practice, especially impressive as the outgrowth of divine direction, and predestined to bear within itself a signal prophecy of that Christ whose disciples we are. It indeed marks a climax of a symmetrical embodiment of the principles of ritualism, omitting none, and combining them in an adroit and impressive equilibrium of worship, art, symbolism, and commemoration.

In art, or the use of decorative methods, color, and appeals to the senses, the Hebrew ceremony was very effective. Such things were consecrated almost by God's word of mouth, so to speak, and their beneficent effects suggested most pointedly in Exodus, chapter xxxv, verses 30–35, while the succeeding chapter speaks of Israel's employment "to work all manner of work for the service of the sanctuary, according to all that the Lord had commanded." The Tabernacle, thus expressly provided for, in its decoration and construction became a work of art, adapted and intended for an ornate and wonderful service. It was a work of art, temporary and provisional, for that glorious Temple of Solomon, whose design and architecture has become an enigma of the world, and synonymous with all that is beautiful and inspiring in architectural work. Much of the popular conception as to the unique beauty of Solomon's Temple is probably gross exaggeration, but that in its execution artistic perfection was sought for is unmistakable. Gold and silver, brass and valuable stones, were devoted to its use, and a great altar, as the apex of its devotional expression, commanded the throngs who filled it. In dress the artistic impulse was not forgotten. The " sons of Aaron " wore a special apparel, and the white cassock which overhung their under garments " was gathered round the body with a girdle of needlework into which, as in the more gorgeous belt of the high-priest, blue, purple, and scarlet were intermingled with white, and marked in the form of flowers." * Levites, a subordinate and sacred order, assisted the priests in the services of the temple, clad in different raiment, while the glorious vestures of the high-priest shone resplendent with gems, and spoke to the worshiper a language of the deepest symbolism. Music assisted in the temple service, and great choruses rendered the moving and triumphant hymns of Israel. The eye was arrested by the sacrifice, the ascending smoke, the flame, the moving priests, the motion of the celebrants, the luster of lights, the wreaths of fragrant incense, and the pontifical splendor of the high-priest.

These were all decorative and art effects; they dominated in the service, and gave it a wonderful realism.

---

* Smith's *Dictionary of the Bible*, article on Priest.

In symbolism, the Hebrew Church was a representative of its holiest and most valuable uses. The many less important and perpetually recurring symbolic acts are lost sight of in the thrilling intensity of prophetic allegory in the triple sacrifices—the Self-Dedicatory, the burnt offering ; the Eucharistic, the meat and the peace offering ; and the Expiatory, the sin and trespass offerings—a series of symbols whose historic impressiveness should apparently deter any one from casting slurs upon the great symbolic acts and usages of the Church to-day. In commemorative exercises, the Hebrew year, filled with its festivals and the great pictorial representation of the exodus from Egypt in the Passover rites, was especially eloquent. The festivals connected with the institution of the Sabbath, the great feasts, as the Passover, the feast of Pentecost, of Weeks, Wheat-harvest or First-fruits, the Feast of Tabernacles or Ingathering, and the solemn Day of Atonement. In the element of adoration, the ritual of the temple breathed a spirit of devout homage, and the special acts of abasement performed by the priest, the fasts, prostrations, etc., all point indisputably to the use of a most reverent demeanor in the worshipers, whether or not these external indications were invariably accompanied by any spiritual delectation.

We have omitted any examination of the religion of Rome and Greece, in the light of our claim that the great religions of the earth which are primary, self-evolved (unlike Protestantism, which may be considered reformatory, secondary, and sporadic, its existence being determined by the existence of the abuses it

4*

*originally* protested against, and by the length of time required for the weakening of the force of inherited habit and the peculiar frame of mind this *useful* movement has begotten), show more or less clearly the ritualistic *facies.* The reason for this omission is to be found in a brief inspection of the worship of these peoples. It was *largely* derived from Egypt, and it unmistakably bore the impress of a ritualistic cultus, and the impressions made by a brief survey of Egyptian methods in worship would be modified, but not changed, by any examination of that of Greece and Rome, a needless and protracting task. Both Greece and Rome, while they yet retained the semblance of any faith, appealed in their ceremonies to the senses in art, decoration, picturesque movement, and dress, and to the imagination in symbolism; to love and memory in commemorative exercises, and to the emotions in the outward expressions of adoration.

Shall we push this brief survey of religious rites further, extending our view over the more barbarous ethnic forms of worship which precede, and are replaced by, the higher shapes of religious conception? The task is not light, exhaustively treated, though, for the sake of profitably exhibiting the germinal stages of holy services we may, for a moment only, dwell on these embryonic indications of the ritualistic idea.

Mexico and Peru possessed, at the arrival of the Europeans, a semi-civilization which was co-ordinated with a religion of a polytheistic character, wherein the sun and seasons, demi-gods and elements, formed a heterogeneous pantheon, not very illogically combined,

and worshiped with unaffected piety. The worship of
their gods, rudely symbolized or represented by idols,
was intrusted to sacerdotal orders, and this very fact
almost presupposes the existence of a ritual more or
less excessive. Prescott, indeed, says : "But, although
the Aztec mythology gathered nothing from the beautiful invention of the poet, nor from the refinements of
philosophy, it was much indebted, as I have noticed,
to the priests, who endeavored to dazzle the imagination of the people by the most formal and pompous
ceremonial." * Art, as they knew it, was lavishly employed in their temples ; the great Temple of the Sun,
in Cuzco, Peru, being, as Prescott succinctly expresses
it, "literally a mine of gold," a characterization to
which Squire would seem fully to accede. Everything
glittered with the precious metal, inlaid and overlaid
in and upon the walls and structure of the temple,
whilst the plate, ornaments, utensils, vases, censers,
were made of the same brilliant material. In Mexico,
the temples or towers, with their barbarously ornamented idols, were upon the summits of the pyramidal *teocallis*, where also, under the open sky, the
sacrificial stone was placed, upon which the immola-
tion of human victims took place. The summits of
these earth and brick heaps were reached by winding
ascents, and on them burned fires upon altars, which,
when numerous, sprinkled the blackness of night with
dancing flames. What more effective appeal as a spectacle could have been made to the worshipers, who

---

* *Conquest of Mexico.*

saw the procession of priests, bearing their victims, winding around the lofty pile, and consummating before their eyes, upon its holy summit, the awe-compelling yet beneficent sacrifice, for whose effectiveness as a climacteric, preparations, in some cases extending over weeks, had already whetted expectation.

In symbolism their services and rites were unusually rich; in fact, in the sculptures of Central America, the symbols appear in bewildering profusion. A few instances from the Mexican mythology, as interpreted by Reville,* will illustrate the presence of this element clearly. *Uitzilopochtli* signifies *Humming-Bird to the left*, as in Mexico "the humming-bird is the messenger of spring, as the swallow is with us," or, in other words, it was the messenger of the sun, their sovereign deity, whose human incarnation was represented as a great giant. "He had three great annual festivals." Here we find commemoration, which is repeated and illustrated everywhere, in all the functions and orders of festivals in their religion. The first fell in May, at the moment of the return of the flowering vegetation. The second was celebrated in August, when the favorable season unfolded all its beauty. The third coincided with our month of December. It was the beginning of the cold and dry season. On the day of this third festival they made a statue in Uitzilopochtli's likeness, out of dough concocted with the blood of sacrificed infants, and after many sorts of ceremonies, a priest pierced the statue with an arrow. "Uitzilopochtli would die with

---

* *Hibbert Lectures.*

the verdure, the flowers, and all the beauteous adornments of spring and summer."

Tezcatlipoca was a god of judgment. His statue was of obsidian, his hair was plaited in a tail, and attached to it a golden ear, toward which mounted tongues of smoke, which typified the ascending prayers of mortals. Tezcatlipoca was the winter sun. Opposed to him and his worship was the humane and gentle Quetzalcoatl, who typified the moist and earth-reviving winds of spring. He is the "feathered serpent," or the "serpent bird." His temple was "dome-shaped and covered. The entrance was formed by a great serpent mouth, wide open, and showing its fangs." His priests were dressed in white, and human sacrifice found no place in his worship. The flying serpent typified the subtile movement of spring and moisture-laden winds, like a breath of renovation. His religion spoke constantly of his return to the earth he had left, and his worship was but a symbolic repetition of that expectation—the spring typifying his return; while the oncoming winter-god, Tezcatlipoca, banished him to the sea as the colder seasons came round, in their unvarying resumption of the *rôle* of destroyer and conqueror. The gods of Mexico were numerous, and as each represented some natural principle, force, or quality, we find, both in the order of their worship and the mode of their representation, that symbolism and commemoration which insensibly mingle together in all ritual, and are in some measure fundamentally analogous, are constantly present, while art and pictorial display, though rude, barbaric, and sinister, never disappear. How natural and how inevitable! These wild ethnic religions arose from the personification of natural things and forces, or of the myths of history and individual delusion, and their worship must reflect the thoughts, associations, and results connected with these.

The instincts of human nature respond at once. How dull and unphilosophic and suicidal to repel and banish the exercise of the same feelings, in their refined manifestations amongst Christians, which crave to employ art and its attendant ideas as naturally to clothe the episodes, events, characters, facts, and principles of the origin of their religion as the pagan or the savage, in a rude and often repulsive manner, employs them to remind him of, or to be to him the reflection of, those primal instigations to worship which he received from nature or from man. Religion to the one is a revelation from God, to the other a suggestion from nature or leaders of thought, but with both worship, properly directed, employs similar methods, instruments, aids, and functions, however widely separated in their quality and beauty.

In Peru, the religion involved, in its public service, the same elements of ritualistic pomp and commemorative festival, with loftier additions and a softer, more decent, cultus. Human sacrifices were abolished, but those of animals were used; a priesthood officiated in their temples, at their altars, and a variety of gods clustered around the central object of their adoration— the sun.

When we turn to more savage races—in fact, to the lowest barbarous tribes—we encounter only the primor-

dial instinct of ritualism, entirely undeveloped and uncultivated, because of the absence of those things which
we, in the next chapter, will endeavor to show are the
stimulants and necessary antecedents of ritualistic life.
The religion of the rudest tribes often seems to be a
medley of superstitious practices, perhaps prompted by
craven fear before the terrors of nature or the sufferings
of life, though there may often be mingled with their
feelings something worthier of the name of religion, belonging to unexpressed and half-awakened emotions and
thought, which in the next phase of religious progress
become dogmas or creeds.   Ritualism naturally appears
when a religion, with the fundamental concept of a
creator, has a history, a founder or founders, and involves the theological notion of sin, on the one hand,
and placation, reconciliation, sacrifice, on the other.
The savage has no such helps, and his stupid or half-
animal mind barely touches the realm of religious ideas
at all.   The wild tribes of Africa are in a great many
instances almost without a thought of God, or any other
impression which might properly be called religious.
They have their frights over this and that, their animal
passions and their brutal tastes.   To relieve themselves
of the first, and gratify the latter, they become the vulgar dupes of medicine-men, magicians, etc.   The rites
they perform are apt to be trivial or frenzied exorcisms
of evil spirits, and their system of worship less worship
than grotesque terror before some imagined peril, or
imbecile pandemonia of dancing and singing, with a
prophet or juggler as the celebrant  of uncouth and
hideous offices.

Yet it is easy to discern, in the savage practices
they follow, suggestions of a ritualistic tendency.   The
senses are appealed to, and a drastic application of
some harsh ordeals, or the exorbitant excess of animal
parade and motion, awaken the torpid sentiments of
awe, and impress the savage mind with a sort of visual
realization of the presence of unseen powers.   This is
a very evident indication of that human and natural
desire for a *sensible* help in the processes of supernatural communion, and although a degraded counterpart
of the refined methods of the Catholic Church, is, to
my mind, allied to these latter, and pointedly seems to
me one of many reasons for their defense.

Human nature, in the whole extent of its varied phenomena, has a fundamental unity of emotional design,
if we will trace it, and not be shocked by the repellent
contrasts, as in this case, afforded by the appearance of
the same instinct in outwardly diverse and seemingly
irreconcilable manifestations.   The principles of ritualism, art, commemoration, and symbolism are of course
but confusedly discerned in most cases, if any of them
is at all apparent; but in instances they approach something like a definable differentiation in rude heathen
worship.   In fact, it must be constantly borne in mind
that the ritualism of the Church but carries on, under
the guidance of or in the spirit of a beneficent revelation, the previously developed methods of ethnic worship which human nature has always used, and with
which that revelation of necessity is in accord.

The Fuegians afford an example of a race almost devoid of the religious instinct, or perhaps, more correctly,

an example of its almost complete suppression. A con-
jurer exercises some influence, though slight, over them.
They yield us no clue as to their feelings in religious
exercises.

The Kaffers of Africa have developed a number of
mysterious practices, which are connected with their
religion, but .necessarily are most concerned with their
present fears and hopes, and they have a very rude cosmogony. They believe in an after life, reverence spirits,
and offer sacrifices. They offer sacrifices to spirits for
a great variety of purposes, and rites and ceremonies
attend these, as in the case of a sacrifice for sickness.
Again, the Feast of First-fruits, when "no Kaffer will
venture to eat the produce of the new year until after
the festival. The feast lasts for several days, and in
order to celebrate it the whole army assembles, together
with the young recruits who have not yet been intrusted with their shields." * The prophets also assemble ; a bull is given, which is caught and strangled by
the warriors in a peculiar manner. The bull, when dead,
is opened by the chief prophet, who mixes the gall
with medicine, which he gives to the king and his
counselors. Dancing, drinking, and eating ensue, and
are continued for several days ; then the king enters
on the scene, dances a furious fandango, and, seizing a
green calabash, dashes it to the ground, thus opening
the harvest.

Their prophets or priests are medicine-men, seers,
doctors, etc., and an order set apart, consecrated, as it

* *Uncivilized Races of the World.* The Kaffer. Rev. J. G. Wood.

were, by strange tests and signs. They have their official dresses, each worn at different rites or offices, and
however grotesque or rude they may appear to our
eyes, they are the analogues of any special vesture in
the Church, and doubtless exercise a similar influence
upon devotees, though immeasurably different in its
character. Their prophets and prophetesses work their
charms and divinations under terrific excitement, and
employ artificial and theatrical adjuncts to heighten
the effect, which is very successfully accomplished.
Their funeral rites are elaborate in case of the death of
a great personage. In all this there is little or nothing beautiful or touching. Their natures are coarsely
moved by grotesque, *bizarre*, and startling methods, but
there is evinced the intuitive use of sensible images and
acts which to them may express some chain of ideas.

Amongst the Bechuanas of Africa very little evidence
of religion is found, except a few singular rites practiced
at funerals, and their blind credulity in the legerde-
main of their sorcerers, while devotional exercises seem
unknown. Amongst the Damaras ceremonials and
usages of a semi-ritualistic character prevail. Thus,
they have a sort of sacred fire, which is kept burning in the chief's hut, or outside of it in fair weather,
of which the chief's daughter is the priestess or *on-
dangere*. She sprinkles the cows with water, ties a
sacred knot in her apron if one of them dies, and when
the village is moved she goes before with a burning
brand lit from the consecrated fire, and this fire is distributed to other villages. Its extinction is regarded
with dismay, and sacrifices are offered to avert calamity.

The funerals of their chiefs are accompanied with ceremonies. In Balonda idols are first met, and their appearance is associated with a belief in a Supreme Being
and immortality of the soul. Ceremonial is rudimentary, but in funerals a pictorial representation is adopted,
as "a man in a strange dress covered with feathers
dances with the mourners all night. He is supposed
to be the representative of the Barimo or spirits." A
great number of puerile and intricate ceremonies prevail amongst other African tribes, of which the New
Moon ceremony amongst the Fans is most interesting.*
They have for us only this general interest, that they
indicate the universal instinct for form in acts of worship or any serious procedure involving communication
with the supernatural. They are silly, empty, and stupid forms, as such, but they are forms with a ritualistic
aspect, and have a philosophical significance in connection with our wish to show the universal prevalence of
form in human religions, however degraded or exalted.

Amongst the Ogboni we encounter a rather more
developed religious practice. They have a pantheon,
with major and minor deities. It consists of numerous
gods, over whom reigns Ovisha Klá. He has a symbol
which is a ship. The next is Shango, who is said to
have a palace of brass and ten thousand horsemen, presides over lightning and fire. His symbol is a small
wooden bat, and his devotees carry a leather bag. Then
comes the Father of Secrets, whose worship is an esoteric and occult practice, to whose strange methods only

---

* *Uncivilized Races of the World.* The Fans. Rev. J. G. Wood.

males are admitted. This Ipa has for his emblem a
palm with four holes. He has a keeper or acolyte.
His priests are known by necklaces made of beads
twisted with ten large white and green beads. There
is a god, or Ovisha, for children, and semi-human
deities succeed, with appropriate legends and observances.

Amongst the Congo negroes polytheism is established, with an influential priesthood governed by a high
priest or Chitome. The Chitome regulates ceremonies,
and is himself the object of superstitious reverence. A
sacred fire burns always in his house, whose very embers
are accounted precious. Next to the Chitome comes
the Nghombo, whose gait is required to be peculiar and
appropriate. Coronations of their kings are conducted
by the Chitome, and involve as much magnificence as
the tribe can afford.

Turning from the savages of Africa to the aborigines
of the South Sea Islands, we find in Tonga a great ad-
mixture of civil and religious ceremonies, which display
the picturesque or suggestive features which rivet the
attention through the senses, and teach a lesson or revive the memory. In the great Feast of Inachi, in Tonga, or Feast of First-fruits, we find a ceremonious procedure of a very elaborate and instructive character. The
yams whose products are to be used in the feast are
different from the ordinary yams, and are planted about a
month earlier. When mature, the king informs the high-
priest, or Tooi-tonga, that they are ready, and the Tooi-
tonga appoints a day. "The day before the ceremony of
Inachi the yams are dug up and ornamented with scarlet

streamers, made of the inner membrane of the pandanus leaf." * They are so entwined over the yam as to produce a checkered pattern. All night long the conch-shells are blowing, announcing the approach of the great festival, while the men sing, "Rest! doing no work," and the women respond, "Thou shalt not work." The next day the ceremony begins, and the people assemble from all parts, dressed in their best. They carry the yams to the center of the village, where they are deposited with much ceremony. Here are laid a number of poles, eight or nine feet long, upon each one of which a yam is slung. The chiefs and other dignitaries now repair to the grave of the last Tooi-tonga and await with bowed heads and clasped hands the approach of the procession. The long retinue, carrying the yams on the poles, approaches, each man appearing exhausted, as a *symbol* of why great thanks should be offered to the gods. "As the men come to the grave, they lay the poles and yams on it, and seat themselves in order before the grave, so that they form a line between the chiefs and the yams."† An oration is then made, wherein the gods are thanked for their bounty, and prayers for its continuance made. Offerings are brought forward in great quantity. Kava drinking ensues, and a speech from a presiding officer explains to the people the rite, and exhorts them to good conduct.

The Tongas have many other ceremonies, for which they have developed a special aptitude; such are the

---

* *Uncivilized Races of the World.* Tonga. Rev. J. G. Wood.
† *Ibid.*

thanksgiving to the god of weather, the Tapu, funeral
of the high-priest, the Tooi-tonga, and others.   The
Tahitians also display this tendency, and ceremonies
amongst them merit notice.   Their god of war, Oro, is
an important deity, whose worship prevails throughout
the Society Islands.   To him was dedicated a sacred
inclosure of very considerable size, and built of huge
blocks of coral stone.   Within this a small house served
as the place of residence for the god, and near it an
altar of sacrifice upon which human victims were immo-
lated.   No particular ritual seemed used.   Other gods
were worshiped, but their worship is uninstructive for
our purposes.   One god, Tane, has some rites connected
with his worship which partake of a spectacular character.   This is the dressing of the god, which, very absurd
in itself, manifests dimly the ritualistic notion.   The
god is brought out of his house with four lesser gods
about him, and while the chiefs of the tribes stood near
their tutelary deities, the priests clustered about the
image of Tane.

" The old garments were then removed, and examination made
into the interior of the idol, which was hollow, and contained various objects, such as scarlet feathers, beads, bracelets, and other
valuables.   Those that began to look shabby were removed, and
others inserted to take their place, and the idols were then invested
in their new robes."   " The feathers attached to these idols, and
placed within their hollow bodies, are mostly the two long tail-
feathers of the tropic bird, white and broad toward the base, and
narrow and scarlet for the remainder of their length.   When the
gods are newly dressed, it is considered a meritorious act for any
one to present fresh feathers in lieu of those which have been deteriorated by age.   After the old garments are unrolled, the feathers
are placed inside the image, and a corresponding number of old

feathers taken out, and presented to the devotee, who values them beyond all things, as partaking of the sanctity which surrounds the original idol. These feathers are then carefully wrapped with sennit, so as to cover them, with the exception of a little portion of both ends, and they are then laid before the idol, while the priest recites a prayer, in which he beseeches the god to transfer his sanctity to these feathers, which from that moment become minor gods." *

It would be tiresome to pursue these comparisons and studies in the religious practices of these lower races. They represent to us the graded state of ritual practice from almost nothing, existing where religion seems scarcely to have established a recognized cult, to more elaborate ceremonial observances connected with polytheism, idolatry, and superstition. Incidentally we may note that much further interest might be imparted to many of these aboriginal practices were we furnished with any close and sympathetic study of their rites, prepared by some one gifted and capable of penetrating the genius of their minds. Such work as Mr. Cushing has done for the Zuni religion is an example of close and fraternal study of Indian worship, which is sadly needed elsewhere. And here, amongst the Zunis, in whose minds has developed an imaginative faculty, who have something of a cosmogony, and whose art feeling was approaching a creative state, ceremonies embodying almost the cardinal ritual principles are described. Ceremonies and rites, mysteries and masonry, abound in their religious and tribal organization. Mr. Cushing has at some length described their singular fetiches, whose significance is of a high symbolic character, and

* *Uncivilized Races of the World.* The Society Islands.

in the following words he alludes to the "day of the council of the fetiches," or the worship of the Prey beings:

" On this occasion is held the grand council of the fetiches. They are all taken from their place of deposit and arranged, according to species and color, in front of a symbolic slat altar on the floor of the council-chamber, in a way I have attempted to indicate as far as possible by the arrangement of the figures on the plate, the quadrupeds being placed upright, while the eagles and other winged fetiches are suspended from the rafters by means of cotton cords. . . . The ceremonials last throughout the latter two-thirds of a night. Each member on entering approaches the altar, and, with prayer-meal in hand, addresses a long prayer to the assembly of fetiches, at the close of which he scatters the prayer-meal over them, breathes on and from his hand, and takes his place in the council. An opening prayer-chant, lasting from one to three hours, is then sung at intervals, in which various members dance to the sound of the constant rattles, imitating at the close of each stanza the cries of the beasts represented by the fetiches.

" At the conclusion of the song, the ' keeper of the Deer Medicine,' who is master-priest of the occasion, leads off in the recitation of a long metrical ritual, in which he is followed by the two warrior priests with shorter recitations, and by a prayer from another priest (of uncertain rank). During these recitations responses like those of the litany in the Church of England may be heard from the whole assembly, and at their close, at or after sunrise, all members flock around the altar, and repeat, prayer-meal in hand, a concluding invocation. This is followed by a liberal feast, principally of game, which is brought in and served by the women, with additional recitations and ceremonials. At this feast, portions of each kind of food are taken out by every member for the Prey gods, which portions are sacrificed by the priests, together with the prayer plume-sticks, several of which are supplied by each member." *

It is vain to pursue this topic further, and in the

---

* *Ann. Rep. Bureau of Ethnology*, p. 32. Washington, 1880–1881.

field of examination we have just left we run the risk of being by some misunderstood and ridiculed because of the childish and apparently barren illustrations we encounter of formal worship. Yet our position is plain, and to ourselves seems unassailable. We find that savage races possess those instincts which, under the incentives and nurture of a historical religion and an ardent acknowledgment of God, originate ritual in its higher, appropriate, and helpful forms. That it appears amongst them under grotesque shapes, or that in some cases only rude demonstrations, as it were, of animal excess are to be referred to the ritualistic idea, is in no way destructive of our claim that ritualism is an implanted necessary tendency which human nature follows, and displays it all the more perfectly as its religion rises in the scale of thought, and embraces more completely the widest possible range of human feeling and aspiration.

These rude, primordial displays of sensual and violent pageantry or form are no more worthy of contempt and dismissal, as having no reference at all to the inviolate cravings and desires of human nature, than the ear-splitting and stridulous music savages produce is, because it seems to bear no discoverable relation to the symphonies of a Beethoven or the songs of Mendelssohn.

The evidence of the principles of ritualism we have endeavored to follow out has been confined to their appearance in religion, but we might have pursued it further in ceremonial government generally, where art, commemoration, and symbolism are more or less influ-

ential.   In religion, these are made helpful and subordinate to adoration or worship.   In civic matters, in the
army, in any public celebration, in decoration, these
perennial factors of ritualistic life appear.   There they
are not quarreled with, because they represent seriously
nothing but good taste, but in the Church they are
associated with ideas or creeds and claims which many
heartily disavow.   In the next chapter we will attempt
to show how ritualism arises, limiting, as here, our consideration of the subject to its religious aspect.

# CHAPTER III.

## PREDETERMINING CAUSES OF RITUALISM, AND THEIR INFLUENCE IN RELIGIONS OF THE WORLD.

THE origin of ritualism in religion is not accidental nor forced. Ritualism originated neither by chance nor device, in the first instance. Ritualism implies simply a constitutional inherent necessity in men to express their feelings in an outward sensible form, which to them fitly excites or responds to the emotions, or relieves, in the expression, those emotions by which they are possessed, or expresses an idea or fact otherwise mentally recalled but not felt. The need felt of ritualism, which is its logical origin, is instinctive; accident or device may largely influence its subsequent growth.

Now, this granted, it does not follow that ritualism appears instantly in response to such natural feelings; on the contrary, in many demonstrable cases, ritual is composed of borrowed usages, which usages may have originated quite accidentally, or under very opposite conditions to those in which they are summoned to do service as visible signs of an inward or mental state. Herbert Spencer, in his study of sociology, has shown, it would seem in many cases clearly, that in a primordial militant state of society, when tribe was arrayed against tribe, nation against nation, and warfare was the business of life, many ceremonial prac-

tices, as between the higher and lower, were or are borrowed from the similar acts displayed by conquering
races or kings toward their prisoners. The acts of a
militant society, he contends, were perpetuated in the
ceremonial observances of an industrial society.

For instance, in the matter of obeisances, Spencer *
finds, or thinks he finds, that primarily they represented
the attitudes of the conquered toward the conqueror,
from which arose those similar ones which show the
subjection of the slave to the master. As representative may be taken the people of Tongataboo, who
" show their great chief the greatest respect imaginable
by prostrating themselves before him, and by putting
his feet on their necks," and Spencer adds, "among
historic peoples this position, originated by defeat, became a position assumed in acknowledging submission."

Abridgment of the earliest types of obeisance follows, and we reach the posture on the knees, with or
without the head touching the ground, so " kneeling is
and has been, in countless places and times, a form of
political homage, a form of domestic homage, and a
form of religious homage." Then, he thinks, genuflec-
tion on one knee (?) follows, then simply bending the
knee, as amongst the Japanese on meeting, or among
the Chinese, as a specified form of obeisance. We then
arrive at bending of the body simply, with various
modifications, as joining the hands, placing the hands
on the knees, etc., and finally reach, in this process of
attenuation, the courteous nod of modern society.

---

* *Principles of Sociology.*

Spencer very truly remarks that "along with the act expressing humility, the complete obeisance includes some act expressing gratification," as joy at the presence of the one saluted, or love for him. Thus kissing becomes united with the obeisance, and kissing the feet and the hands expresses subjection or love. Dancing, as a spontaneous effort of delight, enters in the list of obeisance signs; and as the earliest prostrations soiled the body by the adhering dirt, Spencer makes, somewhat fancifully, it appears to us, the custom of putting ashes on the head a derivative habit. Again, as the conquered surrenders his property, his adornments, his raiment, to the conqueror, so all forms of uncovering the body, from the bare head and naked feet of penitents to the polite salute of lifting the hat, are traceable to aboriginal expressions of personal subjection. Spencer even traces, but by a very feeble assumption, handshaking to these forms—indeed, many of Spencer's deductions in this chapter on obeisances seem forced. It certainly does not appear plain that all ceremonial acts originated in this way, nor is it in reason to think so. A varied retinue of emotions rush forward to claim our consideration as adequate in themselves to supply ritualistic acts almost *de novo*. However, as many rites are, and certainly religious ceremonial is, an expression of reverence and affection, it is in the highest degree congruous and fitting that many of their features should be taken from practices which in war indicated the subjection of the conquered to the conqueror, or in tribal life the love of the subject for his master. What could be more natural? Men struggling, or even mildly impelled, to express certain feelings naturally use those acts which they elsewhere, under coercion, were forced to employ as an expression of an assumedly similar frame of mind. This is by no means equivalent to saying that the rites evoked those feelings of which later they became the expression. They were utilized to aid the tension of mind produced by a desire to publish certain feelings or ideas, but the emotions they gratified anteceded and prescribed them. Certainly the *sermo corporis* of Cicero, which tells to the eye the state of the mind, is an intuitional act, and all rites and ceremonies are initially so ; their elaboration is the consequent result of several influences, all of which are not uniformly or equally good. Now Spencer probably insists that religious observances or ceremonials were derived from the acts expressive of subjugation, which the prisoner went through before his master, and that priestly and class pride, animated by a narrow and intolerable spirit of repression and ignorance, encouraged this primary motion toward ritualism.

Granting this, a doubtful position, it would appear, in many cases, how it affects the position of the ritualist injuriously is difficult to see. Whatever abuses a true thing undergoes in no way detract from the ideality or beauty or value of the principle it stands for ; and though natural, human, and indestructible instincts are perverted, or lured into a delusive gratification, it does not fault or impair or reproach those instincts. Any just impulse in men may at any time be confronted by crafty and wicked motives in others, and be used for meretricious or selfish ends. And this must naturally

occur at periods of history when passion is dominant, a
rude system of manners prevails, learning is monopo-
lized, and personal despotic governments, either in
tribe or state, control civilization.

Again, it is true that the medicine-man of the wild
savage is an impostor, and it is also equally true that
he is in part self-imposed upon. The Egyptian priest
did exalt his office by mummery and an artificial
assumption of mystery, but in all this he was half
dupe himself; the Turkish dervish does surrender
himself to a fit of half-assumed frenzy, but awes his
disciples in an exhibition by which he is himself impressed; the Buddhist monk assumes Nirvana, and
comes out of it perhaps better in pence, but also more
convinced in faith ; and so the Indian, the Egyptian, the
Turk, and the Buddhist find a response, perhaps, nay,
certainly, in the grotesque or solemn evolutions of their
ceremonies, to their emotional and religious cravings,
which ceremonies, inadequate or puerile to our eyes,
struck chords of feeling capable of endless progression
in culture and true religious development. Ceremonies
may have been multiplied for the amusement or benefit
of potentates, dignitaries, and priests, and the enslavement of the superstitious populace, but they perpetuated a strain of feeling which, whether mischievously
played with or not, remained and remains powerful and
comprehensive. The ritualistic movement of this day
is a healthy reassertion of an inextinguishable characteristic of human feeling, but addresses and interprets that feeling by the light of history, intelligence,
and Catholic tradition. For the position is inexpug-

nable that rites, at least in religion, could not have
arisen by purely arbitrary enactments, if they did not
please and arouse and stimulate men's hearts, and that
hence they are a natural phenomenon, and correlate
and correspond to something in human nature requiring them.

We are not anxious yet to prove them desirable,
strengthening, or weakening, or to assume the high
ground in their defense which God's Revelation appears
to us to permit; we are here only concerned with supporting the view of them as inevitable, inherent, and
universal in human society, and therefore, of course,
have nothing to say as to the kinds of rites or choice in
rites, consequences, or tendencies.

It may be safely assumed that ritualism and ceremonies arise in response primarily to a desire, con-
sciously recognized or not, for some outward acts
which will serve as a means of expression, and will
stimulate and gratify the attention and heart. Let us
now examine under what conditions ritualism becomes
developed, elaborated, intricate, and imposing, limiting
now, as heretofore, our attention to religious rites. The
progressive changes by which religious rites pass from
barely animate expressions of human feeling into spectacular exhibitions, where technicalities of color, dress,
position, movement, and speech are addressed to the
minds of auditors, and form an appeal not only to the
feelings, but to the memory and faith and taste, as we
have noticed in the last chapter, seem to depend, first,
upon the assumed more or less absolute presence of
the object worshiped, in its person or in its sacraments;

secondly, upon the epochal phenomena or facts, the historical ideas and incidents, so to speak, connected with the origin and growth of the religion concerned ; thirdly, upon the ability of contemporaneous culture to furnish materials for adornment ; and fourthly, upon the more or less impressionable character of the worshipers. Besides these natural normal stimulants to ritualistic observances, there enter in the ambitious, selfish, or superstitious designs of individuals to whom the religion they thus adorn is of interest or profit.

Here it is well to emphasize some considerations that will doubtless save reader and author from a mutual misunderstanding. All religious rites and ceremonies are probably the work of individuals, but of individuals, in one instance, moved by a strong personal desire to assist themselves and others, which desires have really an ethnic value, and reach a universal need ; and of individuals, in the second instance, who, recognizing the singular efficacy of rites and ceremonies, devise them, not under the stimulus of an innate craving or eagerness for their use, but for the ends of roguery or provisional expediency in blinding the vulgar and stultifying thought, as with Mormonism.

Let us not be tripped in our inquiry by being told that all ceremonies are the inventions of a few, and therefore valueless; doubtless they are, but so are forms of government, schools of art, methods of expression, lines of action; with these latter they are practically the work of the masses, because, when intelligently presented to them or formulated for them, they are applauded, indorsed, and perpetuated. The question really is—as inventions of a few, do they possess the characteristics of permanency, and are they truthful to man's nature? And we do not see that the intervention of authority, prescribing adherence to certain rites, etc., alters the case. It may temporarily establish obnoxious rites; it could not permanently institute the ritualistic system everywhere and for all time.

Now it is difficult, or perhaps tedious, to eliminate from rituals, ceremonies, etc., those practices which have a deceiving aim or a positively degrading object, and it is also not less difficult to discriminate between the varying degrees of badness in such ephemeral inventions. Catholics are concerned practically with that problem to-day. Amongst savages, the medicine-man, for instance, who in a certain sense shows the religious phase of the tribe, resorts to wretched tricks for his trade of divination, and whatever of ritualism enters his performance is barely more than a thin veil to the designs of a lucrative rascality. But the religion here concerned is so equivocal, and the terrors and superstitions of a Hottentot, while ethnologically important, are so primordial and rude, that it cannot be demanded that we push our inquiry amongst such classes. Besides, we have elsewhere shown (Chap. II.) that ceremonies exist amongst wild men, and that their influence is very considerable, whether used for good or bad purposes. We see in these aboriginal worships the crude, disjointed, inchoate clamorings of nature in man for an outward type, symbol, or process of worship, and we again discover their complete absence, along with that of any religion at all. Ritualism assumes a comprehensible shape as a religion displays ideas, and it develops by a law of sequence which no religion, of any universal application or permanency, can withstand. In attempting to catch some glimpse of the stages of its development and the laws they suggest, we shall limit our investigation to the creeds of Egypt, India, China, Arabia, Persia, and Judea.

We have indicated the four important influences whose variously combined actions produce ritual in religion, viz.: First, the presence of the divinity or divinities worshiped, either actually or vicariously, in a sacrament or institution of religion. Second, the historical events or periodical phenomena connected with the religion. Third, the state of contemporaneous culture. Fourth, the psychological nature of the worshipers. Springing directly out of the first of these, and itself exacting special consideration, is the influence of the priestly function. It may be objected that we have not completely taken into account the various causes for the use of rites, and it will be prominently insisted that the chief cause of secular rites prevails in the genesis of religious rites, viz.: a design for distinction or separateness of the exercises, or the celebrants, from all ordinary occasions or officers. While we have not expressly called attention to the force of this feeling, we certainly have indicated its auxiliary influence, inasmuch as the rites described have invariably been pointed to, as intended to dignify and distinguish the services and the *servers* of religion, and we shall, in the brief discussion following in the next paragraphs, see how this design for distinction or separateness of the religious exercises or the religious celebrants arises somewhat as a secondary consequence upon the inception of rites in religion.

The first influence enumerated above is "the presence of the divinity or divinities worshiped, either actually or vicariously, in a sacrament or institution of religion." It is very apparent that this forms, perhaps, the principal incentive to rites, and embraces the most satisfactory plea for their justification. The presence of deity crushes and appalls, or inspires and transfigures, and the mind in either case, though with different feelings, resorts to the mediation of rites to exalt its worship to some pitch of intensity, beauty, and solemnity commensurate with the transcendent moment. In this way the *priestly function* arises, or the office and station of a separate class who ministrate under special prerogatives, powers, and vows before the deity, or dispense the sacraments in which the divine power resides. Here the design of distinction or separateness enters at once, and this fertile source of rites has led, in some religions, to a wild excess of superstitious bigotry, the arrogance of sacerdotalism, and a baneful surplusage of ecclesiastical pageantry. The priestly function we defend, and find it intimately woven with the texture of catholic Christian faith, and it must be regarded as highly determinative of ritualistic procedure. It is not discussed in this chapter, but is reserved for separate treatment in Chapter IV.

The second influence conducive to ritualistic observance is the historical incidents or periodic phenomena connected with a religion. This arouses commemorative zeal, and the pious heart, dwelling with delight upon the scenes and events, cycles and lessons, of the past of its religion, surrounds their chronological return with pictorial beauty, emblematic services, and ritualistic observance. This natural instinct, stultified and repressed, destroys the reality of a historical faith, though it may also, by a perverse self-indulgence, fill worship with fictions and sentimental invention. The third, and a subordinate, influence to ritualistic worship is the state of contemporaneous culture. It is certainly obvious that the condition of taste and the state of art must seriously affect the implements, so to speak, and material at the command of the ritualist for his devotional purposes. The gradual growth of architectural magnificence, and the development of painting, music, and art, certainly, in the Middle Ages, did, and to-day, if allowed to, will contribute to the ritualistic life in the Church in a very marked and perfectly natural measure.

The fourth agency instanced is the mental or emotional tendencies of the worshiper as effective upon his ritualistic bias. This is unquestionable. It exerts the same influence in religious activities as it does in social or domestic life. A cultured and trained nature, craving and accustomed to beauty, demands a beautiful treatment of its religion, if it has any, and if it has been influenced by the preceding considerations or other motives to accept ritualism, will make its worship rich and expressive, and will delight in doing so.

Turning to the history of ethnic religions to trace the growth of ritualistic devices and spirit under the influence of these four agencies, we may not fully be able to delineate, even approximately, the gradual changes which they induced, nor to disengage at all the varying play of one or the other influence, separately predominating at different periods, and of varying value in different religions. The best permitted to us to do, under the limited resources that we command for this analysis, is to show that these causes were effective and real, and that, where they cannot be minutely detected, they are strongly suggested.

The early Egyptians, whose Asiatic origin seems to be generally conceded by scholars, possessed, even in the first historical or legendary notices the world possesses of them, a fairly well-developed religion. It seems to have originated in a form of Sabaism, or star and planet worship, which, involving more and more philosophical ideas as to the origin and relation of things, and imbued with a spirit of pantheism, gradually brought the distant objects of worship into visual nearness, by signs and idols, and multiplied the occupants of their pantheon by the idealization and apotheosis of natural principles.

Mythology wove a tissue of events and personages, and royalty, half confounded with divinity, mingled its conquests and personal ambition with the complex retinue of the Egyptian Olympus; for, as Wilkinson observes, " The Egyptians, in process of time, forsook the pure ideas of a single deity, by admitting his attributes to a participation of that homage which was due to the divinity alone." But this process of impersonation, eventually leading to a most expanded idolatry, amplified ritual observances, and greatly multiplied them. This was inevitable. The worship of the distant heavens brought no sense of a personal presence to the worshiper, and evoked no expression of personal appeal or reverence, as if to a present power. When the gods were brought to the earth by the canonization, so to speak, of the functions of nature, then worship assumed an intricate character. Thus, in the history of Osiris, the beneficent principle of Egyptian philosophy, in which history the great gods figure, we find, according to a very probable interpretation, that, quoting Wilkinson,* " Osiris was the inundation of the Nile; Isis, the irrigated portion of the land of Egypt, where those vapors were nourished; Nephthys, the edge of the desert, occasionally overflowed during the high inundations; Anubis, the son of Osiris and Nephthys, the production of that barren soil, in consequence of its being overflowed by the Nile; Typho, the sea, which swallowed up the Nile water; the conspirators, the drought overcoming the moisture, from which the increase of the Nile proceeds; the chest in which Osiris's body was confined, the banks of the river, within which it retired after the inundation; the Tanaïtic mouth, the lake and barren lands about it, which were held in abhorrence, from their being overflowed by the river without producing any benefit to the country; the twenty-eight years of his life, the 'twenty-eight cubits to which the Nile rises at Elephantine, its greatest height;' the 17th of Athor, the period when the river retires within its banks; the Queen of Ethiopia, the southern winds, preventing the clouds

---

* *The Ancient Egyptians*, Vol. III., p. 79.

being carried southwards; the different members of Osiris's body, the main channels and canals by which the inundation passed into the interior of the country, where each was said to be afterwards buried." This was more and more extended, and animals became the visible exponents of certain powers; in fact, the myriad activity of nature was responded to in the fecundity of invention of the Egyptian mind. The divine principle was made actually *present* in the spectacle of nature's phenomena, and ritual enlarged its scope with the multiplication and presence of their gods. It is quite true that the learned still held the doctrine of a single God, and that much of their worship was the carefully constructed art of priests, who deceived or amused the populace, and that often for excellent reasons. What we wish to show here, however, is not affected by these considerations. Ritual arises primarily under the stimulus of the supposed presence of the god worshiped, or the multiplicity of his functions.

The second influential factor in the determination of ritualistic practice is the history of the religion, viz., the story of its origin, the story or fables of its founders, participants, and defenders. This naturally produces ritual, by an instinct of commemorative desire. The facts, the incidents, in the history of a religion certainly should be treasured by the faithful, and must be inwoven in the progress of their liturgical or ritualistic observances, with their customary rites. In Egypt, these commemorative festivals were well marked. We have already seen that. Osiris was supposed to have visited the earth, "but upon the story of his imaginary life on earth were engrafted numerous allegorical fables," and yet this story, which may be considered the central testament of Egyptian faith, whatever allegorical or metaphysical allusions it bore to the initiated, formed the *raison d'être* of a series of observances, festivals, and ritualistic commemorations. Plutarch instances the Festival of Paamylia, as kept in honor of the birth of Osiris, and adds :

" From the manner of celebrating it, it is evident that Osiris is, in reality, the great principle of fecundity. They, therefore, carry about in procession, and expose to public view, a statue of this god, with the triple phallus, signifying that he is the first principle, and that every such principle, by means of its generative faculty, multiplies what proceeds from, or is produced by it."

And, again, we learn, that—

" The myth of Osiris, in its details—the laying out of his body by his wife Isis and his sister Nephthys, the reconstruction of his limbs, his mystical chest, and other incidents connected with his myth—are represented in detail in the temple of Philæ."

The legend of Typho's shutting up Osiris in a chest on the 17th of the month Athyr was recalled by a ceremony of four days, which not only memorialized this story, but, in the fashion of the double and symbolic characters of Egyptian worship, typified : first, the falling of the Nile, and its return in its own channel ; second, the ceasing of the north wind ; third, the lengthening of the nights, and decrease of the days; and fourth, the destitute condition in which the land was left.

" Upon the 19th of the month Pachon, they march in procession towards the sea, whither the *stolistæ* and priests carry the sacred chest, containing a vessel of gold, into which they pour some river water, and all present exclaim, 'Osiris is found.' Then, throwing fresh mold into the water, and mixing with it aromatics and precious incense, they make an image in the form of a crescent, which is dressed up and adorned, to show that these gods are the powers of earth and water."*

The myths of the Egyptian religion were based upon the revolving retinue of natural phenomena, and the involution of fancy and fact, bearing upon the ordinary events of the seasons and the peculiarities of their geographical position, which composed their religious system, directly involved a perpetual reference to the periodicity of meteorological occurrences, and the periodicity of these was virtually the history of their religion. Thus it came that "the *history of the gods* was embodied in the daily life of the people" (Clarke). The history of a religion, its annals and narratives, plainly affect its ritualistic life.

The third influence heightening ritualistic practice is the state of contemporaneous culture. This means the artistic character of the age, its facility and force, as well as its kind of artistic expression. Of course, the *tone* of ritualistic observance will be greatly modified by the æsthetic or art element in a race. Its influence is secondary, but it has much to do with the actual superficies of rites, their sensible beauty and impressiveness. In Egypt, the cultivation of the arts did not reach that development attained by the Greeks, but a versatile ability, which adapted itself to music, painting, architecture, and sculpture, was possessed by them, and

* *The Ancient Egyptians*, Vol. III., p. 78

the services and character of their temples were lofty and imposing. And as they reached new excellencies of execution, we must believe they added new beauties and features to their temples and service. The kings of Egypt represented the people's culture, and their innovations upon, or enrichments of, the ritual and the architecture of Egyptian religion must be regarded as the standard of the nation's taste. They were constantly erecting monuments to themselves, their victories and deeds, which entered into the service of the national religion from the demi-theurgic character of the kings themselves. Their stupendous tombs—the Pyramids— exercised an influence on their worship, as each was attended with some great ceremony. They built temples and instituted services, and their acts of worship constantly maintained a sumptuous ritual. The Egyptian ritual, as shown in its vast temples and their adornment, reflects the cultus of the race. We find its elements grandiose and solemn. Their art was that of the monolith and monument, and enormous chambers of stone, avenues of pillars, and retinues of variegated functionaries combined in the offices of a religion which from king to peasant permeated every position and duty of life. Their festivals were numerous, their priests powerful, their pantheon crowded, and consequently their ritual redundant and intricate.

The fourth influence that sways and directs the growth of ritual is the psychological nature of the people amidst whom it arises. This, of course, is intimately dependent upon the last consideration—that of contemporaneous culture—for it is the mental counter-

part of the artistic taste and skill of the people, or their
power of objective expression.   Its influence is obvious; as it shapes the people's acceptance of this or
that dogma, it helps to create dogma, tradition, fable, or
creed, and these in turn, of necessity, react upon the
ritual.   The Egyptian mind seemed deeply impregnated with a profound love of the erudite and symbolical; they interpreted nature as the diversified manifestation of God.   This tendency, as we have already
abundantly illustrated, affected their ritual profoundly.
It gave them a multitudinous theogony; it invested
every change in natural phenomena with a sacred
meaning; it involved ascriptions of praise and offerings
of sacrifice and erection of temples to many sorts of
gods; it crowded their art with symbolism, their temples with strange figures and combinations of figures;
and it made the life of the nation a semi-divine one, as
if it itself were but one of the many states of the demi-
urge who animated all creation.   Therefore it may be
claimed—apart from the priestly function treated in
Chapter IV.—that the *real presence* of the deity worshiped, the *history* of the religion, the *condition of contemporaneous art*, and the *inherent mental or emotional
proclivities* of the race have effectively influenced ritualistic life in Egypt, have nurtured, propagated, and produced it.

Let us turn to Brahmanism, to discover in that religion the work of the same set of agencies.   We shall find
here the growth of ritualism and its institution depend-
ing upon these four factors, viz.: the presence of the
deity, the variety or duplication of the gods adored, the

history of the religion, the narratives, fables, incidents, and epochs of its growth, and, as secondary agents, the progress of the race in the arts, and its mental tendencies. In the oldest Vedic age the worship of Indra prevailed, a monotheistic and very simple form of worship. "The religion of the Vedas was one of odes and hymns, a religion of worship by simple adoration" (Clarke). Yet this early age was not devoid of ceremonial life; libations, the moon-plant rite, and sacrifices prevailed. The Bràhmanic age ushered in a more advanced worship. Ceremony began to appear as the religion grew older, as its history developed, and as the cultus of the time favored it. In the laws of Manu we discover the ritualistic practice beginning to assert itself, albeit in foolish and trivial observances. We read there:

"The most excellent of the three classes, being girt with the sacrificial thread, must ask food with the respectful word Dhavati at the beginning of the phrase; those of the second class with that word in the middle; and those of the third with that word at the end."

Again:

"If he seek long life, he should eat with his face to the east; if prosperity, to the west; if truth and its reward, to the north."

"When the student is going to read the Veda, he must perform an ablution, as the law ordains, with his face to the north; and having paid scriptural homage, he must receive instruction, wearing a clean vest, his members being duly composed."

"A Brahman beginning and ending a lecture on the Veda, must always pronounce to himself the syllable ôm; for unless the syllable ôm precede, his learning will slip away from him; and unless it follow, nothing will be long retained."

"The triliteral monosyllable is an emblem of the Supreme; the suppressions of breath, with a mind fixed on God, are the highest devotion ; but nothing is more exalted than the gáyatri ; a declaration of truth is more excellent than silence."

The age of philosophy succeeded; the psychological instincts of the people, which were favorable for the growth of idealism and a vague and metaphysical cosmogony, prepared the way in a measure for the adoption in their religion of ideas which enriched and elevated it, and which were also responded to by an increase of ceremonial observance. The Hindoo Triad or Trinity followed, and though in part devised by the Brahmans to unite a divided orthodoxy against the incursions of Buddhism, its nature was correlated with deeper needs of the Indian mind, which found expression in part in this conception.

Brahma, the creator, Vishnu, the destroyer, and Siva, the restorer, converged in their deified alliance the ideas of their minds as to the triple agencies involved in the spectacle of the world about them. Immediately there clustered about these a series of legends and fancies, partly freaks of imagination, partly thoughts rooted in Hindoo consciousness, which required a sensible representation, and led on the religion into the devious paths of an intricate ritualism. The avatars, or incarnations of Vishnu, brought their gods to them in reality, and extended and diversified their scope. Clarke says, "All the efforts of Brahmanism could not arrest the natural development of the system. It passed on into polytheism and idolatry." Then the innate artistic impulses of the people and their brooding mysticism asserted themselves, and the great temples and elaborate erections we have alluded to sprang into shape, and their ritual became deeply symbolic. It is needless to follow the contemporaneous phenomena of their religion. We have glanced at it in Chapter II., and we have seen that, though a degraded form of religious practice, it involves distinctly the ritualistic *facies*, embodying in its ministrations and outward form the ideas of the priestly function, adoration, art, commemoration, and symbolism.

This assertion receives support from the observations of Mrs. Leonowens, from whose last work, *Life and Travels in India*, a few lines may be acceptably quoted. On page 169 she writes:

"Every act of the Brahmanic ritual is symbolic. Thus, in the evening of the same day, after sunset, the bridegroom sees his blushing little bride alone for the first time ; he takes her by the hand, seats her on a bull's hide, which in its turn is symbolic of several spiritual and physical facts, one of which points to his power to support and protect her."

Again, page 229:

"We rose at dawn next morning, to see this Hindoo community perform in one body, on the banks of the Krishna, the peculiar ceremony of worshiping the sun. The people literally lined the banks of the river ; their faces were turned up to the sky, and as they stood in rows on the steps leading to the water's edge, the effect was very impressive. They then simultaneously filled their palms with water, snuffed it up through their nostrils, and flung it toward the north-east, repeating certain prayers. After this they all proceeded to stand on one foot, then on the other, each holding in his hand an earthen bowl filled with clarified butter, with a lighted wick in the center. Then they all together saluted the mighty luminary, with folded hands raised to their foreheads, and then marched toward the west in imitation of his path through the heavens ; which terminated their sun-worship for the day."

The festival of the *Holi* is one in which the temperament of the race, their æsthetic proclivities, sense of,
and delight in, motion, color, and fantastic revelry,
are displayed in a bewildering and mad excess. Mrs.
Leonowens, describing the popular festival of the *Holi*,
" held in honor of Krishna's sportive character, on the
night of the full moon in the month of February," says:

" That evening we went out on the banks of the Godaveri to see
the termination of the festival, and it is simply impossible to describe the wild enthusiasm of this vast concourse of people. The
banks of the river, the steps of the numberless temples, the courts
within courts, the shrines, the altars, the great halls and music-gal-
leries, with forests of carved pillars, were closely packed with
countless throngs of white-robed priests, half-naked gossains, or
sparkling dancing-girls, while thousands of men, women, and
children lined the banks of the Godaveri, eager and enthusiastic
participants in the gay, bewildering scene. As we stood gazing
at the strange spectacle we heard the wild, discordant sounds of
various musical instruments, the shrill blast of innumerable conch-
shells, and the deafening beat of the tom-toms, whereupon huge
fires began to blaze almost simultaneously from shore to shore at
regular distances, and everywhere round them groups of strangely
dressed boys performed weird circular dances, holding each others'
hands and going around them ; then suddenly letting loose, they
darted and leaped round and round one another, and round the fire
at the same time. This dance is ostensibly performed to commemorate the dance of the god Krishna with the seven gowpiahs or
milkmaids, but there is scarcely a doubt that this festival originally
meant to typify the revolution of the planets round the sun."

Monier Williams, in his introductory observations
(*Religious Thought and Life in India*), in a few paragraphs
states the steps of change which led from a somewhat
abstract form of faith to ritualistic Brahmanism, and
unconsciously describes the play of those influences we
have indicated. He says : " Vedism was the earliest

form of the religion of the Indian branch of the great Aryan family—the form which was represented in the songs, invocations, and prayers collectively called Veda, and attributed to the Rishis, or supposed inspired leaders of religious thought and life in India. It was the worship of the deified forces or phenomena of nature, sometimes gathered under one general conception and personified as one God.

"Brahmanism grew out of Vedism. It taught the merging of all the forces of nature in one universal spiritual being—the only real entity—which, when unmanifested, was called Brahm (neuter), when manifested Brahmā (masculine), and when manifested in the highest order of men was called Brāhmana. Brahmanism was rather a philosophy than a religion, and in its fundamental doctrine was spiritual pantheism.

"Hindooism grew out of Brahmanism. It was Brahmanism, so to speak, run to seed, and spread out into a confused tangle of divine personalities and incarnations. The one system was the rank and luxuriant outcome of the other. Yet Hindooism is distinct from Brahmanism, and chiefly in this, that it takes little account of the primordial, impersonal being, Brahm, and wholly neglects its personal manifestation, Brahmā, substituting, in place of both Brahm and Brahmā, the two popular *personal deities Siva and Vishnu.*"

In turning to China, we encounter the spectacle of a nation, heathen in spirit, indulging in a variety of worships, and affecting indifferently Buddhism, Taotseism, Confucianism, and Christianity. The state religion of China, indeed, represents a mingled worship of a great

6

number of gods and objects. It is deeply affected with superstitious observances, and, regarding the emperor as the "vice-regent," high-priest, and mediator between his subjects and the higher powers, has involved itself in a cycle of heterogeneous ceremonial.

It is not easy to trace the rise of a religion so ancient, its incipient tendencies, its gradual change, or to draw conclusions as to the initial conditions of its rise and progress. It seems that students of the religion of China consider its primitive form to have been the worship of a pure intelligence or *Shangti*, that it was lost, or became deteriorated and merged into a sort of pantheism, wherein heaven, earth, and terrestrial gods are included and propitiated. This, as in the case of Egypt and India, involved more or less the presence of the gods worshiped, and their multiplication assisted in the growth of ceremonial observance or ritual. "The objects of state worship," says Williams,* "are chiefly things, although persons are also included. There are three grades of sacrifices, the *great*, *medium*, and *inferior*, the last collectively called *Kiun-sz'*, or 'the crowd of sacrifices.' The objects to which the great sacrifices are offered are only four, viz., *tien*, the heavens or sky, called the imperial concave expanse; *ti*, the earth, likewise dignified with the appellation imperial; *tai miao*, or the great temple of ancestors, wherein the tablets of deceased monarchs of this dynasty are placed ; and lastly the *shiĕtsik*, or gods of the land and grain, the special patrons of each dynasty. The medium sacri-

* *Middle Kingdom*, Vol. II., p. 195.

fices are offered to nine objects; the sun, or 'great light,' the moon, or 'night light,' the manes of the emperor and kings of former dynasties, Confucius, the ancient patrons of agriculture and silk, the gods of heaven, earth, and the cyclic year." Then follow, as objects of worship, the patron of the healing art, and the innumerable spirits of deceased philanthropists, eminent statesmen, martyrs to virtue, etc., the clouds, rain, wind and thunder, the five celebrated mountains, four seas and four rivers, famous hills, watercourses, flags, trivial gods of cannon, gates, queen goddess of earth, the north pole, etc., etc. Naturally, by a process of personification so comprehensive, the Chinaman brings his gods into a physical proximity with himself, and the self-protective partition of ritual observance, which insensibly rises or is constructed between the worshiper and the *present deity* under these circumstances, has developed its ceremonial *facies* in China.

There has also entered the second incentive to ritual, history, and what is here conjoined with it and produces analogous effects, viz., the periodicity of natural phenomena, when the latter have been embraced in the religious cultus of a race. Thus the tutelar deities of cities are especially invoked and worshiped upon the solstices, equinoxes, new and full moons ; the winter solstice is the great day of the state worship, and the general worship of ancestors takes place one hundred and six days after the winter solstice. Confucius, as nearly as anything, forms a deified human agent in the state religion, and to him some fifteen hundred and sixty temples are dedicated. This involves historical allusion in connection with his life, and then follows the celebration of events as holy-days, a ritualistic feature.

The culture and artistic tendencies of the race are at once involved in the perpetuation, elaboration, and decoration of the ritual thus incepted, and the peculiar and unique gifts of the Chinese are strikingly displayed in the adornment and construction of their temples. Captain Loch, speaking of the temple at Shanghai, as quoted by Williams,* says:

"Pillars of carved wood support the roof, fretted groups of uncouth figures fill up the narrow spaces, while movable lattices screen the occupants from the warmth of the noonday sun. Nothing can surpass the beauty and truth to nature of the most minutely carved flowers and insects prodigally scattered over every screen and cornice."

In the hall of ancestors attached to private houses, banners and lanterns and colored designs are employed, while their skill in painting on rice paper, their sculpture in granite, their work in bronze, green-stone, and ivory, full of *bizarre* and grotesque outline and action, enrich their temples and give the artistic element to their religion. Their artistic peculiarities have been described in these words: "If the romantic and the old-fashioned attract our fancy, the Chinese can point us to an exhaustless store in the recesses of their vast empire. A lack of science and of conception is seen in all their buildings, but fancy seems to have had free license to gambol at pleasure ; and what the architect wanted

---

* *Middle Kingdom*, Vol. II., p. 202.

in developing a scheme he made up in a redundancy of imagination."

The psychological instincts of a people lead to some form of symbolism, and this completes the ritualistic creation, investing it with a poetic depth, and apprehensive and sensitive spirituality. This appears seldom very beautifully in the ethnic religions, excepting Christianity, though some adumbration and suggestion of it whispers of that heart of poetry which beats in the human breast everywhere. Williams calls attention to the omnipresent symbolism of the Chinese, but it is often a formal and puerile iteration of conventional signs. It appears in the decorative features of their religion as well as in other ways, and improves it with a certain warmth of imaginative feeling. The Chinese, as a recent American has borne witness, are not a deeply religious people, yet they illustrate the rise and fruition of the ritualistic tendency as a spontaneous instinct, awakened under given conditions, which, as they are more or less present, give to religious practices a more or less ceremonial character.

Turning now to Turkey, to find the evidences of those influences which determine the rise of ritualism, we find the task difficult and partially impracticable. In describing the outward characteristics of ritualism, we found that Mohammedanism presents very imperfectly the ritualistic idea, though ceremonial observance and artistic beauty are found in that religion, the latter in architectural adornment very markedly. We can now understand why this is so. We will see that the priestly function is absent, though the dervish seems to be assuming that *rôle*, and through him it may yet be introduced into Islam worship. Secondly, no multiplicity of objects is worshiped, no God or vicarious presentment of God is present with them in their mosques. But a commemorative character was given their religion at once after the death of its founder, and in place of a god in their temples, they have succumbed to the substitution of places and things.* Their mental traits and fine fancy have been brought into play, and psychological attributes have at times invested Mohammedanism with an unconscious and sweet symbolism. These last three influences have alone been concerned in the formation of the structural features of Islamism, and their effects are evident.

It must be remembered that Mohammed arose at a time when the Arabs indulged in a most expanded and unrestrained idolatry. The Caaba of the Arabs was the center of their religious creations; pilgrimages to it formed the first indispensable article in their religious outfit. " Each tribe," says Ockley, " either found or introduced in the Caaba their domestic worship ; the temple was adorned or defiled with three hundred and sixty idols of men, eagles, lions, and antelopes ; and most conspicuous was the statue of Hebal, of red agate, holding in his hands seven arrows without heads or

* To-day, in the language of the Rev. F. S. De Haas, the tomb of the Prophet '· is in the south-east corner of an old mosque, inclosed with a silver railing, and overhung with a green velvet pall richly wrought in gold and silver. Suspended over his grave is a gorgeous chandelier, a present from the sultan, hung with sparkling prisms. Large wax candles stand in golden sockets on the right and left, and the whole effect is most solemn and impressive."

feathers, the instruments and symbols of profane divination." (*The Rise and Fall of the Saracen Empire.*)

Mohammed embodied the spirit of revolt and rejection, which, united to a majestic egotism, inspired his system with very different principles, and made it, in a measure, a canonical protest against ritualism and superstition. Ritualism could with difficulty insert itself in a religion which places God at an enormous distance from the worshiper, and unites with that conception no associated manifestations of his person which could be attached to earthly surroundings or scenes. "What object," asks Ockley, "remains for the fancy, or even the understanding, when we have abstracted from the unknown substance all ideas of time and space, of motion and matter, of sensation and reflection?" But it is difficult to circumvent human nature. Where the God was absent the Mussulman inserted the Prophet, and natural instincts did the rest; and though no images and no liturgy are employed by Arabs, signs and symbols, attitudes and commemoration, art and motion are, and they group themselves about the human form of their religious founder, Mohammed, while the growing ascendency of the dervish, with his intoxicating dances and abstruse rites, bears witness to the presence of an inner, suppressed craving in Moslems for the sustaining beauties of form and the pleasing speculations that accompany the celebration of availing offices.

The Moslem found in art some relief from the barrenness of an anti-ritualistic religion, and he grouped commemorative exercises around the founder of his

faith.   In art those elemental incentives of psychology
and mental traits, which we have instanced as effecting
race distinctions in ritual, introduced frequently such
features of ritualism as have to do with the external covering or tabernacle of the worshiper, the temples and churches of worship.   The mosque, and the
loveliness and exquisite intricacy and perfection of
Moorish adornment, was a real ritualistic or ceremonial
sign ; that is, the art nature of the Moor, as far as the
formal restrictions of his creed permitted, invested his
religion with shapes of beauty.   Ritualism does not
produce art, but it fosters it, and art instincts superin-
duce ritualism.   A race so intellectually and emotion-
ally numb as not to respond to the prompting of the
love of beauty is fatally secure against ritualistic devices; but no race is absolutely insensible to it, and so,
in various and characteristic ways, ritual, if it had any
*raison d'être* in a religion, has been helped and modified by art.

Truly, in the Moslem faith the process of enrichment,
except in architecture, seems to have been almost arrested, if there were at any time any such movement
strongly developed.   There are a few formal ceremonies, and some festivals and fasts, and a few impressive customs.   Five times a day the faithful Moslem,
turning his face toward Mecca, the home of his
Prophet, after cleansing of his hands, offers the pious
ejaculation of his faith; and thus, at dawn, at noon, in
the afternoon, at dusk, and at the first watch of the
night, revives the thought of his great Prophet and
teacher in his origin at Mecca.   At these times, in the

cities, the green-robed muezzin from the mosque towers calls to prayer. A fast each year, of thirty days, is observed.

"During the month of Ramadan, from the rising to the setting of the sun, the Mussulman abstains from eating and drinking, and baths and perfumes, from all nourishment that can restore his strength, from all pleasure that can gratify his senses."

Mohammed also instituted fast days on the 13th, 14th, and 15th of every month, when Moslems should abstain from food and drink. These days were called the "naked" days. Sprenger says* that Mohammed early discovered the value of set festivals and seasons of Christians, and in making his fasts he copied their example. Ramadan was, according to the Moslems, the month in which God completed the publication of his work of salvation, an imitation of the Christian's fast for his redemption, and of that of the Jews for their deliverance from Egypt. The festival of *Yd*, or the Feast of Offerings, was an occasion commemorative of victory, and on the morning of the festival every one, slave and free, women and children, young and old, brought fruits, or wheat, or rosin. When the alms were collected the believers formed a procession outside of the last house of the city, to indicate their willingness to begin a pilgrimage. Then the Prophet put on his festival array, a sort of winding cloth infolding him from his shoulders to his legs. Before him was borne a dish brought from Abyssinia. A prayer was spoken, with some deviation from the customary liturgy, and a sermon followed, after which two white

---

* *Das Leben und die Lehre des Mohammed.*

6*

and black-spotted rams were brought before him, and he slew one for the horde of the faithful and the other for himself and family. The flesh was cooked, and the feast ended with a love feast, to which also the poor were invited. This festival, later, appears to have been replaced by the month of fasting, Ramadan. Certainly these are tokens of Mohammed's own appreciation of ceremonial usage.

Again, the pilgrimages to Mecca are invested in the Moslem mind with the efficacious sanctity which a Romanist imparts to his journey to a healing shrine. They are essentially ritualistic in spirit, and have developed and strengthened as an inherited custom, under the influence of commemorative feelings surrounding the life and home of their religion's founder. This custom is in strict parallelism with similar ones established in religions pronouncedly ritualistic. As the Rev. Mr. Kennedy says,* "Judaism was greatly strengthened by the people, according to the divine command, going up thrice every year, at appointed times, to the place where the name of the Lord was, and by then repairing in vast numbers, once a year, to their sacred capital, after they had become widely scattered among the nations;" and thus, with identical results and intentions, "the Mohammedans, by long journeys and perilous voyages, make their way to Mecca and Medina, their sacred cities, and make it a point to be present at the most sacred season, when many thousands are assembled."

But the psychological, emotional or mental traits of

---

* *Life and Work in Benares and Kumaon.*

the worshipers, which secondarily influence religion, have played their part in the growth of Moorish religious art. In Mohammed's first mosque the front wall extended from east to west, as the Moslems in prayer looked toward Jerusalem. The principal entrance was opposite this wall; there were two towers, one of Grace, the other the Prophet's tower; along the forward wall (north) the ground was raised, and only over this part was there a roof, so that two-thirds of the place of worship was under the sky. And Sprenger says, from whose work the above was taken, "This is the plan of all the mosques in India which I recall. This simple temple was also the copy of the most artistic buildings in the world." But how sumptuously enriched and majestically enlarged this toy model became, when, by the process of artistic growth and ethnic development of taste, the race's inherent powers of construction were called into action, and Moslem temples were erected, which, as Bishop Heber says, look as if "built by a giant and furnished by a jeweler." Witness the Mosque of Taj, the Pearl Mosque of Agra, and the Tomb of Akbar at Secundra.

The power of the Moslem to respond to this ritualistic impulse came with an improvement in his workmanship, and obeyed, as we understand it should, the tendencies of his cultus and nature. In India and in Spain the beautiful fabrics of his architectural and decorative skill fascinate and entrance. No iconoclasm of the Moslem law could repress the desire for beauty, and his religion largely absorbed and appropriated his efforts to satisfy it.

F. Marion Crawford, in an article on the Mohammedans in India,* characterizes Moslem art as follows, in a
comparison between it and Hindoo art :

" Greek and Hindoo temples look broad ; Gothic and Mohammedan churches look high. Where the Hindoo would place a
couple of large pilasters thickly carved with a redundant mass of
idol-symbols supporting a square stone cornice, the Moslem builds
a springing arch, twice the height of the Hindoo erection, and
tapering away to a point. Where the Indian carves a rich confusion of grotesque figures, the Mohammedan gives his chisel full
freedom in the creation of every species of tracery and so-called
arabesque ; for the Islamite is as strictly forbidden to make to himself images of living things as the Hebrew."

Again :

" Wherever there are Mussulmans there you will find their graceful minarets and mosques, their domed sepulchres and solitary
tombs, their light balconies and pointed doorways, contrasting with
the heavy architecture of the Hindoos."

The influences which shape and bring to perfection,
as well as to gross extravagance and disastrous vulgarity,
the ritualistic tendencies of worship, are certainly discovered in the phases past and present of Islamism, and
though confronted and restrained by uncongenial religious formulæ, have, notwithstanding, exerted no incon-
siderable effect upon its forms.

In the Persian faith we find the complete configuration of a ritualistic creed, and we need scarcely take the
trouble to penetrate the vicissitudes of its history to
discover the rise of ritual under the influences we have
indicated, as the formal pattern set up in its sacred

* *Harper's New Monthly Magazine*, July, 1885.

books involves this idea in all its fundamental forms. The early Persian faith was invaded by Magian rites and injuriously affected by their polytheistic and idolatrous notions, though *pari passu* it assumed a more highly ritualistic character. Zoroaster taught a very beautiful and pure faith, and his creed and practice were chaste, elevating, and attractive. It was monotheistic, and typified to the senses the supreme and subtile power and genius of its divine idea by fire. It assumed the existence of two antagonistic principles—

"These are the Spento Mainyush (the increasing or creative spirit) and the Angro Mainyush (the decreasing or destructive spirit). God (Mazda), through the agency and interaction of these two spirits, is the causer of all causes in the universe. He is the creator as well as the destroyer of all things. These two causes have been working under one Almighty, day and night, and have been creating and destroying ever since the universe began."*

Again, to explain the infirmities, disabilities, sins, and imperfections in the world and man, Dr. Haug, as quoted by Karaka, says:

"Having arrived at the grand idea of the unity and indivisibility of the Supreme Being, he undertook to solve the great problem which has engaged the attention of so many wise men of antiquity, and even of modern times, viz., how are the imperfections discoverable in the world, the various kinds of evils, wickedness, and baseness, compatible with the goodness, holiness, and justness of God? This great thinker of remote antiquity solved this difficult question philosophically by the supposition of two primeval causes, which, though different, were united, and produced the world of material things as well as that of the spirit."

* *History of the Parsees*, Vol. II., pp. 186, 187. **Karaka.**

Many other beautiful speculations, philosophic dogmas, and a variety of imaginative sentiment and thought are included in the body of the Parsee faith. We are here concerned with its aptitude to assume and emphasize ritualistic methods. And this aptitude arose primarily from its assumption in its worship of a symbol which sensibly impressed the worshiper with the *presence* of his God.

That symbol was fire. Though Karaka indignantly denies that the Parsees in any sense worshiped the fire in their temples, it is incontestable that the swaying flames were not a symbol in its simplest form, but conveyed by a sort of reflection the attributes of God to their minds, and through long usage had assumed a sacred special and deified character. It would seem that the Magi had impressed a more positive significance upon this symbol, and given it a semi-adorable character—a character it doubtless has to-day with the less refined and educated. In this way a ritual was almost self-created, and, if not, must shortly have arisen. The sacred fire was to be watched and nourished, and a class, somewhat restricted, for that service must be established, viz., the priests. The fire, although a symbol, sanctified the house in which it burned, and was approached in prayers with solemnity and ceremony. The fire of the temples exacts itself a ritualistic process for its perfecting. Karaka says : *

" The sacred fire burning there is not the ordinary fire burning on our hearths. It has undergone several ceremonies, and it is these ceremonies, full of meaning, that render the fire more sacred in the eye of a Parsee. We will briefly recount the process here. In establishing a fire-temple fires from various places of manufacture are brought, and kept in different vases. Great efforts are also made to obtain fire caused by lightning. Over one of these fires a perforated metallic flat tray, with a handle attached, is held. On this tray are placed small chips and dust of fragrant sandal-wood. These chips and dust are ignited by the heat of the fire below, care being taken that the perforated tray does not touch the fire. Thus a new fire is created out of the first fire. Then from this new fire another one is created by the same process. From this new fire another is again produced, and so on, until the process is repeated nine times. The fire thus prepared, after the ninth process, is considered pure."

This sacred fire, however its use was interpreted as a symbol, occupied that place in the Parsee worship which brought it in strict analogy with the presence of the deity in other religions, and promoted and sustained a more or less ritualistic worship by the working out of that sequence of acts which we may call a law, by which, under the assumption of the presence of his god or any vicarious representative of that presence in his worship, the worshiper throws up before him, or surrounds himself with, a structure of rites which stimulate and preserve such feelings as are suitable, and help him to realize the presence he adores.*

The history and incidents and personages of the Parsee creed provided ample material for the perpetuation of the same in the minds of their believers, by com-

---

* Dr. Spiegel (Karaka), speaking of the liturgy of the Visparad, says, its contents "are almost exclusively an invitation to Ahura Mazda, the good genii, and other lords of purity to be present at the ceremonies about to be performed." In these instances a supernatural presence at least presided.

memorative services, and these accumulated as new teachers chose to repeat or emphasize some forgotten or flattering episode.

New Year's Day, or *Pateti*, is a day of especial solemnity or significance, being the day on which one prays to God for absolution from sins committed during the past year. Rapithvan is the third day of the first month, and is solemnly celebrated in honor of the archangel who presides over light and fire. Khordad-Sal is " observed as a holiday in honor of the revelation of *Ahura Mazda* to Zoroaster, and of the anniversary of the birth of the Prophet " (Karaka).

The Gahambars, which fall six times in a year, are intervals which indicate various seasons and events, as when the angel ruling over wealth is invoked, the season of the harvest, in summer, at the creation of trees, the creation of animals, and when winter vanishes, at which time the souls of the departed are prayed for. The *Atash-Behran Salgari* is celebrated in honor of Hormasji-Bamanji-Wadia, whose sons, on his decease, built him a great fire-temple. "On this day the 'dastur,' or high-priest, performs the Jasan ceremony in the presence of Parsees, who assemble in large numbers in the fire-temple, and a sermon is preached at the conclusion of the ceremony."

Another festival derives its character from a famous king who introduced it; the anniversary of Zoroaster's death is observed; another is claimed for the departed, and the pious invoke their memory and pray for them. Yet another, partially derived from Hindostan, is a day of propitiation to seas and rivers. Another is dedicated to the honoring of fire, while another is "in honor of the spirit who rules over the animal kingdom. It falls on the second day of the eleventh month, both of which have the same name, Behman. During this month, the Parsees feed stray animals or those that are brought to their doors, with grass, and other similar food. On this day the Parsees abstain from eating animal flesh " (Karaka).

It is indicated, in this rough summary of some of the Parsee festivals, that, besides practices of a dogmatic character, many of them arose in the history and progress in time of their religion, a fact very clearly realized upon reading the history of these people and their Persian ancestors.

The last influential factor in the growth and nurture of ritual is the imaginative characteristics, psychological tendencies of the race, and these, as is obvious, will be, in all that appertains to art or creative thought, much modified by the occupation or prosperity of a race. Ritualism in its religion is often synchronous with the apical periods of a nation's prosperity and power. An aptitude for symbolism is essential to the growth of ritualism, the religio-poetical aspect of worship.

In the Parsees we fail to find those intense artistic natures which engender form and poetry of action or sound, though in color, in an appeal to the eye and sense of smell, through the beauty and fragrance of flowers, powders, perfumes, and dresses, they delight.*

* It is not meant that the Persian race is deprived of executive artistic talent. The beautiful carpets, exquisite needle-works, damascened, carved, and engraved metals, attractive pottery, are eloquent witnesses to their

The Parsees' temperament encouraged symbolism. It would be tedious to enumerate evidences of this last in detail. It has been elsewhere referred to (Chapter II., p. 72), but perhaps a passage from Karaka's work, describing the investiture of a child with the "sudra," may prove interesting as illustrative of this tendency.

" The 'sudra,' which is always worn next to the skin, is made of fine linen gauze or net, while the 'kusti' is a thin woolen cord, or cincture, of seventy-two threads ; these threads represent the seventy-two 'has' or chapters of the sacred book of the Parsees, called *Yazashne.* The 'sudra' means 'the garment of the good and beneficial way.' The 'kusti' is passed round the waist three times and tied with four knots, two in front and two behind, during the chanting of a short hymn. At the first knot the person says, 'There is only one God and no other is to be compared with him ;' at the second, 'The religion given by Zoroaster is true ;' at the third, 'Zoroaster is the true Prophet, who derived his mission from God ;' and at the fourth and last, 'Perform good actions, and abstain from evil ones.'"

Much of their symbolism is very superficial, and they indulge in a weak parade of amiable superstitions.

The present communities of Parsees have passed through the heaviest tribulations, persecution, defeat and exile have crushed them, and though now gaining, as they have been for some time past, in material prosperity, they are an isolated group, and receive no stimulus from the age or their occupation to indulge in architectural splendor or elaboration of pictorial ceremonial. Perhaps, under no circumstances would

chaste and delicate sense of ornamentation and design. Indeed, it is a familiar assertion that the Moor and Arab derived their ornamental arts from these skillful and experienced workmen.

they now do so. Their character seems calm, limpid, peace-loving, and gentle, their minds cautious, conservative, and commonplace. Their ritual is pitched upon a low key, though it does bear all the significant marks of ritual as such. They are, indeed, devout and moral to a very admirable degree, and their religion agreeably responds to their loving and ingenuous natures.

In the days of Persia's glory under Cyrus and Darius, with the stimulus of a great national prestige and the pride-loving influence of royalty, their art became pretentious and massive.

"Before the time of Alexander they had reached a degree of perfection in architecture and sculpture which can still be appreciated in the magnificent ruins of Persepolis, the style of which at once recalls the well-known sculptures from Nineveh. Probably nowhere else does a more splendid monument of former grandeur now exist. The tomb of Cyrus, the ruins of Pasargardæ, the Takht-i-Sulaiman, the Naksh-i-Rustam, and other remains show, moreover, that during the same period the artistic skill of the Persians was not confined to Persepolis alone." *

The ancient Persians employed color to a very great extent, and Fergusson says, † they "built their principal mosques and palaces with walls composed of ill-burnt bricks, which they either plaster and paint, or ornament with glazed tiles of the most brilliant colors and elaborate patterns." Again, he describes the Persian as one who "revels in color and ornament, and leaves form to take care of itself. The gorgeous splendor of a passing pageant is to him a nobler conception than the eternity of a pyramid." The architecture

---

* *Persian Art*, p. 2. R. Murdoch Smith.
† *Palaces of Nineveh and Persepolis Restored.* J. Fergusson.

of Persepolis, with its temple-palaces, the propylæa, its
stately colonnades and stairways, the structures of Nineveh, the remains of the sculptures of the colossal bulls
and other figures, surrounded with emblematic signs,
all furnish striking evidence of the artistic temperament and mental traits of the Persians, which permits
us to conclude that they used spectacle effects and
poetic allusion in their worship, that the attributes of
a lively and somewhat grandiose imagination was
theirs, and that their ritual reflected its character.
Fergusson, quoting from the Dabistan, describes a
capital instance of these qualities:

"On each day of the week in those appropriated to each planet,
the king exhibited himself from a lofty *tabsar*, or window, front-
ing the temple of the planet, whilst the people, in due order and
arrangement, offered up their prayers.   For example, on Sunday, or
*Yak shambah*, he showed himself clad in a yellow *kaba*, or tunic
of gold tissue, wearing a crown of the same metal set with rubies
and diamonds, covered with many ornaments of gold from the *tabsar*, the circumference of which was embossed with similar stones."

And again :

"In front of each temple was a large fire-temple, so that there
were seven in all ; so that each fire-temple was dedicated to one
of the seven planets, and in these they burnt the proper perfumes."

Symbolism prevailed, and, in short, the taste and
character of the. Persian people enriched and influenced, as we claim, their religious ritual.

In Judaism we seem to find a very notable and especially instructive example, illustrating, though in an
arbitrary, yet none the less impressive, manner, the
laws, or, at least, two of them, which govern the development of ritualism.   These two laws are, first, the

ritualistic influence of a historical past in a religion; and, secondly, the ritualistic influence of the *presence* of divinity, or God or his representative, in its services.

The Jews were a chosen people, and destined to form the vessel in which, to later ages, should be carried the knowledge of the truth, as they were also to form a symbol of the Christian life, and to include in their history and historic leaders types of that life by which the values of all lives shall be measured. Their growth and vicissitudes, from the first call to Abraham to their enslavement in Persian bondage, through all the romantic, thrilling, and strange episodes and exigencies of their wonderful career, form mysterious, beautiful, and prophetic pictures of that spiritual pilgrimage upon which each soul is started at its entrance upon the world. Shall we not then realize that the advent of ritualism in their religion, synchronous with conditions similar to those under which it has appeared in other religions, gains a serious significance as a natural phenomenon when directed by divine agency?

The progeny of Abraham, Isaac, and Jacob maintained the worship of the one invisible God for all the long years during which the character of the people of Israel was forming and their numbers increasing. The residence in Egypt, from their entrance under Jacob to their departure under Moses, is measured by hundreds of years.* In all this time their worship,

---

* " While some assign the whole duration of four hundred and thirty years to the captivity in Egypt, others include the residence of the patriarchs, two hundred and fifteen years, within this period."—Milman, *History of the Jews.*

scarcely formed at all, maintained a simple and unobtrusive character. The latter part of this period, when under the strong leadership of Moses they effected their escape, is marked by a series of extraordinary events, culminating in the slaying of the first-born of Egypt, and the institution of the Passover. Then followed the Exodus, the passage of the Red Sea, the organization of the Israelites, the delivery of the law, and thus, after a history which formed a substantial religious recollection, and was involved in the growth and strengthening of their faith, *God began his residence in a vicarious manner amongst them,* in the Ark of the Tabernacle, and then, and only then, under an arbitrary enactment, began a ritualistic government in their Church, the institution of a priesthood, and the use of periodic festivals. The court of the tabernacle, and the tabernacle, are erected, and upon them is expended all the artistic power they commanded, and lavished all of their most precious possessions.

"The interior of the tabernacle was hung with curtains of the finest linen, and the richest colors, embroidered with the mysterious figures called cherubim. The tabernacle was divided into two unequal parts : the first, or Holy Place, thirty-five feet long ; in this stood the golden candlestick, the golden altar of incense, the table of show-bread. The second, or Holy of Holies, seventeen feet and a half in length, was parted off by a veil of the same costly materials and splendid colors with the rest of the hangings, and suspended by hooks of gold from four wooden pillars, likewise overlaid with gold. The priests who were to minister in this sumptuous pavilion-temple were to be without bodily defect or mutilation ; they were likewise to have *holy garments for glory and for* beauty. Aaron and his sons were designated for this office. The high-priest wore, first, a tunic of fine linen, which fitted close, and without a fold, to his person, with loose trousers of linen. Over this was a robe of blue, woven in one piece, without sleeves, with a hole through which the head passed, likewise fitted close round the neck, with a rich border, and reaching to the feet, where the lower rim was hung with pomegranates and little bells of gold, which sounded as he moved. Over this, again, was the ephod, made of blue, purple, and scarlet thread, twisted with threads of gold. It consisted of two pieces, one hanging behind, the other before, perhaps like a herald's tabard. From the hinder one, which hung much lower, came a rich girdle passing under the arms, and fastened over the breast. It had two shoulder-pieces, in which were two large beryl stones, set in gold, on which the names of the twelve tribes were engraved. From these shoulder-pieces came two gold chains, which fastened the pectoral or breast-plate ; a piece of cloth of gold, a span square, in which twelve precious stones were set, in four rows, each engraved with the name of one of the tribes. Two other chains from the lower corners fastened the breast-plate to the lower part of the ephod. The head-dress of the priest was a rich turban of fine linen, on the front of which appeared a golden plate inscribed ' Holiness to the Lord.' Such were the first preparations for the religious ceremonial of the Jews. As this tall and sumptuous pavilion rose in the midst of the coarse and lowly tents of the people, their *God seemed immediately to take possession of the structure* raised to his honor." *

Symbolism of the most profound kind pervaded the propitiatory and eucharistic sacrifices. And now their history, their relations to God through revelation and experience, were solemnized and commemorated in the ritualistic feature of festivals. The Sabbath was celebrated, the Feast of Trumpets, the beginning of the old Hebrew year ; the Passover, when " on the first evening they tasted the bitter herb, emblematic of the bitterness of slavery; they partook of the sacrifice, with their loins girded as ready for their flight; they eat only unleavened bread, the bread of slavery, as prepared in the

---

* Milman, *History of the Jews.*

hurry and confusion of their departure ; " the Pentecost, by which they commemorated the delivery of the law; the Feast of Tabernacles, at the end of vintages, when the branches of the trees were bound together in a rude semblance of the tents the Israelites had dwelt in in the desert.

It is needless to say that the tendencies and peculiarities of the Jews, the subordinate influence in ritualistic development, did not so plainly affect the actual features of their public worship. The " wise hearted " men who " wrought the work of the tabernacle " doubtless were skillful artisans, whose skill reflected not only the practice of the Egyptians, but also appealed to the tastes and illustrated the designs of the people, yet the directions were themselves minute, and deviation from them might have been regarded as dangerous or sinful. However, in the case of this wonderful worship, the concordance of its spirit with the temperament of the people was necessary, and the details of the law, and God's commands to Moses, were all intended to bring the people to a certain preordained state of feeling. The " dramatic union of music, singing, and dancing " in Israelitish worship was a national habit, and was engendered in their disposition. When we peruse the wonders of, and the wonderful events connected with, the erection of the temple by Solomon, its marvelous splendor, and the majestic ceremonial of the installation of the Ark in it, with the stupendous and inspiring climax of the descent of fire upon the sacrifices, we find all the same powerful incentives to ritualistic service repeated, redoubled, and extended.

It would be unwise to extend these examinations further. The rise of ritualism, which itself involves the use of art, commemoration, and symbolism, has been brought about in the chief religions of the world by, first, the assumption of the presence of divinity, more or less actual ; second, the possession of a history which incorporates the religion's epochs, events, personages, and teachings ; third, the development of those poetic feelings, emotional desires, mental traits, and psychological instincts which, varying in different races, and changing with the ages, everywhere influence the externals of ceremonial in a ritualistic direction.

# CHAPTER IV.

## THE PRIESTLY FUNCTION.

PERHAPS no profession or calling in life has in these modern times been subjected to more, or more seriously meant, disparagement than the priesthood. The Puritan, of course, regards him as a menace to society, a contradiction, and an impostor; and the learned and philosophic historians or critics of a broad school discover in him a relic of barbarism, whose antiquity alone makes him respectable. His obnoxious ambition, his self-stultifying ignorance, his chagrin at the rise and dissemination of learning, have been gleefully pointed out, until the "terrors of priestcraft" in college orations have sickened the ears of more than six generations of undergraduates, and the cheap reputation of the popular pulpit exhorter has sensibly waned since he won his spurs by an attack on the "effete institution of the priesthood." But the priest stays, and, under the beneficent watchfulness of God, his office will never become vacant nor his place before the altar empty.

The superb vituperation of Voltaire, the numberless insinuations of Buckle, the analytical and scrutinizing condemnation of Lecky, the cold sarcasm of Mills, have all spent their impotent force upon the priest, and he yet remains, an ordained officer of God, responsible to God, and warranted by all the analogies

of nature and the instinct of races. What is a priest?
In a literal sense its meaning does not clearly, at first,
indicate its office; it is a *presbyter*, or simply an *elder*,
as the allied term *sacerdos* was one who had to do with
sacred things, as, also, *hiereus;* while the Hebrew *cohen*
meant a ruler or chief councilor, terms in themselves
indicating a supervisional character or disciplinary
power. The priestly office assumed special privileges,
special powers, and became invested with an objective sanctity, when some particular inalienable duty or
function, as, for instance, the idea of sacrifice, is conjoined with it; when we find that upon the *cohen*, the
*hiereus*, the *sacerdos*, the *presbyter*, as being the oldest,
the right of offering sacrifice was bestowed. But additional interest—in fact, the supreme and technical value
of the office—is implied when we find it reserved to a
class, whose continuity is provided for in some way, as
by inheritance, relationship, or ordination. In Egypt
certain families became formally the possessors of this
office; it resided solely in their members; they founded
priestly castes. Amongst the Jews, " Moses and Aaron,
of the tribe of Levi, as the elders or leaders, administered the sacred and the temporal affairs of the nation. In course of time Aaron was divinely invested
with the dignity of elder-in-chief in things divine, and
became not only the high-priest, but the father of a
priestly and ministerial line, whose rights were to be
inalienable so long as the Jewish dispensation should
last. These were the *cohens* by excellence, and as sac-
rificing was the chief function which they had to perform, to the word *cohen* (priest) the sacrificial idea

became inseparably attached." * That the order was necessarily perpetuated in the Christian Church, that its continuance, propagation, and stability were divinely prepared for, we may be able to point out later; but first a few words as to the inherent applicability of the idea of priest, and its natural analogies, and the in· evitable influence and effectiveness of this office, the priestly function, upon and for the enrichment and elaboration of ritual.

Religion is a binding back; it implies a separation, a sundering at some time between men and a primal good; it is a process devised to effect reunion, to restore the harmony of the world, and to unite the affec- _ tions and souls of men with the Supreme Excellence it adores. This is more or less clearly recognized in all religions, and even the most anthropomorphic and debased instinctively assume the element of antagonism or alienation between the gods and men, which must be overruled or dissipated. A process, a law of procedure, an established system of more or less technical exclusiveness, must be instituted, by which this restoration and reunion can be effected. This is a system of religion, and its followers not only assume its necessity, but they also accept its provisions, upon the natural inference that it is desirable for them to become reconciled to God, with the attendant pleasures and happiness flowing from such amity. This law, however, has its interpreters, the system its executants, the process its professors—in short, the religion has its priests. The

* "Genesis of Priest," *The Living Church*, Vol. VIII., p. 679. E. Ransford.

implication of the word varies with the greater or less solemnity of the function the priest is expected to discharge. It may be attenuated in significance to the scarcely separative insignia and power of a Methodist preacher, or it may be enlarged and dignified so as to invest its holder with the supernal and cosmopolitan prerogatives of a pope. Of course, in any just sense, the Methodist preacher is not a priest, and never can be ; he is a simulacrum, baseless and unreasonable, from our point of view.

In connection with our explanation of the causes leading to the rise of ritualism, we have pointed out the growth of the priestly function in a ritualistic direction with the assumption of the presence of Divinity in religious worship. The priest then becomes the immediate and intimate avenue of approach to the terrestrial manifestations of God ; he is given the power of self-perpetuation ; he is enveloped and displayed in a certain atmosphere of veneration. His official acts have a religious significance ; they become availing offices ; they impart the blessing of consecration. As the channel through which the efficacy of supernatural grace becomes active, he is a peculiar and sacred personage, his life an exemplary and formal one, his opinions theological and authoritative.

Now, this conception leads at once to ritualistic methods and breeds the ritualistic habit, and there is a very strikingly close relation between the predominance of the ritualistic character of a religion and the importance and power of its priesthood.

Hence, we may assume that where the priesthood is

found a ritual will be found too, and, further, we are entitled to say that if the institutions of Christ created a priesthood, they *pari passu* implied a ritual. And before looking for the office of the priest in those religions in which we find the ritualistic *facies* or expression, we wish to call attention to the fact that a belief in the presence of Divinity, either actually or vicariously, in sacraments or in offices of grace, naturally begets the priestly function; and that whereas the argument is safely urged, that if Christ instituted priests he also accredited ritual, it is further insisted that if Christ promised his presence in his sacraments, or any one of them, he warranted the institution of priests, and if he warranted it he gave it. Elsewhere (Chap. V.) we have attempted to show that the same incitements to ritualism exist in Christianity as in other religions, and amongst them the promised presence of Christ in the Eucharist, which we say implies the priestly function and the priesthood. Therefore, before looking for the traces and evidence of the priest in the great religions, let us endeavor to understand how a belief in the presence of Divinity originates the priestly function.

The presence of God in a sensible form, however apprehended—as in sacraments, or veiled in a fire or in an image (idolatry)—is so extraordinary and impressive that the rites accompanying worship under such circumstances must be celebrated by a special order of men; the phenomenon must be surrounded by every attendant feature of ceremony which will distinguish and memorialize the occurrence, and amongst these is the use of an elevated, consecrated order of celebrants.

Their differentiation from the common groups of devotees and worshipers, at first almost instinctive, becomes more and more marked as the ritual becomes elaborated—a process which their own institution hastens—and, as an inevitable consequence, they assume technical powers, prescriptive rights, in short, they become essential parts of the ritual, without whom the ritual itself is ineffectual. They now are enveloped in the ritual, which they amplify and sustain. Their hands, their voices, their persons are essential to *empower* the *visible sign* with its qualitative attributes. The *presence of God is summoned through their acts.* This marks the apogee of the priestly function; it is not by any means always so advanced, but this is the logical outcome of its inception; and we believe, in the Christian Church, the Catholic party is justified in claiming for the priest just this office. Only this radical distinction is to be borne in mind—the resident power of consecration in the Christian priest was conveyed by Christ in ordination, and has been ever since perpetuated in the same manner, by, as it were, a species of perennial self-propagation.

It may be urged that the savage sees his god in his fetich, and requires no priest to come between him and it. This is true, but the savage worship of a pocket idol is not representative of public worship or a religious cult. It is a private devotion, an almost secular matter. And it must be also remembered that we have not claimed that the priestly function precedes the assumption of the divine presence; it grows out of it very naturally, but marks the subsequent stages of ritualistic development, in fact, it comes into prominence with a higher grade of worship. Whole races or tribes worship their present deities without a priest, but, as their religious system advances, the priest will most certainly become evolved, and occupy an interventional place, separated from the body of believers, and invested with singular and hypostatic powers.

The priestly function appears in various phases of development in the great religions, but reaches in only a few the fullest growth. The semblance is more or less shown, even in non-ritualistic worship, though, of course, its most characteristic forms are associated with religions of the highest ritualistic type.

In Brahmanism, in India, the various forms, sects, and schools which collectively represent that religion contain some equivalent for the priest, but differently conditioned in each. As soon as the necessity for sacrificial acts was recognized, the development of the priestly function was hastened, and assumed enormous proportions in the end. The varying qualities and objects of sacrifice served to strengthen and enlarge the idea of sacrifice in general, and, quoting Monier Williams:

" All this involved the elaboration of a complicated ritual, and the organization of a regularly constituted hierarchy. To institute a sacrificial rite, and to secure its being carefully conducted, with the proper repetition and intonation of innumerable hymns and texts from the Veda, and the accurate observance of every detail of an intricate ritual by a full complement of perhaps sixteen different classes of priests, every one of whom received adequate gifts, was the great object of every pious Hindoo's highest ambition." *

---

* *Religious Thought and Life in India,* Part I., p. 23.

In Hindooism we find a priestly order instituted by one of its great teachers, Sankara, who exercised the right of self-ordination. " These establishments had a complete ecclesiastical organization and a regular provision for self-perpetuation, so that the spiritual powers of the first head of the community were transmitted by a kind of apostolical succession, through a line of succeeding heads, regularly elected." * This is a mark of priestly character which advances the conception to the highest point of objective value. It assumes the possession of an inherent virtue in the priesthood, which becomes the legacy of their successors. Again, in the Vaishnava sects, the religious teachers are not only regarded as wise, but as in some sense possessed of the essence of divinity, and they officiate in special ceremonies. Lines of succession of the priesthood are insisted upon in various sects, and are claimed with the greatest confidence. In the Sikh sect the priestly function appears, and the act of consecration in the baptismal service of the sect is not omitted, a realization of the priest's higher executancy. In addition, the ordained religious teacher, or *Gum*, possesses peculiar powers, and bestows a special value upon his religious acts through his official character.

It is easily seen that in the forms of Brahmanism the priestly function appears, and in varying measure reflects that personate and unique nature of the priest which is its highest form, and which has really been only completely realized in the Catholic priest, whose

---

* *Religious Thought and Life in India,* Part I., p. 23.

7*

acts, under the Christian dispensation, and *by its law*, possess an incommunicable efficacy.

In Buddhism, although the priest assumes an elaborate development in its later and composite phase, and naturally, as this late phase has the ritualistic *facies* well marked, yet in the church, as founded by Gautama, and in the monastic order whose superior he was, slender provision is made for the priestly function. Gautama founded an order of monks whose actions and thoughts were regulated by an exhaustive code. They were all, however, equal, and the rites they administered related to the admission of new members in their order. Yet some relation had to be established and maintained between the order and the world, whose lay forces formed a part of the Church. The order had been commissioned simply to teach the truth, but this very position of teacher instituted a relation which required but a few years and a few congregations to elevate into a relation of priest and people, and such it practically became. Buddha, himself, was intent upon preaching and practicing a certain pure philosophy, conjoined with moral and benevolent precepts for good living, but he had no thought and made no preparation for sacramental uses or institutions. His vision of bliss and his promise to the world was "that he would yet in this life apprehend the truth itself, and see it face to face." But he left an order which preserved intact the doctrines he gave, and which was intended to be a moral community of the most rigid and comprehensive exemplariness, and this order became the custodian of the doctrine, and in reality represented to the world a priesthood, a discipleship, with power and knowledge to teach, though they had no deputed power in sacramental offices. The order was open to all, but a process by which the postulants were indued with membership must first be submitted to.

> "The ceremony of initiation is completed in two grades; there is a lower, to a certain extent preparatory, ordination, Pabbajja, *i. e.*, the outgoing; and a higher, Upasampadâ, *i. e.*, the arrival. The Pabbajja is the going out from a prior state, from the lay life, or from a monastic sect holding another faith; the Upasampadâ is the entry into the circle of the Bhikkhus, the fully accredited members of the Buddhist order." *

As Dr. Oldenburg remarks: "The outer forms were most simple; the old order was wont, when it undertook ceremonial operations, to express what had to be expressed with bare, business-like precision, and nothing more."† It was a voluntary adhesion to a code, not a change or superinduced efficacy through an ordination. The absence of ritual at this point in Buddhism re-enforces our position that ritual is chiefly sustained and nourished by a doctrine of a divine presence in a service. It corroborates it, because the very opposite and obvious position, that Buddha could not be present with his disciples, was inimical at first to ritualistic growth. Buddha had entered Nirvana, was lost to human appeal, companionship, or recollection. Hence also the priestly function, which arises, as we have indicated, with the assumption of the present divinity, was here absent, at least at first. The inevitable course of events that lead

---

* *Buddha : His Life, His Doctrine, His Order*, p. 347. H. Oldenburg.
† *Ibid.* p. 439.

up to it followed, and as Buddha became an idol and a present deity, his monks became priests.

The successive incarnations of Buddhisatwas, or Lamaism, supplied at once the necessary starting-points for ritualism in the direction of the priest, and the priest came. As Markham says : *

" Since the original scriptures had been conveyed into Ceylon by the son of Asoka, it had been revealed to the devout Buddhists of India that their Lord had created the five Dhyani or celestial Buddhas, and that each of these had created five Buddhisatwas, or beings in the course of attaining Buddha-hood. The Tibetans took firm hold of this phase of the Buddhistic creed, and their distinctive belief is that the Buddhisatwas continue to remain in existence for the good of mankind, by passing through a succession of human beings from the cradle to the grave. This characteristic of their faith was gradually developed, and it was long before it received its present form ; but the succession of incarnate Buddhisatwas was the idea toward which the Tibetan mind tended from the first."

The Lamas became great high-priests and popes ; their persons were sacred, their acts momentous, their will inviolate, they conferred the heritage of their supremacy on their successors, they were " venerated as God's vice-regents through all the eastern countries of Asia, endowed with a portion of omniscience, and with many other divine attributes." (Bogle.)

It is needless to pursue this further. The priestly function appears in Tibetan Buddhism, and also in China, markedly. It is of no consequence, or it is irrelevant, that the priest of Buddha is uninteresting or ridiculous, that his practices are mummeries, his life

* *Narrative of the Mission of George Bogle to Tibet, and of the Journey of Thomas Manning to Shusa.* Introduction, p. 45.

often a grotesque exhibition of superstition. The abstract conception of a priest finds a rude and repellent embodiment in this worship, but still an embodiment. In China, where Buddhism prevails extensively, we find the Buddhist priest fully developed, and of his temples and their worship this word-picture from Williams's *Middle Kingdom* gives probably an accurate impression:

"There stood fourteen priests, seven on each side of the altar, erect, motionless, with clasped hands and downcast eyes, their shaven heads and flowing gray robes adding to their solemn appearance. The low and measured tones of the slowly moving chant they were singing might have awakened solemn emotions, too, and called away the thoughts from worldly objects. Three priests kept time with the music, one beating an immense drum, another a large iron vessel, and a third a wooden ball. After chanting they kneeled upon low stools, and bowed before the colossal image of Buddha, at the same time striking their heads upon the ground. Then, rising and facing each other, they began slowly chanting some sentences, and rapidly increasing the music and their utterance until both were at the climax of rapidity, they diminished in the same way until they had returned to the original measure. In the meantime some of the number could not retain their curiosity, and, even while chanting and counting their beads, left their places to ask for books. The whole service forcibly reminded me of scenes in Romish chapels ; the shaven heads of the priests, their long robes, mock solemnity, frequent prostrations, chantings, beads —yea, and their idol, too—all suggested their types or their antitypes in the apostate Church."

In the national religion of China we find the priest represented by the emperor, in a very majestic and impressive manner. He represented the summation and concrete expression of priestly power to the Chinese.

" The prime idea in this worship is that the emperor is *Tien-tsz*, or ' Son of Heaven,' the co-ordinate with Heaven and Earth, from whom he directly derives his right and power to rule on earth among mankind, the one man who is their vice-regent, and the third of the trinity (*san tsai*) of Heaven, Earth, and Man. With these ideas of his exalted position, he claims the homage of all his fellow-men. He cannot properly devolve on any other mortal his functions of their high-priest, to offer the oblations on the altars of Heaven and Earth at Peking, at the two solstices. He is not, therefore, a despot by mere power, as other rulers are, but is so in the ordinance of nature, and the basis of his authority is divine. He is accountable personally to his two superordinate powers for its record and result. If the people suffer from pestilence or famine, he is at fault, and must atone by prayer, sacrifice, and reformation, as a disobedient son." *

When we turn to Egypt, the inquiry, so far as any uncertainty may be felt as to its results, may be almost dismissed. The sacerdotal character of that religion has been one of its most prominent traits, and one which helped it to assume a very ritualistic and elaborate character. The deities of Egypt dwelt in the temples, and the intervention of priests sprang, by an organic religious law, into being in their service. The priestly function in Egypt was so inordinately prolix as to originate five orders: first, the prophets, the highest in the hierarchy; second, the " divine fathers," of inferior rank; third, the purifiers or washers; fourth, beloved of God; and fifth, the incense bearers and superintendents of the temple. The priests were involved in the texture and processes of the general government, they were the advisers of the king, the judges, and state of-

---

* *The Middle Kingdom*, Vol. II., pp. 194, 195.   S. W. Williams.

ficials. The king himself, by birth and position, was enrolled in the priestly order. The priests offered sacrifice in the temples, and were attached to various deities, but their prerogatives and general position varied with their rank. The highest order became invested with the portentous power of interpreting the will of the gods, they were the custodians of the mysteries, and alone possessed the hidden and esoteric wisdom of these strange rites. Their conduct was rigidly ordered, and all the circumstances of ordinary life regulated by a code of exclusive and stringent provisions. They embodied the spiritual aspects of Egyptian life, they conferred vitality to the Egyptian ritual, and were half absorbed in the miraculous and absolute nature of the gods.

In Mohammedanism, as we have seen its anti-ritualistic genius, it will not be expected that the priest will be very prominent, if, indeed, discernible. He must assume small proportions and be entirely divested of those inherent virtues of office which make his religious acts sacramentally efficacious. Indeed, a religion wherein ritualism only reaches some of the earlier decorative stages, and has not arisen as a logical necessity, would scarcely have originated the priest. The Ulema, in Islam, are the expounders or preachers, and they pretend to monopolize the learning and meaning of the Koran ; they are divided into *Imams*, or ministers of religion, *Muftis*, or doctors of the law, and the *Kadis* or *Mollahs*, or judges. Yet the imam has been designated as a priest, and his functions in some respect suggest the appellation. The ceremonies of circumcision, marriage, and washing and burying the dead are performed by him. He ministers in the mosques and conducts services. Though he does not consecrate a sacrament or minister to a present god, his acts do possess to the pious and orthodox Moslem a particular sanctity, and he satisfies, in a meager and helpless sort of way, the need men feel for a special and ordained ministry. But though the regular channels of Mohammedan religious culture and ministration have not supplied their worship with a priest, the irresponsible but successful rise of the dervishes has partially, though irregularly and grotesquely, answered that need.

The talented authoress of *Twenty Years' Residence among the People of Turkey* says:

"The dervish's title to reverence does not, like his rival's, rest upon his learning and his ability to misinterpret the Koran; it rests on his supposed inspiration. On this ground, as well as on account of his reputed power of working miracles and the general eccentricity of his life, he is regarded by the people with extreme veneration."

The story is told by the authoress of a wild and "hairy sheik," who stopped the Sultan Mahmoud and denounced him on his way across the bridge of Galata, and who was summarily executed for his insolence. A soft radiance was imagined thereafter to shine over his tomb, and "the fool" is still venerated as a saint. It impressively illustrates the influence these men have on the popular mind, and the character of that influence. It is inceptively sacerdotal, or, at least, that element is not undistinguishable in it.

There are many orders of dervishes, and their tenets

and ceremonies vary in great detail. Their functions seem to be to supply a sort of religious stimulation, and their exhibitions are often fraught with savage and unnatural demonstrations, though in other cases they become graceful and impressive. The priestly function, having no aliment in the conceptions of the Moslem faith, has not distinctively arisen therein, but these wayward and eccentric extravagancies, like the suggestions of ritualistic methods in their worship which we have looked at, *possibly* indicate the perturbed sense of the people seeking some such satisfaction.

In Judaism, as the direct precursor, signal, and type of Christianity, we find the priestly function most conspicuously shown. As soon as Divinity, in its mysterious and symbolic forms, dwelt among the Jews, then the priest came, and in the hallowed union of his functions with the divine influence, inspired the formation of an extended ritual. The priests of Judah were the "sons of Aaron;" they belonged to the tribe of the Levites, they became sanctified for their calling by the selection of God, and were reserved for the ministrations of his temple. The Levites formed a consecrated tribe from which, by selection, the priests of God were chosen. The Levites were solemnly dedicated, but the priesthood "involved a yet higher consecration." They became the intercessors for the people, and constantly represented to God their dependence, in their sorrows and in their joys, while they conducted those symbolic sacrifices which kept alive the sense of sin, the need of penitence, the actuality of propitiation. Their induction into office was minutely symbolical.

" Their old garments were laid aside. Their bodies were washed with clean water, and anointed with the perfumed oil, prepared after a prescribed formula, and to be used for no lower purpose. The new garments belonging to their office were then put on them. The truth, that those who intercede for others, must themselves have been reconciled, was indicated by the sacrifice of a bullock as a sin-offering, on which they solemnly laid their hands, as transferring to it the guilt which had attached to them. The total surrender of their lives was represented by the ram slain as a burnt-offering, a 'sweet savor' to Jehovah. The blood of these two were sprinkled on the altar, offered to the Lord. The blood of a third victim, the ram of consecration, was used for another purpose. With it Moses sprinkled the right ear, that was to be open to the divine voice, the right hand and the right foot, that were to be active in divine ministrations. Lastly, as they were to be the exponents, not only of the nation's sense of guilt, but of its praise and thanksgiving, Moses was to ' fill their hands ' with cakes of unleavened bread and portions of the sacrifices, which they were to present before the Lord as a wave-offering." *

Nothing that we might think could be devised that would preserve their type unchanged, was omitted. Their form became stereotyped, petrified, and thus the lofty considerations and offices inseparable from their caste were so stamped upon the Jewish mind, and have been so permanently displayed before the world, that it is unlikely that at any time will they become obliterated. They were continued in the Christian Church by a natural reassumption of the same functions ; in fact, they were but the precursors of a ministry, compared with which their office was an ephemeral type, and in comparison with whose sacrifice theirs was but a fleeting symbol.

---

* Smith's *Dictionary of the Bible*, article Priest.

In the religion of Zoroaster, the Parsees have maintained a sacrificial officer, a priest, though not wearing the same striking and sacerdotal marks of pre-eminence which the Jewish *cohen* assumed. He ministered before the sacred fires, and was in a sense a selected deputy of the people, to implore and intercede, and to present to the *presence* of the *god* thus typified in flame, their votive gifts and offerings.

" The priesthood is a hereditary profession among the Parsees. The priest does not acquire his position from sacerdotal fitness, or superior learning. Strictly speaking, he cannot be called a spiritual guide. The son of a priest is also a priest, unless he chooses to follow another profession, which is not prohibited to him. But a layman cannot be a priest. They resemble the Levites." *

The priest amongst the Parsees is qualified for his office by two grades of ceremonies, those of Navar and of Maratab, both of which are preceded by the Bareshnum ceremony. In this latter, purity of body is attained.

" In order to attain to the priestly dignity of a Navar, the candidate goes through two periods of retreat with Bareshnum, six days of retreat at his own house, and the final initiatory ceremony, which lasts for four days in the fire-temple." †

To enable him to take part in the higher rituals, the priest must pass through the ceremony of Maratab.

The priest thus ordained officiates at various ceremonies, and in the investiture of a child with the " sudra," in marriage, at death, at the consecration of a

* *History of the Parsees*, Vol. II., p. 235. Karaka.
† *Ibid.*, p. 238.

" tower of silence," and in the preparation of the Homa drink, figures in a *rôle* which distinctly reflects the technical characteristics of the priest as conceived in more ritualistic religions.

We have examined the traces and appearances of the priestly function, in those great religions which have most deeply affected and penetrated human thought and character, and we find that they are none of them entirely devoid of its evidence.

It would have been an easy task, though unnecessarily lengthening an inquiry too generally understood even to need so much elucidation, to have pointed out the priest in the Scandinavian religions, in the worship of Greece and Rome, in the ferocious rites of the Aztecs, and the more peaceful and attractive forms of the Peruvian aboriginal cult, and to have indicated his shadowy approach in the medicine-man and juggler of the savage. Everywhere the priest idea in some measure prevails, and, with its greater or less development, the ritualistic tendency appears in greater or less force. The priest presumes a presence of Divinity, before which he ministers; he represents the eternal verity of man's sin, probation, and reconciliation with God. He must enforce an ideal of living while he assumes the sacred functions, the virtue of whose operation he dispenses to the people. His position is hierarchical, and he brings into religion a reflection of that system of orders and grades which the whole natural world promulgates and shows. The priestly function cannot be divorced from any religion which recognizes man's prostrate state, and which affirms that it possesses a process by which fallen man can not only rise, but be renewed and remade. That profession is made in Christianity; the priest is an essential part of that process, he has been provided for it by its Founder, he is involved in the evolution of Christian doctrine, and as the whole truth as it is in Christ pressed upon the world the recognition of its Saviour's presence in the Sacrament of the Holy Communion, the priest rose in the strong light of that radiant faith, and, mingling with other thoughts and incentives, gathered in the worship of the Church the beauty, of the world's art, the melody of its music, the contemplative poetry and inspiration of its symbolism, the piety and sweetness of its grateful commemoration. The priest must be a ritualist, and if Christianity contains a priest, it must assume ritualism.

The priest illustrates the narrower and more correct use of the term "ritualism" also, to which we alluded in Chapter I., p. 4. He it is who becomes a type of the strictest formalism, and uses forms of words, which as used by him secure certain virtues, evoke or precipitate certain properties. This feature of ritualism is quite obvious in all ethnic religions, and very noticeable in the ritualistic churches of Christianity. It is not indicated in this book as a special principle of ritualistic or ceremonial life, as it is really embraced in those we have mentioned ; or, more accurately, it is involved in the priestly function as an incentive itself to ceremonial worship. The range of the priestly function is indeed shown by the number and character of those things which the priest alone does or says, and, in the general discussion of ritualism as an objective phenomenon, they can be legitimately referred to its art element, its symbolic or its commemorative characters, as they heighten more or less exclusively one of these features, or assume a divided nature amongst all.

# CHAPTER V.

RITUALISM A NECESSITY IN THE CHRISTIAN CHURCH.

THE fact of the ritualistic life in the Christian Church is self-evident ; the Roman and Greek churches are ritualistic, and we have seen in Chapter I. that they both afford means for determining the elements of ritual in general. We are here desirous to show that this ritualistic life *belongs* to the Christian Church; has developed with its development and strengthened with its strength; that it is inherently necessary in the Church; and that, if the fact of its universality in the religious phenomena of the world everywhere is acknowledged, as we think the previous chapters show it should be, and if we can establish that Christianity, as we have received it, supplied and supplies the identical conditions under which we have seen it, ritualism, arise in these other religions, then we believe not only the expectancy of finding ritualism in Christianity is justified, but that Christianity without ritualism is in an abnormal, factitious, and temporary state; that Protestantism, as a body of opinion, has put itself in dangerous antagonism with the laws of religious development in human nature, and must either return to the abandoned terrors of ceremonial and churchly life, or, in its progressive attenuation of belief and practice, succeed in extirpating the most noble and refining features of Christian worship, to the vulgarization of thought and feeling.

This defense is written in justification of that Catholic movement which has put the Anglican Church in its
right position as the truest representative of Christian
belief and practice, as the Body of Christ, as the single
embodiment of religious thought which is adequate to
perpetuate the historic and spiritual reality of Christ's
Word, and to harmonize that Word, in its varied aspects,
with the varied phenomena of modern thought—in short,
a Church indefectible in the long run in its teaching
and authority, and to-day extending, under the guidance of the Holy Ghost, to erring man, as well as it
can be offered, the salvation of body and soul in Jesus
Christ.   That Catholic movement which has placed the
Anglican Church in its commanding and royal position
is essentially ritualistic.  We have spoken to prove that
in this it is not simply defensible, but that, in its mission to restore Catholic doctrine in the Church, it must
involve ritualism as an essential, as knit in with the
elements and texture of its teaching.   It is not desired
to imply, though we run the risk of such misrepresen-
tation, that Catholic *power* cannot exist without ritualism—it has been kept through many weary years of the
Church's existence; but we do mean that without ritualism Catholic doctrine runs a great danger of being obscured, weakened, explained away, or rejected.   The
creed, the orders, and the sacraments give Catholic
power, and the Church has never lost these, though it ·
has in many places succeeded in stripping itself of all
beauty and all zeal.
    We have said that in this chapter we propose to
show that ritualism belongs to the Christian Church,

and must be and is maintained there, and that without any considerations at present of its moral fitness or influ-' ence, or its inherent beauty and truth. The argument we employ to establish this is twofold : first, the *argumentum de natura rerum in religione*, or an argument based upon the very nature of things in revelation, outside of which nature of things no one can succeed in inaugurating any permanent issue in the Church. Secondly, the *argumentum de facto*, or the argument based upon history, viz., the recorded events and changes in the Church's life.

The outline, or scheme of thought, embracing the use of these double arguments is as follows : We have seen that ritualism exists more or less fully in all religions (Chap. II.). This establishes a *prima facie* argument that it will arise in Christianity. We have seen that the general provocations or causes of ritual are : first, the assumption of the divine presence, actually or vicariously, in sacraments involving, secondarily, the priestly function (Chaps. III. and IV.); secondly, memorable events in a religion invoking commemoration (Chap. III.) ; thirdly and fourthly, nature, temperament, talent of the race employing the religion, for expression, artistic, musical, or symbolic (Chap. III.). If it is shown that these causes for ritual actually exist in the Biblical Christianity, as recorded and described by the apostle, then we have established a rational basis for expecting that ritual will arise in Christianity exactly as under these same conditions it has done so elsewhere. Observe, we are not engaged at present in justifying ritualism on expedient or general grounds.

Part II. of this book deals with that. We are simply
employed now in showing that it must have arisen in
conformity with all natural procedure, elsewhere examined in other religions, because, as Christ finished
his work, he left it charged with all the necessary
forces to effect its (ritualism's) inception and growth.
Finally, we beg the attention of those readers who, because they do not find ritual expressly described or
figured in the Bible, nor any very express evidence of it
in the first years of the Church's life, conclude it is
mischievous and intrusive. Really, this is, in the light
of what we know, inconclusive. The absence of all
ritualism, or evidence of it, in the Bible, or in the succeeding years of the young Church, scarcely should attract the skeptical attention of any philosophic student
of this question. Putting aside the meagerness of our
knowledge of that early service, and the attitude of ex-
patriation assumed by Christians, which made them at
first a secret society, it did not belong then or there.
It was a mark of the developed Church, itself as much
an example of evolution and growth as a crustacean or
a tree; it signified its maturity, its permanent form.
The Church is a product of growth, under the divine
germinating and fructifying influence of the Holy
Ghost, which same influence acts, as it must ever act,
in accordance with the constructional lines of man's
nature. The principles of ritualism, the seeds of its
deathless power, are buried in the soil of human nature,
and that human nature is inherently in accord with the
preaching of Christ's Word; and that Word, supplying
those very conditions necessary for the germination of

the ceremonial principle, will bring the same to an objective existence, as surely as under favorable surroundings the sun's rays will fetch the sprouting plumule of the wheat grain to the surface of the ground—a grain which the careful sower may have planted weeks or months before. It is and was and will be of no value as a counter argument to assert that ritualism did not at once define the outlines of the early Church. It could not, during the lives of the apostles; it would have been disorderly and unnatural, out of place and premature. This has been realized by the sectarian historians. Dr. Schaff * says: "The Church, too, in the first century, was as yet a strictly supernatural organization, a stranger in this world, standing with one foot in eternity, and longing for the second coming of her heavenly bridegroom." It is of import, and this involves our first argument, to prove that the dispensation of Christ did provide the normal stimulants to ritualism, its logical antecedents and premises, and thereby, as all of God's creation is a consistent unity, a regulated and interbalanced whole, did justify, indeed, provided expressly for its later rise.

God, in the dispensation of Moses, it is conceded, anticipated the dispensation of Christ, and prepared and directed an elaborate chain of events, as well as raised a significant line of personages, which were, all together, events and persons, signals and types of the coming advent of the Son of God. For "Israel, besides being a civil polity, was a theocracy; she was not merely a

---

* *History of Christianity*, Vol. II., p. 134.

nation, she was a Church.   In Israel religion was not, as with the peoples of pagan antiquity, a mere attribute, a function, of the national life.   Religion was the very soul and substance of the life of Israel; Israel was a Church, encased, embodied, in a political constitution." *

The covenant with Moses established the Church of Israel, whose outlines and features were to be reflected· in the Church of Christ, however obscured the objective resemblance might be.   This was a logical necessity. The type and the antitype must conform, and conformity of the spirit means, not in a slight measure either, conformity of the body.   The rigidity of the formal arrangement of the Jewish Church and worship, though, as we have seen (Chap. III.), strictly explainable, as far as its ritualistic features go, upon the assumption of the same processes being present which engendered ritualism elsewhere, was a safeguard against the dangers of change, variation, and inexpressiveness.   The sign given was neither uncertain nor unsteady.

The strict continuity of the Jewish and Christian Churches, and, therefore, the strict parallelism of their dominant constructive features, has been set forth by Cardinal Newman with striking distinctness.   It establishes a *prima facie* evidence that ritual must enter into the texture of the Christian Church.   We quote liberally from his strong and eloquent plea : †

" Let it be observed that if the prophecies in their substance certainly have had a literal fulfillment, as I think any one might see who considered the matter, so that the Jewish Church and Chris-

---

* *Sermons,* The Divinity of our Lord.   Canon Liddon.
† *Sermons bearing on Subjects of the Day,* by John Henry Newman.

tian are really one, then this will follow, viz., that that very appearance of separation and contrast between them, which I grant does exist, does but make it more necessary that there should be some great real agreement and inward unity between the one and the other, whether we can discover what it is or not, on account of which they are called one. What has taken place in the Christian Church is, of course, no fulfillment at all of promises made to the Jewish, *unless*, in some very true sense, they may be called one Church. The greater the difficulty on the surface, so much the firmer and stronger must be the principle of continuity and identity within, to counterbalance it. And what are these points of intimate union between the Church in her Jewish and in her Christian form, it is, of course, important to inquire.

"Not only do forms and ordinances remain under the Gospel equally as before, but, as is plain from the very chapter on which I am commenting, what was in use before is not so much superseded by the Gospel ordinances as changed into them. What took place under the law is a pattern, what was commanded is a rule, under the Gospel. The substance remains ; the use, the meaning, the circumstances, the benefit is changed ; grace is added, life is infused ; ' the body is of Christ,' but it is in great measure that same body which was in being before he came. The Gospel has not put aside, it has incorporated into itself the revelations which went before it. It avails itself of the Old Testament, as a great gift to Christian as well as to Jew. It does not dispense with it, but it dispenses it.

"It seems, then, that making what allowance we will for the changes which were introduced by the Gospel, which in point of knowledge, grace, and influence upon the world were incalculably great, and cannot be overrated, yet, as regards the substantial form of religion, ecclesiastical order, ritual, polity, observance, the change was not considerable.

"Again : under the Jewish law, the ministerial office was continued by a succession ; it was not committed to men here and there, as it might be, but passed from father to son. The carnal form of this ordinance is now at an end, but the succession remains ; spiritual sons succeed spiritual fathers. As, under the law, each preceding generation of priests begat the following, so each generation ordains the next under the Gospel. Again : the Jewish temple is abolished, because the true and spiritual temple, the communion of saints, has been established by Christ. Yet though the type is at an end, the precept remains. Temples are to be built to God's honor under the Gospel, and to be consecrated, and to be treated as his dwelling-places, and in other respects, as far as suitable to be conformed to the model of that ancient building once commanded. Once more : under the law there were altars and sacrifices ; these very altars, these very sacrifices, have come to naught, for they were a shadow of good things to come ; but still altars and sacrifices endure, though with a different virtue and a different purpose ; they are part of that body which is of Christ. He has taken possession of them, and made them spiritual."

Now, the central physical feature of the Jewish worship was the presence of Jehovah in the shrine of the ark, in the Holy of Holies of the temple. Whatever that manifestation might be, it was assuredly a fact, if the attestation of Scripture amounts to anything, and although this appearance became intermittent in the process of time, God yet held these sacred precincts as the site for revelations to men ; and here came to Zacharias, at the very inception of the Christian dispensation, the supernatural vision and message concerning John the Baptist. God, as Jehovah, resided in some mysterious way, yet actually, in the Jewish Church; God, as Christ, it is legitimately, compulsorily inferred, dwells in some mysterious, yet actual way, in the Christian Church. This must be a fair inference. Does Christ warrant it? And, first, does Christ speak of a Church or does he define a ritual?

In the momentous and beautiful scene when Jesus, with his disciples, came into the coasts of Cesarea Philippi, and talked with his disciples about himself, and Simon Peter confessed him, he uttered these impressive words: "And I say also unto thee, That thou art

Peter, and upon this rock I will build my *Church;* and the gates of hell shall not prevail against it."* (St. Matthew, xvi. 18.) This establishes the inference of a Christian Church. Christ had not revealed previously the character of his bequest to the world. He had preached and cured, and sown wide-cast the seeds of his most beneficent influence. As death approached, and the outline of the invisible Church began to stir the vision of his prophetic glance, he mentioned, for the first time, what that bequest would be, what he lived to accomplish and testate. The outlines of the Church were never inflexibly drawn, but there were furnished the needful apparatus or equipment for its birth and progress, the orders, the sacraments, and the formative influence of Christ's person and teachings, acts and miracles, in all their catholic diversity of implication and application. Now, it is not necessary to ask for repetition, reiteration, and emphasis of this expression of Christ. His words on any subject have not commonly been subjected by believers to an incredulous criticism because of their infrequency. They have all been regarded as important. We must conclude that a Church based upon some functional offices, and having some inherent power, was founded by Christ, for we learn that the disciples shall baptize all people, and preach the Gospel, and commemorate the Passion in the Eucharist. The very fact, however, that he himself

---

* The Roman perversion of this passage to authorize papal usurpation is easily corrected ; the rock alluded to is the confession Peter has just made, not Peter himself ; were it Peter, the original would read τῷ Πέτρῳ, whereas it is τῇ πέτρᾳ.

does not rigidly define it, save in some essential elements, is evidence that having gathered together and influenced the separate elements, he knew they would themselves, under the guidance of the Holy Ghost, combine and segregate, and form a Church more technically limited. If, then, Christ left a Church, or the beginnings of a Church, which, irresistibly, through the divine motion imparted to them, developed a perfect Church, the next question to be answered is : Does he dwell in that Church, and how?

The Jewish Church possessed a residential character as the home of God on earth; its antitype must even more touchingly and literally possess its Founder in itself. It is significant to refer to the much-abused text: "Lo, I am with you to the end of the world." Of course it is quite intelligible that such an expression could be understood to refer simply to a protective spiritual supervision and sympathy, but it is intrinsically improbable. It must be remembered that believers accept Christ as the Son of God, his mission as the most stupendous and revolutionary human society has ever encountered; that his words are deeply freighted with meanings and suggestions of the most solemn sort, and that such a promise, under the circumstances, implied a definite and positive personal assistance. It was a logical and appropriate expectation that, as God dwelt visibly with his chosen people in the past, Christ should inhabit the fair mansion of the Church which his death had consecrated, and which became the teacher of the world through an intussusception, in its spiritual form, of his own spiritual nature.

" For the children of the Spirit, the eternal Christ lives now not less truly than eighteen hundred years ago. Did he not say : ' I will not leave you comfortless, I will come to you ' ? And how ? Of what kind was this world-enduring presence to be ? Politicians are present after death, by the laws or dynasties which they have established. The intellectual survive by the force of the ideas to which they have given currency. The good live yet more nobly by the persuasive beauty of their examples. Was the presence of Christ to be of this description—a presence not of his person, but of the natural effects of his historical appearance—differing in degree, but not in kind, from the posthumous presence of kings and wits, and eminently good or bad characters ? No. It was to be a real but a spiritual presence. It was not to be, as some Socinianizing theologians have imagined, a presence of the Spirit, substituted for the presence of the Saviour. The Spirit is emphatically the Spirit of Christ, because he is the minister of Christ's supersensuous presence. The second Adam is himself a 'quickening spirit.' Christ is eminently present with us by the presence of his Spirit. We do not see him, but he has not left us. He is with us invisibly, but as truly as he was in the streets of Jerusalem, or on the shores of the Lake of Galilee, and the children of the Spirit see him, contemplate him, cling to Him, as did the disciples of old." *

But there can be to human hearts no spiritual reality without its sign, its physical counterpart, and the indwelling of the Christ-life in the Catholic Church must be typified and signalized in some material form, just as the pillar of smoke and fire were objective evidences of God's presence to the ancient Jews. Man is a body as well as a soul. It is common, but erroneous, to speak of man's body as related to his spirit only as is the casket to the jewel which it contains, or only as a prisoner to the walls of his dungeon. As a matter of fact, the personal spirit of man strikes its roots far and deep into

---

* *University Sermons.* Canon Liddon.

8*

the encompassing frame of sense with which, from the
first moment of its existence, it has been so intimately
associated; in a thousand ways, and most powerfully,
the body acts on the soul, and the soul on the body.

It is urged that, through the refining intellectualism of
the day, the increasing mental apprehensiveness of the
race, no sign, no outward symbol, is needed that Christ
may be considered as present with us without some
outward form as with it. This is a radical contro-
version of a fact. Nothing is so present to us as when
its presence appeals to us through the senses, and it is
simply obstinacy, and an obscuration of truth, to say
it is. The question as to whether it is more difficult to
apprehend Christ through a form as present, when that
form offers no adequate representation of himself, is irrelevant or worthless, because, as a matter of *strict evidence*, Christ, the Master, is a hundredfold more present *actually* to a devout Catholic than he has ever been
to the most fervent divines of Protestant doctrine. It
is simply a scientific necessity, arising from the constitution of human nature.

But how did Christ, if he did at all, provide for the
fulfillment of his promise: "Lo, I am with you to the
end of the world"? He provided exactly what the
necessity of the case required, and gave it a pathetic
intensity of meaning by associating it with that very
act of outward propitiation, *i. e.*, his death, which
forms the hope and the remembrance of the human
race, the basis of Christian doctrine, the stigma and the
glory of the world, and is interwoven in the tissue of
history as a fact and as a mystery. He instituted the

office of Holy Communion, which became an extension of his death, and formed the *visible process*, to every believing soul, by which redemption by His death once for all became the particular possession of each at any time. The language of Scripture is not obscure, it is not even equivocal.

" And as they were eating, Jesus took bread, and blessed it, and brake it, and gave it to the disciples, and said, *Take, eat ; this is my body.*

" And he took the cup, and gave thanks, and gave it to them, saying, *Drink ye all of it ;*

" *For this is my blood of the new testament*, which is shed for many for the remission of sins."

But more expressly in St. John we have the famous passage (vi. 47–58):

" Verily, verily, I say unto you, He that believeth on me hath everlasting life.

" I am that bread of life.

" Your fathers did eat manna in the wilderness, and are dead.

" This is the bread which cometh down from heaven, that a man may eat thereof, and not die.

" I am the living bread which came down from heaven : if any man eat of this bread, he shall live forever: and the bread that I will give is my flesh, which I will give for the life of the world.

" The Jews therefore strove among themselves, saying, How can this man give us *his* flesh to eat ?

" Then Jesus said unto them, Verily, verily, I say unto you, Except ye eat the *flesh* of the Son of man, and drink his blood, ye have no life in you.

" Whoso eateth my flesh, and drinketh my blood, hath eternal life ; and I will raise him up at the last day.

" For my flesh is meat indeed, and my blood is drink indeed.

" He that eateth my flesh, and drinketh my blood, dwelleth in me, and I in him.

" As the living Father hath sent me, and I live by the Father ; so he that eateth me, even he shall live by me.

" This is that bread which came down from heaven : not as your fathers did eat manna, and are dead : he that eateth of this bread shall live forever."

What mountainous obstinacy it is to explain away and reject these words, and what a dangerous occupation, too.

The simply commemorative doctrine, as usually accepted by Protestant churches, does seem from every point of view a most shallow and futile theory. It reduces a saving office to a platitude of invention which is scarcely ingenious. Let any one read Candlish's explanation of "Our Participation in Christ's Death," *et seq.*, in the Lord's Supper, in his *Christian Sacraments*, and note how one who, I presume, is a representative Calvinist, fritters away all meaning, dignity, and power in this enriching central sacrament of the Christian Church, and yet, in his effort to put some accordance in his views with the plain Scriptural language, as well as give it some solemnity of character, creeps along the outside of the true Catholic teaching, and consumes page after page with theological trivialities and wordy distinctions which are practically meaningless, though they serve to hide the truth.

Let us fortify this position, viz., the Real Presence of Christ in the Eucharist, by some considerations adduced by eminent and wise and spiritual men in speaking of this sacrament. M. F. Sadler, in a lengthy essay on liturgies and ritual,* says, speaking of the elements:

---

* To be found in a volume entitled *The Church and the Age,* which is composed of a number of elaborate essays on ecclesiastical and related themes.

" As mere emblems, they would have a wondrous sacrificial expression, but they are more than emblems.   They are identified in
some infinitely mysterious but real way with his own sacrificial
body and blood.   Of no sacrifice of old could God say, ' This is my
body : ' of no blood of lambs or goats could God have said, ' This
is my blood.'   So that though in Holy Communion there is no
death, yet there is that in it which identifies it in a heavenly and
spiritual way with that which it exhibits."

Again,

" This incarnate Word and wisdom of God gives utterance to
the most startling and enigmatical language that ever fell on mortal ears.   With the future of his Church spread out before him,
with a full cognizance of the various ways in which men would
accept or reject, apprehend or misapprehend, his words, he sets
forth that the highest supernatural and spiritual results of his own
mediation are to be brought about by a method which he himself
studiously expresses in terms which seem to describe a physical
process in language taken from the lower world of matter and
sense, rather than the higher world of mind and spirit—in words
markedly and decisively objective, because describing the outward
acts of the body rather than the intuitions of the soul.

" No supernatural results of his mediation go beyond this, that
our very bodies should be raised up to the resurrection of life ;  no
spiritual results can go beyond this, that we should dwell in him
and he in us ;  and yet these two results are made by him to depend not only upon believing in him, obeying him, or pleasing
him, but upon eating his flesh and drinking his blood.

" Before examining whether all, or how far, these words refer to
the reception of the Holy Communion, I would remark that it is
impossible to divest these terms of their deep mystery.   Let any
one attempt to translate them into the language of ordinary spiritual life, by divesting them of what refers to the outward and corporal, and by interpreting them as a simply spiritual process, and
he will be convinced how inadequate any such explanation is to
account for the choice of such terms."

More impressively, perhaps, Mr. MacColl says : *

---

* *Lawlessness, Sacerdotalism, and Ritualism,* p. 268.

"I dare not explain away these solemn words. I must believe that they contain some deep meaning ; for it is incredible that our loving Saviour permitted himself to indulge in language which, if not true in some real sense, is misleading and mischievous. He saw that his very strong and solemn language was liable to be misunderstood by the bulk of those whom he was addressing. But he had not to think of them alone. Numberless generations yet unborn were in his thought, in whose ears those words would sound as the glad tidings of a life from the dead. Like his own Incarnation, it was the lot of the doctrine on which he was insisting to be 'set for the fall and rising again of many in Israel, and for a sign which should be spoken against.' But not one jot or tittle of that doctrine would he explain away. Rather than do so he was willing to risk not merely the desertion of the offended multitude, but of his own small band of disciples. 'Will ye also go away ?' They did not, for they acknowledged that his words were 'the words of eternal life.' But the question clearly implies that he would have preferred their forsaking him to the alternative of watering down the ' hard saying' which had offended and repelled the multitude."

And lastly, Dr. Newman, commenting on the words " For my flesh is meat indeed, and my blood is drink indeed : "

"About these words I observe, first, that they evidently declare on the face of them some very great mystery. How can they be otherwise taken ? If they do not, they must be a figurative way of declaring something which is not mysterious, but plain and intelligible. But is it conceivable that He who is the truth and love itself, should have used difficult words when plain words would do ? Why should he have used words, the sole effect of which, in that case, would be to perplex, to startle us needlessly ? Does his mercy delight in creating difficulties ? Does he put stumblingblocks in our way without cause ? Does he excite hopes, and then disappoint them ? It is possible ; he may have some deep purpose in so doing ; but which is more likely, that his meaning is beyond us, or his words beyond his meaning ? All who read such awful words as these in question will be led, by the first impression of them, either with the disciples to go back, as at a hard saying, or with St. Peter to welcome what is promised ; they will be ex- cited in one way or the other, with incredulous surprise or with be- lieving hope. And are the feelings of these opposite witnesses, discordant indeed, yet all of them deep, after all, unfounded ? Are they to go for nothing ? Are they no token of our Saviour's real meaning ? This desire, and again this aversion, so naturally raised, are they without a real object, and the mere consequence of a general mistake, on all hands, of what Christ meant as imagery for literal truth ? Surely this is very improbable."

Does not this consensus of opinion indicate that Christ's own words can reasonably be understood as at least implying his real presence in the Eucharist ? Now it is not my duty, as an apologist of ritualism to Christian men and women who repudiate it, to explain how this thing is probable or even imaginable. I wish to show that Christ, if the words of Scripture are to be trusted, did permit this unquestionable inference to his followers, disciples, and preachers, that his presence rested in their midst, and that it became visibly local- ized in that mysterious sacrament known as the Supper of our Lord.

But the presence of Divinity forms the first starting- point of ritualism, as we have endeavored to show (Chap. III.); indeed, is always its pervasive and justi- fying provocation. It must have produced the same effects in the development of the Christian Church as it did in other religions, and if it were calculated to produce those effects, it was meant to do so. The unity of human nature is complete. God never in- tended to controvert natural tendencies, nor could he have meant to supply, in the revelation of Christ, stimuli to false and opprobrious methods of worship. Ritualism becomes a logical consequence of Christ's own words.

In the commemorative features of Christ's teachings there is more implied, or, rather, all implied and little or nothing said. The Bible narrative itself, however, em-·phasizes events of our Lord's life, and leaves the ineffaceable impression that these events demand our perpetual veneration and recollection, that they must by some device be constantly recalled. Yet the spirit of commemorative regard, as connecting itself with Christ's life, arises from the abounding and exhaustless beauty and richness of that life to humanity as an example, and from the priceless value it has imparted to all life, by the redemption from sin and death purchased by his death. Christ has taught us the inestimable importance of his relation to us. He has forged the indissoluble bonds that make us a part of himself. He has pictured the affectionate and zealous industry with which he searches for us. If he has taught so pregnantly the sufficiency our insufficiency may discover and take, in his purity and perfection, then he impressed himself on the human heart in such a way that commemoration must arise as a grateful tribute from loving and grieving souls, and it will deepen and expand, and, embracing the outline of his life, incorporate dogmatic statements. In this way Christ, in the Bible, by an indirect though none the less purposed way, evokes the feelings that lead to commemorative offices.

How could it be otherwise? At the moment of his departure, when at the Holy Supper in the upper room at Jerusalem, he gave himself forever to the world, Canon Liddon has pointed out how singularly emphatic is his presentment of himself to his disciples, as if he would stamp his *memory* upon their hearts, with the burning, thrilling pressure of loving and again divine assurance, that he indeed was the Saviour of the world, he says:

" In the last discourse it is his person rather than his teaching which is especially prominent ; his subject in that discourse is himself. Certainly he preaches himself in his relationship to his redeemed ; but still he preaches above all and in all himself. All radiates from himself, all converges toward himself. The sorrows and perplexities of his disciples, the mission and work of the Paraclete, the mingling predictions of suffering and of glory, are all bound up with the person of Jesus, as manifested by himself. In those matchless words all centers so consistently in Jesus, that it might seem that Jesus alone is before us ; alone in the greatness of his supramundane glory ; alone in bearing his burden of an awful, fathomless sorrow."

That wonderful personality was thus impressed, not only on that sorrow-stricken and brooding throng, but it has lain on the heart of humanity with the warm pressure of an actual presence ever since. Surely it was an appeal to every sweet and noble emotion of the throbbing, loving hearts of men. Surely, when Jesus so made himself the heritage of those for whom he died, it were an outrage upon that nature which he addressed, and a direct refusal to obey the promptings of the hearts he stirred, if the age that followed had not, with a tender anxiety and searching care, renewed its memory of himself—the Great Friend—by dwelling on the story of his life, and forming from its history, its meanings, and its uses, the Church's year of festivals and fasts. Christ was himself the token of, as he was the sacrifice for, man's redemption, and he made his life a token and a gift. This logically establishes commemoration, if human impressions, desires, and needs count for anything; if the ideal desires of men's hearts, consecrated by the beseeching provocation of Christ's words, mean anything. It means and leads to this aspect of ritualism, and this commemorative practice, thus implied, is extended properly to the events, personages, etc., and prominent articles of the Christian Church.

Finally, as the last justification of ritualistic practice, we find indicated in the New Testament the priestly function. Was not Christ, in his own person, the High Priest of Humanity? Was he not expected to be, and has not St. Paul designated him as such?

"And as to the priesthood," says Dr. Newman, "far from its abolition, Christ was but to purify and refine it. 'He shall sit as a refiner and purifier of silver, and he shall *purify the sons of Levi*, and purge them as gold and silver.' Nor was he to abolish sacrifice, for the prophet proceeds: 'He shall purge them as gold and silver, that they may offer unto the Lord an offering in righteousness.' And what this offering was to be the prophet tells us, speaking of it as a rite of the Church in its universal or Catholic form."

But Christ's priesthood was transmitted to others by so direct a transmission that the Holy Ghost, on the day of Pentecost, visibly proclaimed the wonderful act of succession. And what does Christ mean when he says: "As my Father hath sent me, even so send I you"?*

---

* St. John, xx. 21.

These apostles became peculiar men ; they represented a reservoir of spiritual plenitude, responsibility, and power, which they deputed to others by a process of physical contact, the *laying on of hands.* Christ deputed them, and them only, to baptize, to preach, to celebrate the mystery of his death. Did he not say: " But ye shall receive power after that the Holy Ghost is come upon you ; and ye shall be witnesses unto me, both in Jerusalem and in all Judea and in Samaria, and unto the *uttermost part of the earth* " ? If the *uttermost part of the earth* means what it implies, the apostles in person did none of them so witness for Christ, but it is certainly true that their line of spiritual influence and power, continued in the Church, has done so. Was not Matthias made the successor of Judas under the bond, "that he may take part of this *ministry* and *apostleship,* from which Judas, by transgression, fell "? Is it not made evident that the authority of Christ remained, in some sort, on earth after his departure? Have words any meaning ? then how shall we interpret, "And when he had said this he breathed on them, and saith unto them, Receive ye the Holy Ghost. Whosesoever sins ye remit they are remitted unto them ; and whosesoever sins ye retain they are retained " ? *

Can any philosophic mind suppose that this authority was limited to the lives of the twelve apostles, but should not continue in a dynasty of which Christ was the head, and which shall be continued through the princes and rulers of the Church till the veil of time

* St. John, xx. 22, 23.

falls from the face of eternity? Was Christ's work temporary, his words fugitive? Is not each and all penetrated with a meaning that speaks to the last days as
clearly, as indisputably as they spoke to the disciples
and friends of his life?

We have said (Chap. IV.) that the priestly function
was the "exercise of special powers in the conveyance
of grace." That function, implicitly and explicitly, according to the Scriptures, was the apostle's. Passage
after passage reiterates this.

Compare St. Matthew, Chap. x. 1–8.
     "      "      "        "    xvi. 18–19.
     "      "      "        "    xxviii. 18–20.
     "     St. Mark,        "    iii. 13–15.
     "      "   "        "    xvi. 15 *et seq.*
     "      " Luke,        "    x. 16.
     "      " John,        "    xiv., xv., xvi.

These last three chapters are filled with unexpressed
but sensible intimations of the special character of the
apostles. See also St. John, xxi. 15 *et seq.*

So far as the life and words of Christ go, as given in
the Bible, it does seem as if the apostles were indued
with the "exercise of special powers for the conveyance
of grace," and it does not seem that, except these and
the seventy, any others were.

This establishes a strong inference that a priestly
function was, no matter if only latently, impressed upon
the apostles; and if so, then *a fortiori*, it was intended
for transmission to their successors, a heritage and
gift as well, to other ages. Later days developed the
character, subdued at first, and this important aid to-

ward ritualistic observance seems thus derived from the language and history of the evangelists.

Finally, on general grounds, we think it was a just and significant provision that ritualism should not, in the proclamation of Christianity through Christ, become obvious or obtrusive. The most ardent and consistent ritualist is certainly also a Christian, and knows that his ritual, however efficacious he may think it is for the preservation of Catholic truth, is not itself a doctrine or a saving ordinance. Christ preached the Catholic truth, and with that preaching he prepared, in many subtilely divine ways, for the growth of a ceremonial Church. The ceremony was not the Word, it went with it ; but the Word of Christ alone manifested itself, incomparable, supernatural, practical, and saving. Nothing was to be involved needlessly at that moment with the wonderful message of Jesus; save Jesus, nothing was to attract the attention of an awakened world. The period was one of exaltation, in which humanity and its sin, unveiled, knelt before the burning presence of the Son of God. But, in the many forces, various influences, unseen voices, that later converged upon the growing nucleus of the Bride of Christ, the Church, those, as we have seen, were not left out which shaped it into an orderly, a stately, a teaching ritual. To what extent, and how actually they can be found in the words and events of Christ's life we have seen, *i. e.*, the expressed presence of Christ in his sacrament, the implied, though not expressed, necessity of commemorative exercises, the establishment of a priestly function, not distinctly asserted to be that at first, but none the less

so, and to become more and more apparent and necessary as time removed the visual recollections of Christ,
that, as they faded away from the quivering memory,
the tranced eyes of men should fall, as it were, upon
that mystery of the Eucharist which in the priest's
hand is the viaticum, and the present extension of
Christ's sacrifice, *et ostium Cæli.*

These influences, never quiet, molded the Church,
and, taken in conjunction with the tastes, habits, and
mental attributes of Jew and Gentile, the last incentives to ritualism, prepared its final form, after less than
two centuries of growth; itself not too long a period—to
shape that divine organism which should contain Christ
to the end of time.

Some further thoughts in reference to ritualism and
its guarantee from Scripture. We have shown how in-
expedient it was for Christ to speak of ritualism. He
apprehended its necessary use and provided the stimuli
for its rise, not for the sake of ritualism, but because
his doctrine directly nurtured and required ritualism.
Ritualism is in Christ's word because Christ's word is
what it is. They that have ears to hear let them hear.

But the inspired word in the New Testament does
elsewhere, more point-device, bring its contribution of
suggestion and description to the support of ritualism.

What is this strange, wonderful work of the Revelations, the last majestic symphony of language and
thought and aspiration and devotion, that closes, as
with a sustained burst of piercing, heavenly music, the
work of God. Here is art, the splendor of form and
color; symbolism, the divine union of thought with

form; commemoration, the imaginative rehabiliment of scenes that the heart loves. It is all shot through and through with the most ardent realization of ritualistic expression, but its tremendous messages, its wild portents and omens, promises and threats, are not belittled nor disguised. The pulsations of its period, the strength of its moral significance, are unarrested and unchanged by an imagery that sustains and advances their august beauty.

What influence the voice of St. John had in forming the outward habits of the Church we do not know, but surely, men will pause, who listen to his voice in that mysterious testament, before, with new sneers and taunts, they insult and mock the services, "ritualistic services," of God's Holy Catholic Church.

Let us now turn from the Bible, having noticed how far it provides for the growth of ritualistic practice, and, turning to the actual profane history of the Church, notice to what extent and how quickly it responded to those stimuli created by Christ.

It is quite logical, we think, to believe that the Church, especially at the moment of its severest trials from hostile attack upon it, by secular force and critical objection, should have received the guidance of God. It is a little difficult to conceive that that guidance would have brought it to an altogether unworthy or questionable shape. And first, it is essential to remember that the Church did not, and of necessity could not, assume its final and permanent type at once. It did not spring into the world full armed and full grown; it submitted itself to the action of those processes of growth which obtain in every realm of nature, and through whose selective and perfecting influences the stable things of the earth are made. As Christ was God, yet underwent, and thus transfigured, the physical changes of natural growth and mental invigoration, so did his Church, and without becoming less divine, conciliate nature, as it is in man, to herself, by passing through stages of development which come under natural law.

Necessarily this was so, as the aggregate sum of thought and inspiration which forms the Scriptures had not been delivered to the world before the end of the first century, when some of the most transforming and deepening messages from God came in the mystic beauty and profound statement of St. John's Gospel, and in the judgment splendor of the Apocalypse. Nor was this all. The history, not recorded in the New Testament, of the first century, after the Pentecostal blessing upon the germinal Church (germinal in a constructive and objective sense), was fraught with special events intended to shape and codify the strengthening body of Christians. The spiritual outlines of the militant Church were all embraced, we must believe, in Christ's prophetic vision, but the physical fabric which built that ideal configuration into the world was only slowly formed. The slightest historical or philosophic or even religious instinct must recognize this. The martyrdom of St. Peter and St. Paul, the terrible and ghastly persecution under Nero, the fall of Jerusalem, and the last utterances of St. John, were all agencies directed toward giving the Christian Church its ultimate shape, and they were, let us note, agencies which tended to build that Church in lines of ceremonial effectiveness. And in this wise. The Church could not early have been given its concrete form, as, indeed, its body of dogmatic doctrine was not then completed; it existed, a *corpus licitum*, but not a *corpus confessum*, and often was a *corpus delicti*. It was a masonry of secret professors of a strange faith, and carried on its methods of religious practice under the frown of the law, and always under the suspicious sneer and half-concealed menace of heathen society. It could not assume, under such discouragements, any conspicuous pageantry, but must court an inconspicuous disguise of simple and indifferent methods. The sacred orders of the ministry had been provided for, and were maintained; the sacraments were venerated and preserved, though their full import, perhaps not then, nor until the body of Revelation was completed by John, was clearly seen. With these precious possessions the fragile and insignificant vessel of the early Church was intrusted. The march of events builded it into a ship of state, whose ample dimensions and firm construction would carry them unchanged and unpolluted to the farthest ages. Those events, we say, tended to build the Church in the lines of ceremonial effectiveness.

The deaths of Peter and Paul, and the persecution under Nero, regarding their influence on the early Church solely from the point of view we are engaged in discussing here, were calculated to not only drive the Christians in upon themselves, clinging with a closer, deeper affection to the faith, but also to make

9

their service more profoundly expressive. It, the Church worship, became all they had; they felt peril and enemies surrounding them; their great leaders were perishing; they must have sought a new consolation and new help in their services. They could not have resisted the natural impulse to commemorate these apostles, and as they remembered those whom they had seen and loved, the effort of affectionate recall threw them back again upon the memory of the One Master. They would instinctively live more directly in his presence and realize his provision for them; the sacrament, doubtless, aside from abuses, became a clearer and clearer symbol and fact of Christ's presence, as persecution robbed the Church of those it had more closely known, and it survived, a substitute for the companionship of men, whose spiritual communion they again realized in this Eucharist.

The destruction of Jerusalem (A. D. 67) was an event which, aside from its terrors and blood-revolting incidents, must have appeared to the early Christians as an astounding fulfillment of the Saviour's prophecy, and impressed them profoundly with a different and more confident attachment to the faith than any they had yet felt. To the Christians amongst the Jews it must have excited a pathetic convulsion of natural feelings when the Holy City, which, perhaps, had been their cradle or the religious center of their hopes and prayers wherever they had dwelt, which held the temple of God, and in which the sacred associations of the past were gathered, should disappear so completely, and amid an awful carnage and scenes of mad and criminal fanaticism. They must have recalled with new affection the movement of the temple's ceremonial, and sought to restore to their memories, as well as to their hearts, some tokens of its liturgical beauty. To the Gentile Christians the destruction must have, in many ways, appealed strikingly, as an end of the past dispensation of Moses and handing over to the Christian faith the solemn claims and responsibilities of the new. They could not have failed, at least, the more studious and thoughtful, to feel that the ceremonial outline of that past system must be resumed, but with new material and on a broader basis, in the Church of Christ. The overbearing magnificence of the temple worship had been swept away, its arrogant exclusiveness confounded, and now the worship of God was alone continued in the new body. This thought of their related offices in the world, their relation of progenitor and heir, in the never-ceasing progress of praise on the earth, this unity of object must have sensibly brought to light a singular parallelism existing in their sacraments, their officers, and their aims, and with this there would have been a natural acquiescence to accept ceremonial usage.

But in St. John, whose influence has so deeply penetrated the Church, and imparted to her the supernal glow of beatification, as if the mystic current of her life, since John spoke, pulsed more closely in unison with the beating of the divine heart of Jesus—in St. John we find the culminating agency which left in the Church the fruitful seeds of catholic and ritualistic life. As Dr. Schaff says:

"He is at once the apostle, the evangelist, and the seer of the new covenant. He lived to the close of the first century, that he might erect on the foundation and superstructure of the apostolic age the majestic dome gilded by the light of the new heaven. He had to wait in silent meditation till the Church was ripe for his sublime teaching." *

The Gospel of St. John and the Apocalypse are charged with that deep spiritual apprehensiveness which gives both an actual and mystic meaning to the sacraments, making both the symbol *necessary* and the virtue imparted *real*. The contemplative and orphic nature of much that St. John has written was well calculated, in conjunction with the superb imagery he employed, to ripen the catholic spirit of the Church until it was ready to appropriate all beautiful devices which could nourish and express its thoughts.

An important fact to be remembered in this connection is this: that both Jew and Gentile converts had come from religions all of whose methods were ceremonial. The beauty and symbolic splendor of the Jewish ritual had been to the devout Jew a perpetual comfort and refreshment, and seemed yet, in the days of apparent decadence, to keep alive the hope of final glory. The heathen, whose temples witnessed the intricate evolution of priests and priestesses, whose walls resounded to the chant of chorus, and on whose platforms and in whose niches the pleasing figures of gods and goddesses stood—such an one, however completely he may have broken away from idolatry and paganism, would have been made, unconsciously perhaps, sensitive to beauty in worship, and responded to its most evanescent phases with real pleasure.

The pagan writers certainly realized the value of sensible helps to the imagination and faith of worshipers, for, says Phidias, as quoted by Neander, " it cannot be said that it would be better for men simply to lift their eyes to the heavenly bodies, and that there were no images at all. All these the man of reason worships, and believes that he beholds from afar the blessed gods. But love to the gods makes every one wish to be able to honor them near at hand; so that he may approach and touch them, offer to them with implicit faith, and crown them." And, again, " it lies in the essence of human nature to endeavor to make present before our senses the absent objects of our love." At first, to be sure, the sense of antagonism, the revolt of mind against everything which had previously helped to enslave the thought in a false and execrable faith, may have deepened a transient repugnance to forms and imagery, which, seen only in the light of their unfortunate association with error and sin, would have taken on a false appearance. Persecution would have only strengthened this abhorrence. Neander refers to this distrust of the first Christians. He says : *

" The use of images was originally foreign to the worship and excluded from the churches of the Christians, and so, in general, it continued to be in this period. The confounding of religion and art in paganism made the early Christians suspicious of art. As at the pagan position, the sense for the beautiful had often appeared at variance with, and even opposed to, the moral taste, so the early

---

* *History of Christianity.*

warmth of Christian zeal was inclined to reverse the relation. The religious consciousness easily took an opposite direction to the æsthetic principle of the ancient world, and the holy disdained the beautiful form which had been allied to the unholy."

Yet the young Church at no time was puritanic or anti-ceremonial, and a return to a healthy delight in beauty would have soon taken place the moment the Church enjoyed its natural freedom.

And now, looking at the infant Church in the first century, before, in fact, it had yet fully responded to all the formative influences called into action by God, we find a ceremonial practice which only needed a wider liberty, less restrained and timid relations with the outside world, for it to ripen with the advance of art and mental refinement into technical ritualism. Dr. Schaff tells* us that the services of the Church were based on the plan of those of the Jewish synagogue, whose worship, he says, "was simple, but rather long, and embraced three elements, devotional, didactic, and ritualistic. It included prayer, song, reading, and exposition of the Scripture, the rite of circumcision, and ceremonial washings. The prayers and songs were chiefly taken from the Psalter, which may be called the first liturgy and hymn-book." Dr. Schaff, whose sectarian sympathies permit him no latitude of interpretation where, perhaps, it is entirely justified, describes the early Christian service as consisting of preaching, reading, prayer, and song, and this latter, he admits, embraced the Nunc Dimittis, the Magnificat, and the

---

* *History of Christianity*, Vol. I.

Benedictus; then there were confessions of faith, the anticipations of the beautiful Apostles' Creed, which in sentiment they exactly prefigured. "Finally, the administration of the sacraments, or sacred rites instituted by Christ, by which, under appropriate symbols and visible signs, spiritual gifts and invisible grace are represented, sealed, and applied to the worthy participators." These sacraments were Baptism and Holy Communion. The first would scarcely have any sensible influence upon the forms of the Church, but the latter, characterized by Dr. Schaff "as the inmost sanctuary of Christian worship," according to the interpretation given of this wonderful rite, would have very essentially affected ceremonial usage. In accordance with what we have seen, if the early Church accepted the virtual presence of Christ in this sacrament, ritualism, in its varied forms, would have followed inevitably. We have stopped to show that this real presence is implied, if not expressed, in the Testament; we shall find that, as we think, the early Church accepted its actuality in a catholic and fervent spirit.

The prominence of this solemn office was plainly recognized. It was a daily celebration, and was regarded as involving the highest, holiest, and most refreshing act of worship possible for man. Neander, dealing with the history of the early Church, speaks of this sacrament in these words, which represent truly to him the attitude of the first Christians toward this mystery:

" The visible Church required visible signs for the spiritual facts on which its inward essence rests. Hence Christ, who meant to found a visible Church, instituted two outward signs, as symbols of the invisible fellowship between him, the head of the spiritual body, and its members, the believers, and of the union of these members not only with himself, but with one another—visible means of representing the invisible heavenly benefits to be communicated by him to the members of this body ; and with the believing use of these signs furnished to the outward man of sense in behalf of the inward spiritual man, was to be connected the enjoyment of that fellowship and of those heavenly benefits."

And again, regarding especially the Lord's Supper, he says :

" Hence Christ said, when he distributed wine and bread among his disciples, that this bread and this wine were to be to them, and consèquently to all the faithful of all times, his body and his blood, the which he offered for the forgiveness of their sins, for their salvation, for the establishment of the new theocratic relation ; and as these outward symbols represented to them his body and his blood, so would he himself be hereafter spiritually present with them just as truly as he was now visibly among them ; and as they now sensibly partook of these corporeal means of sustenance which represented to them his body and his blood, so should they receive him, the Saviour, present in divine power within them for the nourishment of their souls ; they should spiritually eat his flesh and drink his blood, should make his flesh and blood their own, and cause their whole nature to be more and more penetrated by that divine principle of life which they were to receive through their communion with him."

The allusions to the real presence of Christ in the Eucharist, from St. Paul, through the early fathers, are numerous. St. Paul himself speaks of " not discerning the Lord's body ; " St. Ignatius and Justin Martyr confess the presence of Christ in the sacrament. St. Irenæus speaks of the Eucharist as consisting of two things—an earthly and a heavenly ; St. Chrysostom asserts, " the Lord's body, although the nature of bread remains;" and Theodoret, by a subtile penetration of thought, writes of this matter that Christ "honored the symbols which are seen with the title of bread and wine, not changing their nature, but adding grace to their nature." * Dr. Pusey, in his work on the *Doctrine of the Real Presence, as contained in the Fathers from St. John to the Fourth General Council*, concludes his summary by urging that as students of religion have all been accustomed to value ante-Nicene testimony as to the divinity of our Lord, they should accept the same testimony as to the nature of his relation to this sacrament. He says (p. 720):

"The principle of these quotations is one and the same. The argument is valid for all or for none. Either it is of no use to show that Christians, before the Council of Nice, did uniformly believe in the divinity of our Lord, as the Church has since, or it *is* a confirmation of the faith that they did receive unhesitatingly, in their literal sense, our blessed Lord's words, 'This is my body.' . . . Yes! along the whole course of time, throughout the whole circuit of the Christian world, from east and west, from north and south, there floated up to Christ, our Lord, one harmony of praise. Unbroken as yet, lived on the miracle of the Day of Pentecost, when the Holy Spirit from on high swept over the discordant strings of human tongues and thoughts, of hearts and creeds, and blended all their varying notes into one holy unison of truth. From Syria and Palestine and Armenia; from Asia Minor and Greece; from Africa Proper, and Egypt, and Arabia, and the Isles of the Sea; wherever any apostle had taught, wherever any martyr had sealed with his blood the testimony of Jesus; from the polished cities or the anchorites of the desert, one eucharistic voice ascended, 'Righteous art thou, O Lord, and all Thy words are truth.'"

* I am indebted for these citations to the excellent and learned work of the Rev. Arthur Wilde Little, *Reasons for Being a Churchman.*

9*

It is true that many of these utterances were much
later than the earliest days of the Church, but it is also
certain that at that time tradition kept alive the doctrine of the Church, and that, at least, it would have
required many years to have effected a change of
conviction and conception so radical as would have
been that from Zwinglianism, with its colorless common sense and poverty-stricken spirit, to Catholicism.
Nothing would have favored this recent intrusion of a
false body of belief. No. The age exulted in the
thought of the unseen yet present Redeemer, and
hung its sweetest hopes upon that daily *sacrifice*
wherein his propitiatory death was recalled in the symbolic offering of bread and wine. Again, the period of
the first century was one of childhood in the Church, if
we may reverently say so, and the words of Christ
were accepted in no questioning, pseudo-confessing,
and doubting spirit. They were regarded literally, and
without definition, analogy, defense, or offense; they
were taken to be honest-meaning words; and though
all these scruples would come later, there was no
chance for disputation, and no impatience for explanation then.

It is certain, we think, that the worship of the
Church of the first century had assumed a liturgical
character. This liturgical character is well described in
the Rev. Mr. Little's work, and we quote at length his
convenient and expressive defense (pp. 210–213):

" The liturgy, in the strict sense of the word, means the service
used in celebrating the Holy Eucharist. It admits of no doubt that
our Saviour, at the Last Supper, followed the usual ritual of the

Passover, inserting, at the most appropriate places, the eucharistic blessing of the bread and wine, and the distribution of the consecrated elements. It is, moreover, reasonable to suppose that he gave the apostles directions as to the way in which they were to do this." (This last suggestion appears to us sophistical in character.) "Be that as it may, they certainly could never have celebrated that Holy Communion without recalling and reproducing the outline of the Paschal service which the Master had used. His example was command enough, even if he did not explicitly order them to follow it ; and, as a matter of fact, they did follow it. Wherever they went they carried with them the outline of the liturgy, and that, too, based on the Paschal sacrifice.

"Although it was not generally (if at all) committed to writing till in the second century, yet it retained all its parts, and had only verbal differences in the most widely severed portions of the Church. In the great centers like Jerusalem, Ephesus, Rome, and Alexandria the liturgies used bore the impress of apostolic individuality, while still keeping to the general form of Catholic unity. Thus arose four great types of the primitive liturgy, called respectively (*a*) The Liturgy of St. James, used in Jerusalem (and in a slightly modified form in Antioch, known as the Antiochian, Clementine, or Apostolic Liturgy) ; (*b*) The Liturgy of St. John, used in Ephesus, Gaul, Spain, and Britain ; (*c*) The Liturgy of St. Peter, used at Rome ; and (*d*) The Liturgy of St. Mark, used at Alexandria.

"These all have twelve parts or divisions in common. The order in which these parts occur is not always the same. The substance of each is the same ; and even the verbal expression, though not identical, is so similar as to demonstrate a common origin. They differ less from each other than the four great races of men whom God ' hath made of one blood for to dwell on all the face of the earth,' and who may all justly claim a common origin from Noah, by whose sons 'was the whole earth overspread.' After Scripture lessons and a sermon, with which the service usually began, the twelve parts common to all ancient liturgies are as follows :

"I. The Kiss of Peace.
II. Lift up your Hearts.
III. The Tersanctus.

IV. Commemoration of the Institution.

V. The Oblation.

VI. The Invocation.

"(The three last form the Prayer of Consecration, or Canon of the Mass.)

" VII. Prayer for the Living.

VIII.　　"　　"　　" Faithful Departed.

IX. The Lord's Prayer.

X. Union of the Consecrated Elements.

XI. The Communion.

XII. Thanksgiving.

" This is the order of parts according to the Liturgy of St. James.

" The four varieties of the early liturgy are at least as much alike as the four Gospels, which have so much in common that we are sure they are each based on the one oral Gospel which the apostles taught for twenty years before they wrote down the first word. The Apostolic Liturgy is, in its substance, older than the written Gospels and Epistles. St. Paul himself several times quotes from liturgical forms used in the early Church. This fact is clearly shown in Neale's *Essay on Liturgiology* (pp. 411–474), is often alluded to by Conybeare and Howson, and is admirably set forth by a layman of our own church in a most instructive monograph on the Divine Liturgy."*

In direct connection with its liturgical characteristics, and variously affecting and affected by the liturgies, was the sacred ministry, the priesthood of the Church, with its triple order of bishop, priest, and deacon. This fact, of a body of consecrated men, was the suggestive prefigurement of another fact, the possession by the Church of the presence of her Master in the sacrament. We are not contending that that fact was clearly recognized ; its ritualistic influence appears stronger as its theologi-

---

* *The Divine Liturgy in the Book of Common Prayer*, by George W. Hunter.

cal import was more comprehended later; but the orders of the ministry did preserve inviolate *that presence* under eucharistic forms. The ritualistic growth of the Church, we have said, was not to be expected to be completed upon the consummation of Christ's mission. Christ provided all the necessary conditions which should foster and perfect it, and these were all united, interdependent, and prominent amongst them was the priestly function.

It is aside from our purpose to enter into any demonstration of the existence of the three orders of the ministry in the early Church. It has been done so often, and the array of learning, argument, and penetration shown in the task has been so remarkable, that we should only stultify ourselves, even to attempt to examine these conclusions. It is enough for our purpose to quote the excellent and temperate language of the Rev. George Waddington, in his *History of the Church.*\*

"There are many reasons which make it necessary, in the treatment of this subject, to distinguish clearly between what is historically known and what is plausibly conjectured, for it is from the confusion of facts with probabilities that most of the difficulties of this question have arisen. In the first place, it is certain that from the moment in which the early Churches attained a definite shape and consistency and assumed a permanent form of discipline—as soon as the death of the last of the apostles had deprived them of the more immediate guidance of the Holy Spirit, and left them, under God's especial care and providence, to the uninspired direction of mere men ; so soon had every Church, respecting which we possess any distinct information, adopted the episcopal form of government. The probable nature of that government we shall describe presently, but here it is sufficient to mention the undisputed fact, that

---

\* *History of the Church*, p. 41.   Rev. Geo. Waddington.

the religious communities of the Christian world universally admitted the superintendence of ministers called bishops, before the conclusion of the first century. . . . It is also true, that in the earliest government of the first Christian society, that of Jerusalem, not the elders only, but the ' whole Church,' were associated with the apostles, and it is even certain that the terms bishop and elder, or presbyter, were in the first instance, and for a short period, sometimes used synonymously, and indiscriminately applied to the same order in the ministry. From the comparison of these facts it seems natural to draw the following conclusions—that during the lifetime of the apostles they were themselves the directors, or, at least, the presidents of the Church ; that as long as they remained on earth it was not necessary in all cases to subject the infant societies to the delegated authority of a single superintendent, though the instances of Titus and Timothy clearly prove that it was sometimes done ; and that, as they were severally removed from the world, some distinguished brother was in each instance appointed to succeed, not, indeed, to the name and inspiration, but to the ecclesiastical duties of the blessed Teacher who had founded the Church. The concurrence of ancient records confirms this last conclusion ; the earliest Church historians enumerate the first bishops of the churches of Jerusalem, Antioch, Ephesus, Smyrna, Alexandria, and Rome, and trace them in each case from the apostles. And thus it came to pass that, for more than twenty years before the death of St. John, most of the considerable Churches had gradually fallen under the presidency of a single person, entitled bishop, and that, after that event, there were certainly none which did not speedily follow the same name and system of administration ;" and again, " on the other hand, the separation of the sacred order is so commonly mentioned by the early fathers—not by Cyprian only, but by his predecessors Tertullian and Origen—and so invariably treated as a necessary part of the Christian system, that if its origin was not coeval with the foundation of the system, it was at least unrecorded and immemorial."

Of evidences of more formal ritualism, in the first century or immediately after, we have but little. In the family religious symbols first appeared. The Christians had on their goblets the figures of a shepherd carrying a lamb on his shoulder, and Clement of Alexandria says: "Let our signets be a dove or a fish, or a ship sailing towards heaven, or a lyre or an anchor, and he who is a fisherman will not be forgetful of the Apostle Peter, and of the children taken from the water." Religious emblems passed, according to Neander, from the domestic use into churches as early as the end of the third century. "The visible representation of the cross may, doubtless, have early found its way among Christians, both in their domestic and ecclesiastical life. This token was peculiarly common with them. It was the sign of blessing when they rose in the morning and when they retired at night, when they went out and when they came in; employed, indeed, in all the transactions of daily life. It was the sign which the Christians unconsciously made, in all cases of sudden surprise." "The Jewish Christians retained for some time, with the whole Jewish ceremonial law, all the Jewish festivals, although gradually they ascribed to them such Christian import as might naturally present itself."

It is a clear inference from all we have said that we expect to find the Church becoming progressively ritualistic as she grew stronger, and by a natural evolution of feeling develop her inherent nature as prosperity permitted her ample and unrestrained enlargement. In the second and third centuries these early formed tendencies developed, as we claim they ought to have done. They were inherent in the organization of the Christian Church, and it was never intended that they should remain instances of arrested growth, but should bring to fruition their inestimable and divinely planted germs. It is also quite true that errors, those which have led to and have been appropriated by Romanism, were beginning to appear, and, as we have before hinted, the discrimination between Catholic and adequate ritual and Romanistic and exaggerated ritual has been now left to the conservative judgment of the Church, and the religious contest of the future is really between these ·divergent schools of ritualistic practice. Dr. Schaff, whose admissions appear to us valuable, albeit containing suggestions which are injurious, and statements we imagine easily debatable, says, in his *History of Christianity :* *

"In the external organization of the Church several important changes appear in the period before us. The distinction of laity, and the sacerdotal view of the ministry, become prominent and fixed ; subordinate church offices are multiplied ; the episcopate arises;" (This is misleading, the episcopate was already established ; it assumes more importance as the proportions of the Church enlarge.) "the beginnings of Roman primacy appear, and the exclusive unity of the Catholic Church develops itself in opposition to heretics and schismatics."

Again (p. 123), he says truly and suggestively, though his own inferences from the facts he groups there are probably that these results were purely accidental, or, humanly speaking, historical necessities, instead of detecting their *inevitable and predestined connection* with the mission of Christ and the establishment of his presence in the body of the Holy Catholic Church:

" The idea and institution of a special priesthood, distinct from the body of the people, with the accompanying notion of sacrifice

* Vol. II., p. 121.

and altar, passed imperceptibly from Jewish and heathen reminiscences and analogies into the Christian Church."

He indicates, though using language both unfair and misleading, that, as we have said:

" The Levitical priesthood, with its three ranks of high-priest, priest, and Levite, naturally furnished an analogy for the threefold ministry of bishop, priest, and deacon, and came to be regarded as typical of it."

And neither could the

"Gentile Christians, as a body, at once emancipate themselves from their traditional notions of priesthood, altar, and sacrifice, on which their former religion was based."

Renan has observed the same growth and structural elaboration in the Church, and, struck with its extent and power, has called it "the most profound transformation" in history. There was no transformation. It was a growth as absolutely certain, organic, and necessary as the unfolding of a flower, whose plain green sepals inclose the gorgeous colored petals of which they give at first no premonition; and, as in the flower, there was nothing invented, or artificially adopted or tried. In the second and third centuries, Tertullian, Ignatius, Clement of Rome, Cyprian, asserted the sacerdotal character of the ministry. We have shown that the priestly function is evolved from or included in the conception of a divine presence actually or vicariously in sacraments, and that both stimulate and imply ritualism. It, ritualism, strengthened and was permitted to strengthen; it developed the Catholic Church along lines of feeling which no anti-ritualistic cultus could have evoked, much less appropriated and retained.

Episcopacy reached a very complete development in the second century, and, as Dr. Schaff says, " Episcopacy, in the full sense of the term, requires for its base the idea of a real priesthood and real sacrifice, and an essential distinction between clergy and laity." Distinctions and conceptions, before dimly sketched upon the surface of Christianity, became, through the etching action of danger and persecution, firmly and strongly drawn. More than that, gifts and offices sacramentally bestowed upon the Church were understood, elevated, and defended, when the trials of time indicated their value and necessity.

Beautifully Dr. Schaff expresses the just feelings of the fathers of the Church : *

" The fathers of our period all saw in the Church, though with different degrees of clearness, a divine, supernatural order of things, in a certain sense the continuation of the life of Christ on earth, the temple of the Holy Spirit, the sole repository of the powers of divine life, the possessor and interpreter of the Holy Scriptures, the mother of all the faithful. She is holy because she is separated from the service of the profane world, is animated by the Holy Spirit, forms her members to holiness, and exercises strict discipline. She is catholic—that is, complete and alone true—in distinction from all parties and sects. Catholicity, strictly taken, includes the three marks of universality, unity, and exclusiveness, and is an essential property of the Church as the body and organ of Christ, who is, in fact, the only Redeemer for all men."

The ritualistic growth was natural and progressive ; it followed in Christianity the development we have seen it assume in other religions, and under the same incentives. Christianity resembles, upon its terrestrial

---

side, the totality of all religious thought and motion, and on its celestial side penetrates, transfuses, and transfigures these elemental and inherent conditions of religious life with the inspiration and revelation of truth as it is in Jesus Christ.

Now art, symbolism, and commemoration began to play their parts in the elaboration of Christian worship, and, as their action was less impeded by persecution, the results were more and more impressive.

"After the middle of the third century the building of churches began in great earnest, as the Christians enjoyed over forty years of repose, and multiplied so fast that, according to Eusebius, more spacious places of devotion became everywhere necessary. The Diocletian persecution began with the destruction of the magnificent church at Nicomedia, which, according to Lactantius, even towered above the neighboring imperial palace. Rome is supposed to have had, as early as the beginning of the fourth century, more than forty churches. But of the form and arrangement of them we have no account.

"With Constantine the Great begins the era of church architecture, and its first style is the basilica. The emperor himself set the example, and built magnificent churches in Jerusalem, Bethlehem, and Constantinople, which, however, have undergone many changes. His contemporary, the historian Eusebius, gives us the first account of a church edifice which Paulinus built in Tyre, between A. D. 313-322. It included a large portico, a quadrangular atrium, surrounded by ranges of columns ; a fountain in the center of the atrium, for the customary washings of hands and feet before entering the church ; interior porticos ; the nave or central space with galleries above the aisles, and covered by a roof of cedar of Lebanon ; and the most holy altar. Eusebius mentions, also, the thrones for the bishops and presbyters, and benches or seats." *

Commemorative services were early instituted ; they

---

* *History of Christianity*, Vol. II., pp. 200, 201.

grew and formed the Church's year into a cycle, whose rounded beauty expresses the pilgrimage of life, as it does recall the facts of Christ's life. Wednesdays and Fridays were weekly days observed in commemoration of the passion and death of our Lord. Easter, Pentecost, and Epiphany were made into festivals, while the fast of Lent and the observance of Good Friday and Holy Week became universal. In the fourth century the Christmas festival appears. The enrichment of the services continued, and Dr. Schaff has, with, in the main, perfect fairness, traced their liturgical and ritualistic promotion. Liturgies of very composite character were in full use, and the Canon of the Mass, the celebration of Holy Communion was, as Schaff says, "the culmination of Christian worship." They differed in detail in various places ; thus there was the Liturgy of St. James, used in Jerusalem, and in a modified form, under the name of the Clementine, at Antioch; the Liturgy of St. John, used in Ephesus, Gaul, Spain, and Britain; the Liturgy of St. Mark, used at Alexandria. The view taken at an early period of the Eucharist is expressed by Justin Martyr:

" For we use these not as common bread and common drink ; but like as Jesus Christ our Redeemer was made flesh through the word of God, and took upon him flesh and blood for our redemption ; so we are taught that the nourishment blessed by the word of prayer, by which our flesh and blood are nourished by transformation, is the flesh and blood of the incarnate Jesus."

The saturation of the Christian world with liturgical rites at this period, when we have some written records, indicates the earlier rise of these in the first congregations. Dr. Schaff describes the service of the middle of the third century, as follows:

> " The service proper consisted of two principal acts ; the *oblation*, or presenting of the offerings of the congregation by the deacon for the ordinance itself, and for the benefit of the clergy and the poor ; and the *communion*, or partaking of the consecrated elements. In the oblation the congregation at the same time presented itself as a living thank-offering ; as in the communion it appropriated anew in faith the sacrifice of Christ, and united itself anew with its Head. Both acts were accompanied and consecrated by prayer and songs of praise.
>
> " In the prayers we must distinguish, first, the general thanksgiving, the Eucharist in the strictest sense of the word, for all the natural and spiritual gifts of God, commonly ending with the seraphic hymn ; secondly, the prayer of *consecration*, or the invocation of the Holy Spirit upon the people and the elements, usually accompanied by the recital of the words of institution and the Lord's Prayer ; and finally, the general *intercession* for all classes, especially for the believers, on the ground of the sacrifice of Christ on the cross for the salvation of the world. . . . The congregation responded from time to time, according to the ancient Jewish and the apostolic usage, with an audible 'Amen,' or '*Kyrie eleison*.' The '*sursum corda*' also, as an incitement to devotion, with the response '*Habemus ad Dominum*,' appears at least as early as Cyprian's time, who expressly alludes to it, and in all the ancient liturgies."

The formative conditions under which ritualism arises into objective shapes were now fully prepared. The history of the Church, the priestly function, and the divine presence were recognized and valued, and as state protection warranted the most public confession of Christian faith, ritualism more and more illuminated the rich outlines of ceremonial observance, and brought its power of expression in contact with that religious zeal and fervor which craved and used it.

And ritualism, like all healthy ethnic movements, in its discursive eagernes̀s, assimilates everything that it finds which adapts itself to its service. Pagan rites, if expressive, were involved in Christian worship, where they did not taint the latter, nor deflect conviction from the truth; and this, according to all natural law, was inevitable and desirable.

"Christianity could not at once invent a new art any more than a new language, but it emancipated the old from the service of idolatry and immorality, filled it with a deeper meaning, and con-secrated it to a higher aim." (Schaff.)*

The strong springs of sacramental thought were now flowing through the arid wastes of paganism, and the fruitful culture of Christian worship brought in its train the flowers of beauty, of symbolism, of commemoration, the spiritual loveliness of a worship wherein the senses yielded to the soul the homage and the service of their deepest consecration to God.   Lubke says† of this time :

"Christianity begins, amid oppression and persecution, its world-convulsing course, penetrating with its blessed truth slowly but irresistibly the souls of men, and silently creating a new central core of life, shortly destined to reveal itself in triumph, so soon as the rotten shell of heathen living shall crack and fall asunder.   As this new truth begins to leaven the hearts of men, made sorrowful by the departure of ancient glory and the general decay of morality ; as it gives them the beautiful certainty of salvation and redemp-tion, and, in the midst of a universal ruin, strengthens the ever-

---

* See an article by Rev. Heber Newton, in *The Forum*, Vol. I., No. 1, on "Is Romanism a baptized Paganism?"   It contains some excellent thoughts, but, from the low spiritual plane of vision taken, has a debili-tating and deleterious influence, as with much of the writer's work.

† *History of Art*, Vol. I., p. 337.

increasing multitude of the faithful to a confident endurance through trouble and death, the soul of the Christian is irresistibly impelled to give an outward expression to its inmost feelings ; to enhance by a worthy ritual the solemn dignity of divine service ; to bring into the places of public assemblage visible symbols of the joyful certainty of the new covenant ; to give token in the graves of the beloved dead of its confidence in a future eternal reunion."

The Christian Church in art displayed its ritualistic spirit, the latent spirit that can never be expelled from it, because it animates, so to speak, its sensible corporeal life. The Roman basilicas were modified for Christian worship; color, painting, architectural device, symbolic ornament, vestments, processions, the movements and postures and signs of adoration, the succession of festivals and fasts, all brought to its completion that Catholic Church which, mentally perfected to the eye of God, was ushered upon the earth by him in a germinal form of doctrinal truth, to assume, in accordance with the processes of life and growth which prevail throughout nature, and through the evolution of this Church's implanted tendencies, the royal beauty of Catholic worship. That central fact of the Atonement, reiterated, extended, in the sacrament of the Eucharist, became the glowing, magnetizing center of Christian services. It was crystallized in the form of their churches; it became the radiant point in every Christian's life; it was the *motif* and object of all ceremonial splendor.

Lubke, describing the early churches, which were metamorphosed Roman basilicas, says:

" The worshiper, on entering, is irresistibly drawn by the parallel lines of far-reaching columns to the one goal and central point of the whole structure, where the stewards of the divine mysteries serve about the elevated altar, while from the high arch, as well as from the walls of the apse, the revered forms of Christ and his chosen ones shine down upon him with solemn grandeur."

The secondary influences which modify ritualism, *i. e.,* the characteristics, environment, tastes, and inclinations of races, made themselves felt, assisted and varied ritualistic results. Thus we learn that

" Divine worship had developed a particularly splendid ritual with the Byzantines, rendering a building of varied construction necessary, and since the dome did not assimilate well with the parallelogram, the plan of the church now became decidedly complicated. Thus a system of domes and half domes, with every conceivable variety of wall niche pertaining to them, was connected with the most varied designs." (Lubke.)

Later the Romanesque architecture, which greatly modified the Roman basilica, but retained it, arose, and later the Gothic appeared.

Similarly, in liturgies, there was an early diversity of use in separated regions, and also churches and congregations and orders of priests engaged in special works, devoted themselves to the perpetuation of certain memories, or enlisted in peculiar and special efforts of charity or contemplation. The composition of the Church embraced each spiritual activity and nurtured it in unison with all.

The errors of Romanism have a bearing on this subject, but they cannot be discussed here. Romanism is a ritualistic church, and rightly and properly values her ritual ; her corruptions of the faith have only superinduced an hypertrophy of ritual, leading, possibly, to superstition, though not necessarily to idolatry ; but this does not invalidate the claims made here for ritualism. Ritualism is established in the nature of man as an inherent tendency developed under the conditions we have reviewed. Those conditions were supplied in Christianity, as they had been in all religions, and ritualism appeared. We believe that this very fact gives to Christianity a stamp of universality; it has by a revelation supplied man with a religion which restores him to God and happiness without divorcing him from the organic conditions under which his religious nature, in all its other manifestations, has appeared; and this identity of means casts a new, beneficent light over all ethnic worships. It elevates them, establishing a sort of indirect connection of them with the principles and methods of that utterance of God in the world which we call Christianity. They became reflections, distorted and obscure indeed, of that "true light which lighteth every man that cometh into the world."

At any rate, we find in the early Church, which embodies the faith in and the teachings of Christ, this distinct phase, or rather habit, of ritualism, and it developed, we must believe, not arbitrarily, delusively, or wrongly, but naturally, according to law, under the guidance of the Holy Ghost, and was logically implied in all that Christ did and said.

Its concrete appearance was later than the date of those facts and spiritual ministrations that made it possible, but those facts and sacraments which were its logical antecedents were all there before it.

10

# PART II.

## THE

# REASONABLENESS OF RITUALISM.

# CHAPTER I.

## ART IN RITUALISM.

WE have endeavored to demonstrate that there seems to be an inherent attachment to ritualism existing in human nature, and we have reviewed what we consider its characteristics and the predetermining incentives to its rise and extension.·

To the minds of those philosophers who regard the fundamental consciousness and nature of man as inviolate, we think these considerations must form a very effective plea for its (ritualism's) perpetuation, however modified they might wish to make the nucleal creed which it interprets and adorns. And their position is a strong one. If ritualistic tendencies are implanted in man's nature as primordial instincts, it is unwise, if it is not madness, to fight against them. If these tendencies are interwoven with the texture of our psychological being, it would seem as arbitrary to contravene and despise them as to attempt to extirpate the spiritual nature itself, of which they become, from this point of view, the accompaniments.

But there is another line of apologetic defense which we have pursued in this second part of our thesis, and that is to show the reasonableness of the use of the elements of ritualistic practice in Christian worship. Those elements we believe to be art, symbolism, and commemoration, and in this chapter we wish to show, in regard to art, that, first, it is profoundly allied with the religious nature of man, if it is not directly its derivative; secondly, that its expediency in religion—its actual utilitarian advantages—are very great; and, thirdly, that its refining and comforting influence is unmistakable and powerful.

And, first, as to the absolutism of art in its relation to religion. We might at the very outset quote Mr. Ruskin, who,* in discussing the principles of beauty, maintains that art is itself a kind of religion, and possesses the attributes of infinity, unity, repose, symmetry, purity, moderation, each one of which is connected with Deity, as: "Infinity, the type of divine incomprehensibility; unity, the type of the divine comprehensiveness; repose, the type of divine permanence; symmetry, the type of divine justice; purity, the type of divine energy; moderation, a type of government by law." †   It is scarcely necessary to have recourse to this intricate, if not somewhat fantastic (in spite of many beautiful allusions, parallels, and suggestions) analogy to prove the intimate relations of art and religion. Strauss says: ‡ "The function of art in all its branches is, no doubt, to reveal the harmony of the universe, or at least to display it to us in miniature, for though it ever maintains itself amid the apparent confusion of phenomena, it exceeds our comprehension as an infinite whole. This is the reason of the intimate connection which, with all nations, has always existed between art

* *Modern Painters.*
† *Mental and Moral Science*, Vol. I.   A. Bain.
‡ *The Old Faith and the New*, Part II.   Friedrich Strauss.

and religion. The great creations of the plastic arts have also, in this sense, a religious influence. Poetry and music, however, exert the most direct influence of this kind on our inner life." The religious sentiment, as defined by philosophers, involves the play of emotions directly stimulated, elevated, and deepened by the works and processes of art. Thus A. Bain defines veneration, or the religious sentiment, as "constituted by the tender emotion, together with fear and the sentiment of the sublime," and continuing, says, "the composition of the feeling is expressed in the familiar conjunction—wonder, love, and awe."

If the religious feeling is not entirely constituted of, it certainly involves, the tender feelings, together with a more or less pronounced and salutary sentiment of fear and sublimity. The tender feeling arises from love, the sentiment of fear from a sense of sin, and that of sublimity from the worship of the Almighty. Now it is evident that this group of feelings is directed objectively, viz., has to do with an outside object. It is also everywhere conceded that a feeling which has to do with a second person is stronger in the presence of that person than in his absence. It is the especial intention of art in ritualism, which itself we have seen (Part I., Chap. III.) has indeed primarily originated in a sense of the *presence* of the god worshiped, to make us realize the object of our adoration. And the conjunction of music, painting, of the display of the tokens of our faith, of the pageantry of color, with the impressive and solemn action of the service, of the outward signs of reverence, all combined within proper limits, do force upon us, through an appeal to our emotions, to our sense of the fitting, and through the excitation of our imagination, the realization of something worshipful.

The depth and form of this realization will assume greater intensity and reality as the worshiper has already trained himself to believe or think in these matters, having naturally the most profound effect upon those who accept Catholic doctrine. Exactly in proportion to the vividness of this sense of God's presence, will the tender feelings of love, the solemn sense of sin, and the devout attitude of worship be felt and assumed, and the worshiper, immersed in the feeling of the sanctity of God's enveloping spirit, forget everything but that supreme effort of obligatory prayer and praise to which the service is given.

But, furthermore, if art did not improve our devotions by ministering to a sense of the reality of " God with us," it does attune and shape our thoughts harmoniously and sweetly, and so smooths the asperity of momentary temper, so allays the sharp pain of sorrow or despair, so temptingly allures our nature to place itself devoutly before God, so intermingles, through an identity or harmony of their secondary characters, the religious feelings with our æsthetic gratification, that insensibly the aspect of our worship becomes involved in the beauty of the rites used by the Church, and we find the effort of self-concentration and mental attention less artificial and strained, more easily assumed, and yielding richer results.

The idea of art, in its most complete definition, in-

volves a religious or semi-religious aspect. As Bain
says:*

"Art is considered to occupy its proper province when inspiring
sympathy and benign emotions, and lulling angry and hateful passions. Hence it allies itself with morality, being, in fact, almost
identified with the persuasive part of morality, as opposed to the
obligatory compulsory sanction."

Another writer says:†

"Historically, it has always been found that the arts, in their
origin, are dependent on religion. Nor is the reason far to seek.
Art aims at expressing an ideal; and this ideal is the transfigura-
tion of human elements into something nobler, felt and apprehended by the imagination. Such an ideal, such an all-embracing
glorification of humanity, only exists for simple and unsophisticated
societies in the form of religion. Religion is the universal poetry
which all possess." ‡

In an article on "The Decay of Art,"§ the writer speaks
of a certain "analogy between religion and art," as ex-
plaining, possibly, the supposed decay of *both* in an age
progressively materialistic, and says that "the spirit of
exact inquiry and the limitation of our cognitions to
material and demonstrable phenomena is waging war
on that entire range of spiritual faculties, perceptions,
emotions, on which all religious systems have been

---

* *Mental and Moral Science.* A. Bain.

† *Renaissance in Italy.* The Fine Arts, foot-note, p. 8. J. A. Symonds.

‡ Some remarks of Ruskin in his *Lectures on Art*, have a confirmatory
value in this place. He says: "The great arts . . . have had and
can have but three principal directions of purpose—first, that of enforcing
the religion of men; secondly, that of perfecting their ethical state;
thirdly, that of doing them material service."

§ *New Princeton Review*, Vol. II., p. 20. W. J. Stillman.

founded." He perceives, as Ruskin had, the singular unison of certain emotional states and certain forms of physical or art beauty. He says, " that twilight and others of the greater phases of nature, which have a special artistic appeal, owe it not to the fact that they are forms of phenomena, but to the coincidence between them and certain moods which are inherent in the human mind, *i. e.*, to their subjectivity ; just as in a larger way physical beauty owes its fascination not to its being a fact, but to its accord with certain unexplained chords of human emotion." And again, he says, " Art is simply the harmonic expression of human emotion. Where there is no emotion there is no art." Such views imply a close interdependence, which, if not absolute, will always, in the nature of things, appear in practice between art and religion. If certain sensibly beautiful arrangements of color and form are substantially related to certain mental states, and serve to evoke and intensify these latter, it is not difficult to see that such mental states as are religious must have provided for them collateral sensible phenomena which are, so to speak, their functional irritants. These phenomena are embraced in the world of religious art, and they are those which ritualism liberally employs. Indeed, the psychic influence of art in a religious direction, the effect of its products when furnished for such purposes, is obvious, and no one who has encountered them can evade or withstand their power.

The impulse of a religious nature, imparted to genius, originated masterpieces in music, sculpture, and painting, and naturally these masterpieces, presented to the mind, awaken some counterpart or echo of the same feelings which were their inspiration. The influence of the works of the great masters in painting is recorded in every work of European or general travels; it is unmistakable and impressive. Bayard Taylor, before the Madonna della Sedia of Raphael, bears eloquent testimony to the moving power of its beauty. He says:*

" Like his unrivaled Madonna in the Dresden Gallery, its beauty is spiritual as well as earthly ; and while gazing on the glorious countenance of the Jesus-child, I feel an impulse I can scarcely explain—a longing to tear it from the canvas, as if it were a breathing form, and clasp it to my heart in a glow of passionate love."

Hawthorne says:†

" I was a good deal impressed by this picture [the Martyrdom of St. Sebastian]—the dying saint, amid the sorrow of those who loved him, and the fury of his enemies, looking upward, where a company of angels, and Jesus with them, are waiting to welcome him and crown him ; and I felt what an influence pictures might have upon the devotional part of our nature."

And again, in another place :

" Once more, I deem it a pity that Protestantism should have entirely laid aside this mode of appealing to the religious sentiment" [viz., by pictures].

The effect of expressive painting, perhaps, could not be better illustrated than by the story told of the powerful picture of John Huss before his Accusers. The lofty dignity and intrepid bearing of the recusant is so effectively shown that it has been known to soften the feelings and enlist the sympathy of many Romanists

* *Views Afoot.*
† *French and Italian Note Book.*

who saw it, and who had been previously animated by
the strongest antipathies against the famous heretic.
Shelley describes the impression left upon his mind by
a masterpiece of Correggio, which, however indifferently associated with, or suggestive of, a religious mood
to the writer (Shelley), very vividly indicates its effect
upon a mind less skeptical. He says:*

" There was one painting, indeed, by this master, Christ Beatified,
inexpressibly fine. It is a half figure, seated on a mass of clouds,
tinged with an ethereal, rose-like luster; the arms are expanded,
the whole frame seems dilated with expression; the countenance is
heavy, as it were, with the weight of the rapture of the spirit; the
lips parted, but scarcely parted, with the breath of intense but regulated passion; the eyes are calm and benignant, the whole features
harmonize in majesty and sweetness."

Of Raphael's St. Cecilia he writes:†

" The central figure, St. Cecilia, seems rapt in such inspiration
as produced her image in the painter's mind; her deep, dark, eloquent eyes lifted up, her chestnut hair flung back from her forehead; she holds an organ in her hands; her countenance, as it
were, calmed by the depths of its passion and rapture, and penetrated throughout with the warm and radiant light of life. She is
listening to the music of heaven, and, as I imagine, has just ceased
to sing."

Now it will be reasonably objected that the age of
the masters is past, that it will not return, and that
we cannot hope to bolster up our decaying faith by
religious or appropriate pictures of extraordinary or
even moderate beauty. This objection, in the first
place, exaggerates our deficiencies in art; and, secondly,
forms really no impeachment against the use of the

---

* *Shelley's Letters*, Bologna.  † *Ibid.*

painter's art itself, but only raises the important and secondary question, what standards we will adopt for its regulation. Even then we shall find it largely a comparative question. The picture which, to the simple and unlearned or uncultured worshiper, serves its excellent purpose of nurturing his religious impulses through the related emotions it excites, may be as worthy of a place, so far as its immediate effects upon this worshiper are concerned, as the more elaborate and sublime compositions which move the cultured and satisfy the dilettanti. It is safe, or would be, in all cases to insist upon as high a standard as we can attain to in such things, and a critical and even querulous judgment is desirable in their inspection.

But it is more seriously objected by Symonds, in the first chapter of his third part of the *Renaissance in Italy*, that art, or at least painting or sculpture, leads to paganism. He says:*

"When the worshiper would fain ascend on wings of ecstasy to God—the infinite, ineffable, unrealized—how can he endure the contact of those splendid forms in which the lust of the eye and the pride of life, professing to subserve devotion, remind him rudely of the goodliness of sensual existence. Art, by magnifying human beauty, contradicts these Pauline maxims : ' For me to live is Christ, and to die is gain ;' 'Set your affection on things above, not on things on earth ;' 'Your life is hid with Christ in God.'"

And again Symonds says:

"To effect an alliance between art and philosophy, or art and theology, in the specific region of either religion or speculation is, therefore, an impossibility. In like manner there are many feelings

* * *

* *Renaissance in Italy.* The Fine Arts, p. 25.

which cannot properly assume a sensuous form ; and these are pre-
cisely religious feelings in which the soul abandons sense and
leaves the actual world behind, to seek her freedom in a spiritual
region."

This argument, if the author meant it for an argument, against the use of painting or sculpture—only a
part of art as we have used the term—in worship, is
really ineffective, and, in a measure, self-destructive.
It is, we think, sophistical, and unconsciously perverted
by a display of the ultra-Protestant notions in regard to
"purity of worship."

Color, form, portraiture, if dominated in its production by religious feeling, does not obstruct religious
feeling. It is simply a violence to sense and experience to say so. The measure of the impulse, and its
quality, which originate a religious painting of merit, is
an index more or less accurate, according to the conditions of the worshipers, of the feelings it is calculated
to arouse. Neither is it true—and this involves simply
a question of proof, easily answered by observation and
experience—that religious art, in the form of painting
or sculpture, arrests the upward flight of the soul, fast-
ening it to the dross and sights of earth. The stimulus
of art, in this form, truly is not a continuing sensation,
as with music. It does not accompany the spiritual
ascension, as with music, but neither does it clog or
delay that emotional propulsion which "leaves the actual world behind, to seek her freedom in a spiritual
region." It ministers, as it should, to other needs in
worship, as we shall see later, as well as to less ethereal
natures, and it also affords, again and again, a starting-

point, a suggestion, by actually superinducing a spiritual frame of mind, from which the mind passes on in a reverie and dream to that passive form of ecstasy which, Mr. Symonds seems to think, is the only religious aspect of worship. The worship of God is a catholic and rich and wide field of sensation, not limited to the narrow bounds of a circumscribed sentiment. It is diversely varied, and few understand the exact avenue of approach by which their neighbor or friend advances toward God. The provisions of the Church must, therefore, be composite and manifold, that she may entrap all in the golden net of Christ's redemption, and her life must embrace every manifestation of art which touches the heart, or, through the senses, bears in upon the soul the realization of God's nature, operations, and beneficence.

But Mr. Symonds has gone further, and more explicitly defined his scruples. He cites the instance of a painting, I think one of Fra Bartolomeo, of a St. Sebastian, whose fleshly loveliness deranged and imperiled the devotions of some sisters. While there is no citation of evidence to prove this, it can be supposed and understood that the story is altogether true. But this is simply a statement that the art example he finds derelict does not at present serve devotional purposes or assist the spiritual insight or imagination. But art can frame and paint pictures which do. We have just reviewed some of the effects produced by pictures. It is an ineffective plea to urge the abolition of representative art from our churches because, at a time when the *naïveté* and realistic impulse of awakening art produced pictures *comme l'oiseau vole, comme cheval court* (Taine), those were made which suggested improper thoughts. Art does not paganize, if it is Christian art; and beauty of face and form, expression and color, can be devoted as forcibly to evoke the religious sentiment, as it may be to startle and accelerate the irreligious or the impure. The unveiled nudities of mediæval art, which in their inception were born of the best motives, do not form a just ground for wholesale prohibition, and surely the religious world of to-day would not readily part with the vast heritage of devotional portraiture and painting which this same age has bequeathed to us.

"Nothing is useless that gratifies that perception of beauty which is at once the most delicate and the most intense of our mental sensations, binding us by an unconscious link nearer to Nature and to Him whose every thought is born of beauty, truth, and love. I envy not the man who looks with a cold and indifferent spirit on these immortal creations of the old masters—these poems written in marble and on the canvas. They who oppose everything which can refine and spiritualize the nature of man, by binding him down to the cares of the work-day world, would alone cheat life of half its glory." *

The perception of beauty through the eye has not, I believe, been successfully explained on a physiological basis, but must be considered ultimately referable to some correlation of the sensible impressions involved with our mental faculty, and is, in terms of physical science, inexplicable.† Gunther says (*Power of Sound*, p. 185):

---

* *Views Afoot.* Bayard Taylor.

† E. Gunther, in his voluminous work on the *Power of Sound*, pp. 65, 66, has pointed out that our appreciation of beauty of form does not entirely

"In an artistic work, then, it seems as if we may perpetually discriminate an element of law and order, an element of reasonable, striking, and purposeful arrangement, which can be formulated and recognized as within the domain of the general intelligence, from an element of beauty and impressiveness which, in the case of form no less than in that of color, is beyond the scope of reason and of reasoned analysis and argument; and the intuitive perception of which, in each special kind of presentation, seems often connected with some special range or ranges of association dating back, perhaps, to the very dawn of emotional life."

If this be true, our pleasure in the beauty of religious art springs primarily from a mental or psychic movement, and this must depend for its *raison d'être* upon our religious nature (of course, under the tutelage of Christian education), and, therefore, religious art becomes an excitant of that nature, and is logically warranted. For beauty has a diverse or double nature; there is the beauty of form and the beauty of expression, and this latter in a large degree masters and controls the former in religious art. Again, as painting, sculpture, and architecture, aside from their represent-

---

depend upon the abstract elements of form, nor upon symmetry, and that "the attempt to isolate the effects by a simply mechanical isolation of this or that portion of form, yields most disappointing results;" that in our pleasurable perception of the beauty of architectural structure, though "the actual ocular motions are sometimes adduced as having an explicable pleasurable character," they do not explain our delight, as the same muscular movement of the eye is secured by following an exact reproduction of the same lines on a paper or blackboard, and no, or little, æsthetic response is evoked. Again, "gradations of light and shadow," though "they present means of enjoyment much more positive," are less than lines "amenable to the usual physiological considerations of nervous action, as that the condition for pleasure is exercise of function, keeping short of fatigue, and with frequent rests and reliefs of the excited elements."

ative functions, whose advantages we consider later, excite religious feeling; and as " feeling also comprehends within it the contemplative existence of the spirit, and as all spiritual life is subordinate to an idea and is governed by the same, feeling consequently falls under the idea of the Beautiful."* The Beautiful can scarcely, however, in moral or spiritual things, so far as it is artistically present in these, be separated, from the True and the Good, which are immediately suggested, and, therefore, its concrete expression in religious art powerfully contributes to the excitation or renovation of spiritual or moral states of mind. For, says Hand : †

" Both feeling and affection constitute the power of the spirit, which by reason of this relationship can be regarded as a whole. In it unite the ideas of the Beautiful and the Good, and the pleasingly Beautiful becomes valuable, wins our affections, and is *desired* and *appropriated*."

*Il y a un Dieu parce qu'il y a de la vertu, de la beauté, de la vérité.*

Do not these considerations enable us to perceive how inherently, intrinsically, in its proper use, the art of painting is allied to religious instincts, and may afford us assistance in those moments of devotion when the spirit refuses to rise, and the mind, destitute of ideas, nervously searches for suggestions in its surroundings, or clings gratefully to the finer thoughts

---

* *Æsthetics of Musical Art; or, The Beautiful in Music*, Bk. I., p. 100.   Dr. Ferdinand Hand.

† *Ibid.* p. 101.

of other men? For, as Gunther * has suggestively
written :

"From the moment when, as infants, we smiled at a kind face
and cried at a cross one, association, entering into our experiences
of human expression, has largely identified beauty and ugliness
with a sense of right and happiness and with a sense of wrong
and wretchedness, respectively."

The utility and the educational influence of art are
considered later.

" Architecture," says Gunther,† " stands, of course,
on quite different ground from the representative arts,
but in other ways it has most distinct ethical bearings.
The glooms and lights of architecture are literally sympathetic; and they come not as the shifting characteristics of transient and occasional sound forms, but as
belonging to that which really encompasses and shelters
our lives, as brooding companions, the daily visitants of
familiar spots."

Few, perhaps, realize how insensibly, yet certainly,
the influence of building molds the temperament of
its constant beholders and occupants, more especially
those of refined and sensitive natures—an influence
more important and valuable as the character of the
building is that of one built for a serious and designedly
lofty purpose. Who, of Americans, that have sat for
half an hour in the mingling lights, the half gloom, and
the changing shadows of Trinity Church, Boston, but
has felt the elevating power of its simple strength and

---

* *Power of Music*, p. 376.
† *Ibid.*

effective proportions, the poetizing and soothing and spiritual power of its dark and its splendid windows? And, again, who that has been imprisoned within the weary, staring white and rectangular walls of a meeting-house, looking at white glass and green shutters, or that stereotyped terror, the pulpit platform and the preacher's sofa, but must have felt the message of salvation partook of the flatness of the surroundings it was delivered in, and somehow seemed a sort of unlikely thing after all? The mysteries of Christianity keep no longer their recondite and sacred beauty in such associations, and the senses, rudely chilled and blunted, reflect a torpor upon our mental assent. . Such places, it sometimes seems, are the best places to teach irreligion and foment skepticism in.

The attitude and course of devotion are stimulated in a noble church, and the influx of enthusiasm and affection seem better sustained where its parts bear some conjoined and unique expression of religious use and functions. The delight felt in a beautiful cathedral is distinctly religious in character—I speak here of Christian art—it cannot be otherwise; the elements of admiration, seriousness, perception of regulated melodic relations, deepen greatly the inclination to worship.

"For beautiful buildings are not like other works of art, burning messages from soul to soul, too puzzling, and often too rapid to allow thought of other things ; rather their office is to lend grace and dignity to the outer uses of life while harmonizing with its varied inner phases, and to stimulate every strain of worthy emotion by enabling men to breathe at times an atmosphere that belongs to other generations, charged with the memories that turn to hopes, or the hopes that shall turn to memories." (Gunther.)

In architecture, as with painting, we discover primary essential relations with religious exercises, states, and moods. The service of the Episcopal Church is itself a fabric ; in an intelligible sense, it is architectural, and it demands that sort of corporeal environment which only a beautiful building fittingly gives.

It may be remarked that architectural elegance and pretensions have become the property of all denominations. Were this so, it does not modify our claim in this thesis, but is only a striking proof of the wide march of ceremonialism, which is suffusing the general body of Christian practice, and developing everywhere as far as the rules or precedents or sensibilities of the denomination it appears in permits. Of course, much of artistic device recommends itself to Protestantism, and is eagerly assimilated, and though many of its manifestations are ludicrously like domestic decoration and parlor splendor, it is all linked by skeins and lines of thought, which its users sometimes detect, with the *ritualistic idea.*

If we turn to music, we meet a form of art which all religions more or less commonly claim, which affords, indeed, the most inspiriting and remarkable means of religious expression, and whose influence may be justly described as incalculable. It is the language of emotion, and is, therefore, no less truly tributary and helpful as a vehicle of thought, for, as Spencer profoundly remarks, "Thought and feeling cannot be completely dissociated. Each emotion has a more or less distinct framework of ideas, and each group of ideas is more or less suffused with emotion."

The ceremonial revival in the English Church has reinstated music in the religious service, and has effected a return to purer, higher, and richer standards of music as well. It has heartily combated the droll monotony of sing-song psalmody, the bombastic *fioratura* of vocal gymnastics, and the riotous hurly-burly of encampment minstrelsy. It has "in a very few years pulled the wheezy organs out of their dingy nooks, and swept half the old musical-boxes in the land from our churches, concert-singers and all. Then arose the age of white surplices and new hymn tunes, and decent versicles and anthems."* As it has restored the solemn enactment of the sacrifice of Christ upon the altars of the Church, so has it evoked the sublime strains of the great masters of melody and song, and mingled the enchantments of harmony with the invocations and memories and praises of the Church.

"Every lovely fancy, every moment of delight, every thought and thrill of pleasure which music calls forth, or which, already existing, is beautified and hallowed by music, does not die. Such as these become fairy existences, spiritual creatures, shadowy, but real, and of an inexpressibly delicate grace and beauty, which live in melody, and float and throng before the sense whenever the harmony that gave and maintains their life exists again in sound."† If the sense of sight leads us, in its highest uses, to detect a connection between its exercise and the movements of the mind or of the feel-

---

* *Music and Morals*, p. 119.   H. R. Haweis.
† *John Inglesant.*   J. H. Shorthouse.

ings, and, therefore, the inherent appropriateness of its adaptation in religious forms, how much more obvious this seems with music.

"The music of mankind," says Hand,[*] "makes itself known, in the second place, as the immediate representation of the activity of the feelings;" and again,[†] "music immediately makes manifest the feelings without the help of any other means; we recognize feeling as having become sound;" and again, he speaks of the relations of music to that Christian faith our civilization subscribes to.[‡] "Men have sung and made music in all times, but when the Christian religion aroused life into feeling, and filled it with the highest ideal of existence, humanity could find in tones only a sufficient means of expression, and a new art, as a Christian art, was attained to;" and finally, as if in a spirit of profound interpenetration with the genius of music, as we in this latter day recognize it, he says:[§]

"From all that is finite and conditional, the spirit of the Unconditional, the Eternal Truth, the Infinite Freedom, the Godhead, speaks to his heart, and as this spirit becomes one with his own spirit, and he bears it within him, and is penetrated, raised, and blessed by it, this constitutes the contents of his feeling, which then expresses itself in tones. Thus, music truly cannot represent ideas themselves, but it attests the existence of the idea within us, and excites it, raises us above the finite, and secures to us the participation in a life which operates beyond and above the limitations of space and time. That which, in majestic and beautiful music, affects our profounder soul, we term unutterable and indefinable. It is the Infinite itself which receives us, and which we bear within

---

[*] *Æsthetics of Musical Art*, Part I., p. 96.      [†] *Ibid.* p. 105.
[‡] *Ibid.* p. 108.                                   [§] *Ibid.* p. 119.

us. In this elevation above all earthly things, into a region wherein words are no longer sufficient, a magic peculiar to music operates. It makes us free, and tears us from the limits which ideas draw around us ; the spirit then feels itself freed from the conditions of a poor earthly existence."

The Episcopal Church possesses a service and various offices of wonderful beauty ; its service of the Eucharist is an example of Catholic worship, unchangingly beautiful, while the perfection of its Litany has become the theme of the most passionate eulogies. It is enabled with such a service to appropriate the best works of musical art, to invoke and utilize the whole ample and amazingly adequate machinery of musical expression. And this ritualism has urged and prevailed upon it to some extent to do. Have we not reviewed the deep organic rules or laws of music's harmonic union with religious feeling, the common spring of both in our humanity, and the oneness of their emotional aspects ? And in face of all this, must we be told by some rehabilitated convert that its use is prelatical and Romish ? The fervor and imaginative strength of Mozart, Beethoven, Gounod, Handel, Haydn, are available factors in the Church's service, and they are of incalculable weight and value. The musical completeness of the Mass can be appropriated without violence, by the Episcopal Church, and the throb and motion of these masterpieces involved, by natural heritage and propriety, in the pathos and sublimity of her supreme acts of devotion. The beseeching Kyrie, the sonorous and diversified beauty of the Credo, the tearful loveliness of the Agnus and Benedictus, the ecstatic ascriptions of the Sanctus, and the world-enveloping agitation and exultation of the Gloria are all hers, and it is the boast of ritualism that these have been restored to her Catholic worship and possession, without an act of felony, or an acknowledgment of alien tendencies. In the whole subject of music, confessedly the most powerful instrumentality as far as human inventions or designs are concerned, the Church possesses, ritualism has inaugurated new departures in all directions, of the most momentous and energizing practical influence. The lamentable flatness of her hymnology has been replaced by better types of composition, both verbal and musical, the disgraceful and slovenly performances of her singers slowly changed into the exemplary and careful discipline of surpliced choirs, and the forlorn patchwork of musical *pot-pourris* at Church festivals made to give way to the tonic power of a single service unified throughout by the inspiration of a single mind. The revival of Catholic doctrine has necessarily restored the methods of Catholic worship. Music has been reinstated in her unique domain in the Church's service, and all the manifold directions of its influence upon religious natures renewed.

The varied assemblage of acts, vestments, processions, lights, colors, vessels, decorations, which we have hitherto embraced under the term art, and which are commonly regarded as distinctively ritualistic, cannot be so satisfactorily considered under this head, viz., of art's rudimentary union with religion, as under those of utility and educational uses; yet, in a general, though perhaps to many, vague way, it may be.

The religious frame of mind is an exalted one, even in the moments, perhaps, of the deepest penitence and self-abasement, and, at any rate, in the service of worship it should be so.  But the intimate adjustments found everywhere in nature between an animal's organization and the animal's environment may be as confidently expected or prepared in man.  The exalted frame of mind is preserved unshaken, or else the lagging attention restored to its first ardor, when the diversified functions of priest and people are presented, as in the Roman Church, with splendor and harmonious precision.  The mind is insensibly stimulated because of the unusual order of exercises, in which it discovers a *value* similar to that which its own unusual condition, or momentarily assumed state, possesses.  The analogies to this, in social or public life, are numerous.  The gayety of an event, when the hearts of people are glad, is appropriately and very substantially assisted by bright colors, merry signs and sentences, bright music and laughing demeanors; the scene of woe is made impressive by natural and correct accessories.

It appears then, if not fully, partially shown, that art, in its representative offices of painting and sculpture, and its presentative office of music and architecture, has some distinctive claims to be substantially conformable with religion; that it involves many similar strains of feeling; that it is violent and unjust to prohibit their united action or display; that the fundamental principles of emotional development in each are similar, if not identical; and that both admit of their beneficial union.

As a last consideration, in this connection, we may allude to the fact that we have shown or indicated the probability in Chapter II., Part I., that religion and art, in the broad sense used throughout this essay, have appeared together, are associated, have sprouted, as it were, from some primordial root of common feeling, and, however divergent the subsequent growths of both may have been, their stocks were primarily intertwined or confluent. It is, to say the least, unphilosophical to forcibly separate them now ; it may prove—indeed, we are inclined to believe it has proven—criminal as well as calamitous.

In the second place, we would apologize for the use of art in religion, because of its practical benefit, its utility, its measurably great assistance in religious work and Christian civilization. It is very evident to the Catholic Christian, and it might be acknowledged by a large number of the representatives of Protestant Christianity, that the religion of Christ is filled with personality, that a realization of the person of Christ, of the apostles, of saints, of good and bad spirits, of a life of companionship hereafter, of God's love and watchfulness, of Christ's mediation, compose an essential part of it, as necessary, to most people more necessary, than a mental assent to dogma, and that it is far more obstructive and inimical to the approaches of bald skepticism than that mental assent can ever be.   Says Strauss : *

" The other and principal reason of the retrogression of religion in our time we have already discovered in the present inquiry.  It

---

* *The Old Faith and the New.*   D. Friedrich Strauss.

lies in the circumstance that we are no longer able to form so lively a conception of the personality of the absolute Being as did our predecessors."

But the Catholic faith involves more elements, which partake of the nature of *personification*, so to speak. The Catholic personifies his Church—at least, for our expression is perhaps misleading, his Church has an objective reality; is a composition of orders which possess certain efficacious powers; is an entity involving the sacramental presentation of Christ and his sacrifice to the world; is a historic continuity deriving its *spiritus vitalis* from Christ, an afflatus unceasingly prolonged. This condition of mind involves the use of the imagination; these various objective realities, to be distinctly and unceasingly recognized, require the use of an artistic appeal to the senses. Christ, the apostles, the saints, judgment, future bliss, the events of the Bible narrative, are taught and, as it were, materialized to common apprehension most vividly by the use of pictures, of design, of expressive and touching acts of devotional use, of appropriate tokens and decorations; and to what extent the Church's own objective existence is thus revived is almost incalculable. The procession of surpliced choir, the altar, the burning lamps, the vested clergy, the special selections of music, the attitudes and movements, the incense, the advancing and retreating cross, the orders of ministry, and the related functions of all of those officiating, convey an impression of an organic body, of an ecclesiastical structure of magnificence, extent, and power. The Church life seems bodily presented to the worshiper, and he feels a new

sense of its inherited beauties and elaborate construction. But the feeling goes much farther with the
Churchman. His admiration of the order and beauty of
the services is knit in with a recognition of her supernatural office, and the resources of art, well employed,
persistently strengthen and animate his loyalty to
her.

The congruency of our sense with our mind appreciation of ideas, if such a thing can be brought about,
prints those ideas on our mind as nothing else can.*
Ritualism has brought that about with religion. She
has provided a great number of direct appeals—appeals
admirably executed, too—to the senses, while she has
enforced, in words and by· preaching, the doctrines of
which those sensible, sense-moving appeals continually
speak. Nothing could be devised so perfect for preserving and emphasizing an idea. And if Christian
ideas are worth emphasizing or preserving, the use of
art in their illustration will prove unexcelled in its results. And all this because the imagination is enlisted and the doctrines of redemption through Christ

---

* Ruskin offers some valuable observations on this question in his *Lectures on Art.* He says : " There are thus two distinct operations upon our
mind ; first, the art makes us believe what we would not otherwise have
believed ; and, secondly, it makes us think of subjects we should not otherwise have thought of, intruding them amidst our ordinary thoughts in a
confused and familiar manner." Ruskin objects to the first influence, inasmuch as he says : " Our duty is to believe in the existence of divine or
any other persons only upon rational proofs of their existence, and not
because we have seen pictures of them ; " but in the case we discuss here,
the Christian faith is accepted already by the worshiper, upon rational or
so-called rational grounds, and therefore the influence is not meretricious
or deceptive.

are blended with gracious figures, loving faces, soul-stirring music, the warmth and beauty of hearty services. The affections are vividly excited, as they may always be by the use of sensible and touching methods. James Martineau, in describing the "moral resurrection" of Comte, whose natural affections had been captured and overpowered by the "wonderful Clotilde," says* it consisted "in the discovery that the heart is to have the primacy over the head; that the movement of humanity is from the affective life, while the intellectual function is simply regulative and selective." This order of events is not limited to Comte's experience, either. The moral resurrection of most men is effected in a similar manner.

The expediency of the employment of art becomes strikingly urgent when we trace the vital connection between a religious frame of mind and an imaginative one, and when we consider how powerfully the latter is re-enforced in this connection by ceremonial or art usages. We do not mean that an imaginative temperament forms an orthodox mind necessarily, but that religion makes demands upon the imagination if its best results are attained, its truest comforts realized, and, indeed, requires the imagination to substantiate its positions. It must be allowed that belief in Christian doctrine is neither easy nor obvious; the assent to miracles, the acceptance of the entire system of supernatural government, of the office and character of Christ, of the continued power and validity of orders,

---

* *Types of Ethical Theory*, Vol. II.   J. Martineau.

of the veracity of Holy Writ, are not simple affirmations, made by thinking people always, or even generally, with the same sort of certainty with which they repeat their own experiences or believe those of others.

Imagination which can reproduce events, which can carry us beyond the sordid commonplaces of our daily life, which can construct the ideal systems of divine order, which can create a paradise before our eyes, or unveil the mystic splendors of a spiritual immortality, which can paint and draw and breathe the breath of life upon Saviour and apostle, which can link the past with the present and renew the hallowed pledges of childhood in the dusty and stark days of manhood—an imagination which throws around the hard struggle against evil the beauty of a chivalrous warfare for God, and refreshes the fainting heart with the imagery of a supreme crusade—an imagination which thrusts its possessor past the portals of death into another world, and reviews by anticipation the mingled credits and debits of his own account, which fills its neighborhood with the aura of innumerable spirits, or crowds the sanctuary with ascending and descending ranks of angels—such a temperament, more or less developed, is known to be directly helpful to the religious nature of a man, which it not only strengthens but beautifies. It makes our assent to creed more natural and less perfunctory. Also our sensibility, our apt and correct appreciation of moral beauty, is relative to our powers of imagination, for Stewart says,* "what we commonly call sensibility "

---

* *Elements of the Philosophy of the Human Mind.*

(and he especially alludes to moral sensibility) "depends, in a great measure, on the power of imagination." But this is not all; the function of imagination
is not exhausted in raising pictures, or creating forms,
or sensitizing feeling. Something of the service performed by it to the scientist is also rendered by it to
the believer. Tyndall has pointed out the "scientific
use of the imagination," * and has shown how many accepted and established facts of physical science, which
"common-sense" alone could never have credited, are
realized only by the imagination. The same stupid
"common-sense" is to-day perpetually faulting the
Christian with its narrow bigotry and its obtuseness.
Imagination enables the Christian to detect the essential spiritual truth of many dogmatic positions, which,
baldly stated, appear, in ordinary terms, incomprehensible. It dissolves the rigid formularies of the theological definition in the ether of its finer sense, and clothes
the framework of orthodox faith with the investiture of
abundant and expressive imagery; and again, as Tyndall has said, "the speculative faculty, of which imagination forms so large a part, will nevertheless wander
into regions where the hope of certainty would seem
to be entirely shut out."

It, therefore, cannot be questioned that the culture of
the imagination will be found useful in religious education, nor can it be further questioned that the employment of art, ceremonial practices, etc., in worship or
church service, will directly assist the religious imagination. For Doctor Reid says that "imagination properly

---

* *Fragments of Science* (*vide* Essay). J. Tyndall.

signifies a lively conception of objects of sight; the former power being distinguished from the latter, as a part from the whole;" and Addison has also said that "it is the sense of sight which furnishes the imagination with its ideas." Dugald Stewart thinks both too sweeping or too contracted, but that both touch the truth that the *senses* generally excite or stimulate imagination. The repeated pictures of Christ's sufferings, Christ's miracles, Christ's person, the imagery of the Passion, the illuminated presentation of the saints, of the patriarchs, of the events of Bible history, the grand ascriptions of praise, sung from robed choirs in temples of beauty, the attitudes of worship, the motions of reverence, the fragrance of floral decoration and its fitness, the pomp of vestments in the gradations of ministerial office, and the use of color as expressive of grief or gladness, the bodily presentment in sculpture of seer and prophet—all these minister to and nourish the imagination with a rich and plentiful pabulum. Ritualism strengthens and enlivens the religious imagination, and thus renders us less opaque to the Gospel light, and more sensitive to the pressure of the Christ nature. Dugald Stewart thus characterizes the qualities of the imagination:

"The faculty of the imagination is the great spring of human activity, and the principal source of human improvement. As it delights in presenting to the mind scenes and characters more perfect than those which we are acquainted with, it prevents us from ever being completely satisfied with our present condition or with our past attainments, and engages us continually in the pursuit of some untried enjoyment or of some ideal excellence." *

---

* *Elements of the Philosophy of the Human Mind.*
11*

Its value in religion is also similar ; while it integrates and establishes our faith, it extends our scope of desire and gives a wider range to our aspirations.

But the expediency of ritualistic methods in the use of art is again rendered apparent by its associational potency, the efficacy of the same forms to recall the same ideas, and thus by an iteration almost insensible, fix indelibly on the mind religious convictions. The principles and elucidations of the school of " Associational Psychology " will explain our meaning. This school, whose expounders have been Locke, Hobbes, Hartley, Priestley, Darwin, Tucker, Bain, Alison and Mill, affords important suggestions in this connection to the ritual apologist. Ueberweg * defines their fundamental ideas as follows :

" Sensations by being repeated leave vestiges, types or images of themselves, which are *simple ideas* of sensation. Sensory vibrations by being repeated beget in the medullary substance a disposition to diminutive vibratiuncles corresponding to themselves respectively. Any sensations, A, B, C, by being associated with one another, get such a power over the corresponding *ideas a, b, c,* that any one, as A, can excite *b, c, d,* etc. Any vibrations, A, B, C, by association get such power over the vibratiuncles *a, b, c, d,* that any one can excite *b, c, d.* Simple ideas run into complex ones by means of association. In such cases the simple miniature vibrations run into the corresponding complex miniature vibrations. Some of the complex vibrations attendant on complex ideas may be as vivid as any of the sensory vibrations excited by the direct action of objects."

Whether this is entirely acceptable or not, its inherent force is not impaired by any superficial criticism.

* *History of Philosophy,* Vol. II.

An association of beautiful ideas or of theological
verities, in our religious life, with the sense form of service makes those very forms sermons and instructions ;
and here we pass far beyond the mere æsthete, whose
ritualism is a trifle and an entertainment. Particularly
is this the case in the eucharistic office, which, in its
splendor and adjuncts of ceremonial dignity and procedure, reiterates unceasingly the Church's idea of the
real presence. How vividly is renewed the train of
thoughts which should attend the mystery of the sacrament, when the vested priest enters the sanctuary, when
the eucharistic lights are lit upon the altar, and the
impressive movement of the office begins with the simple beauty of Our Lord's Prayer.

Dugald Stewart says :*

"By means of the association of ideas a constant current of
thoughts, if I may use the expression, is made to pass through the
mind while we are awake. . . . So completely is the mind in
this particular subjected to physical laws, that it has been justly
observed, we cannot by an effort of our will call up any one
thought, and that the train of our ideas depends on causes which
operate in a manner inexplicable to us."

The very forms at Holy Communion force out of
our minds irrelevant thoughts, incongruous notions, or
wicked impulses. They act, by the physical necessity
of their associational power, to fix our attention and to
subdue our minds.

It has often been insisted apologetically that the use
of ritual, of beautiful music, vestments, flowers, incense

* *Outlines of Moral Philosophy.*

and lights, all of which we have uniformly considered as art, are a form of offering to God. This can be claimed and urged and felt, but ritualism, as a *fact*, does not rest on this basis solely. Their effect is reactionary; they subjugate and assist our own minds; they refresh our faith, kindle our imagination, and evoke a retinue of salutary thoughts; they italicize a sacred moment and leave it in our memories, a group of benignant and noble thoughts.

Finally, in defense of the art of ritualism, we would urge its comforting and refining influences. How ardently the child enjoys some picture illustrating the story or history it is reading, and how definitely it recurs to that picture as the portraiture of the event, in later years. If the story were sad, a good picture will cause the tears to flow, which might never come without it; and if gay, the jolly illustration will bring laughter where there might have been only smiles. The poor, the obtuse, the cold-hearted, the unsympathetic, the incredulous, the uneducated, are in religion all children; and images, symbols, forms are as gratifying and helpful to them as the picture to the child; they exert a distinctly refining influence, as they bring within the range of their narrow sensibilities and limited sympathies the purposes of Christianity, and the sufferings and person of Christ. Says Lecky: *

" Wrapt in the pale winding-sheet of general terms, the greatest tragedies of history evoke no vivid images in our minds, and it is only by a great effort of genius that an historian can galvanize them into life."

---

* *History of European Morals*, Vol. I., p. 138.

This remoteness of persons and events, the half-grasped outlines of their shadowy shapes, is a constant menace to Christian doctrine; and imagery the substantial presentation of these persons and events is the only adequate antidote to the insidious disease of growing doubt.

We have urged that ritual art builds and develops the religious imagination, and as it does so it elevates and comforts its possessor. It adds a stock of new ideas to his mental cupboard; it expands the periphery of his emotional activity; it fills his mind's eye with delicate and gentle shapes, and lures him upward by the phantom forms of innumerable hopes. Lecky says:*

"Our imaginations, though less influential than our occupations, probably affect our moral characters more deeply than our judgments, and, in the case of the poorer classes especially, the cultivation of this part of our nature is of inestimable importance."

The use of art, of sense-stirring appeals, re-creates religion and enhances its moral suasion tenfold. The unfortunate and dismal barrenness of some Protestant worship is literally appalling. Its *raison d'être* we are not concerned with, neither would we change it in those churches, but the chapters in the first part have shown, we think, how this poverty of ritual is logically implied in the ultra-Protestant position. Religion seems pre-eminently meant for the poor—we speak humanly—and in the poor it often finds its most grateful adherents. But a form of religious worship that does not aim to give the sad occupants of plain or dreary homes, the vexed comrades of misery and vice, something that shall touch their senses and gratify them and delight them—that will go farther and anticipate, by a sort of ideographic spectacle, the wonders and the possibilities of realization hereafter—is a religion that shirks its responsibilities, and can neither be blessed nor fruitful. The author we have quoted above has shown an acute susceptibility in his appreciation, in this matter, of Catholic methods :

" Religion is the one romance of the poor. It alone extends the narrow horizon of their thoughts, supplies the images of their dreams, allures them to the supersensual and the ideal. . . . It is the peculiarity of the Christian types, that while they have fascinated the imagination, they have also purified the heart. The tender, winning, and almost feminine beauty of the Christian Founder, the Virgin Mother, the agonies of Gethsemane or of Calvary, the many scenes of compassion and suffering that fill the sacred writings, are the pictures which for eighteen hundred years have governed the imaginations of the rudest and most ignorant of mankind. Associated with the fondest recollections of childhood, with the music of the church bells, with the clustered lights and the tinsel splendor, that seem to the peasant the very ideal of majesty ; painted over the altar where he received the companion of his life; around the cemetery, where so many whom he had loved were laid ; on the stations of the mountain, on the portal of the vineyard, on the chapel where the storm-tossed mariner fulfills his grateful vow; keeping guard over his cottage door, and looking down upon his humble bed, forms of tender beauty and gentle pathos forever haunt the poor man's fancy, and silently win their way into the very depths of his being. More than any spoken eloquence, more than any dogmatic teaching, they transform and subdue his character, till he learns to realize the sanctity of weakness and suffering, the supreme majesty of compassion and gentleness."

The services of the Church should be both propitia-

tory and edifying, both an offering to God and a delight
to worshipers. They are meant to have an influence
upon those who use them, and a church is to employ
every ability of man's to extend and ennoble his religious capacities. While, in fact, the basis of all worship is
the need men feel of God's protection, alliance, and communion, the choice of the instrumentalities, the means
of worship, so far as any cognizance of them by God is
concerned, is really indifferent, or unimportant; and perhaps the more simple methods are the better, if we consider God's pleasure only in our service. This is really
not a matter upon which any one can speak with safety,
nor, indeed, can discuss at all without verging upon
impropriety and running into futile hypotheses more
curious than useful, as to God's tactual relations with
human beings. We can only infer from God's previous
dealings with men, from analogies and inferences drawn
from nature, and from our own needs, what elements of
expression we can appropriate in our religious practice.
We are just here contending that the use of art, as we
define it, educates and comforts men; if, in conjunction
with this influence, it assists their religious natures, as
we elsewhere claim, it is recommended in the strongest
possible way to man's acceptance.

In Catholic—not necessarily Roman—worship, motions, attitudes, and significant signs are used, as bowing, genuflections, signing with the cross, while in the
practice of the officiating priest, or priests, many more
are employed. These all come under the head of art,
and admit of being considered as such in every place
where we have endeavored to plead for its retention;

but there is a consideration not, up to this point, adduced, which has an especial bearing on some of these things, and can be conveniently referred to here. We mean " the worship of the body." It apparently has become in Protestant usage a habit to think that the bearing of the body is of no consequence in worship, and that a devout frame of mind is entirely consonant with a careless, or even ridiculously incongruous position of the body. This may seem justified by an appeal to " common sense," but it is none the less contradictory to common experience. The movement and posture of the body are distinctly expressive of feeling, and relieve and complete emotional states, as the erect and evenly advancing body excites and satisfies the martial spirit, the varied sinuous and complex gyrations of the figure pleasurably respond to the impulses excited by bright music, and dramatic expression involves the adroit address to the eye of the speaking postures of the actor —

> " *His whole function suiting*
> *With forms to his conceit.*"

The mental attitude of worship is assisted by the devout attitude of the body; the influence of the latter upon the first is direct and unmistakable. It is involved in the congruity of nature and natural action, and its (the body's) auxiliary relations to the mind can be so utilized that the mind's moods convey a new and ample sort of pleasure to its agent, compared with which its previous similar states, unhelped in this way, seem fragmentary and vacuous.

Finally, art may then, in its utilization in religious

processes, without regard to the historico-ethnic considerations adduced in Part I., claim a merciful hearing
from the school of anti-ritualistic Puritanism, on the
score alone that it is fundamentally allied with religion,
that it is highly expedient and profitable, that it is
deeply educational, and comforting in religious growth.
We may be permitted to sympathize with those, who, to
use the characterization of Green,* "started back from
the bare, intense spiritualism of the Puritan to find
nourishment for their devotion in the outer associations which the piety of ages had grouped around it, in
holy places and holy things, in the stillness of church
and altar, in the pathos and exultation of prayer and
praise, in the awful mystery of sacraments," and we
may agree with Story † that, "so long as human nature
remains the same, this splendor and pomp of processions, these lighted torches and ornamented churches,
this triumphant music and glad holiday of religion,
will attract more than your plain conventicles, your
ugly meeting-houses, and your compromise with the
bass-viol." "For my own part," he continues, "I do not
believe that music and painting and all the other *arts*
really belong to the devil, or that God gave him joy
and beauty to deceive with, and kept only the ugly,
sour and sad for himself."

---

* *History of the English People.* Puritan England, John Richard
Green.
† *Robi di Roma.* W. W. Story.

# CHAPTER II.

SYMBOLISM and art are conjoined in a very great measure in ritualism, and symbols are so interwoven with, or so underlie art material, that only a mental dissection separates their kindred parts. The cross, the crown, the gothic arch, the arrangement of nave, choir and sanctuary, the lights, the order of service, incense, music, vestments all speak to the informed worshiper of some doctrine, fancy, or devout aspiration. It is symbolism, indeed, which gives to art its spiritual significance; the sensible aspect of art, penetrated by the subtle effluence of symbolic poety and poetizing, reaches a higher level, and becomes the most legitimate nutriment for our religious natures. Symbolism is thus in a degree, the soul of religious art, the wide and pregnant womb whence new and beautiful art conceptions have continuously sprung.

If art is primarily identified with religion, as its tangible expression, and having arisen through similar emotions, symbolism is as much so, for symbolism is the poetry of religion, its vocabulary of signs and signals, its effort to read in circumambient nature the mystic recognition of its own universality. If art is expedient because it realizes and perpetuates our faith, symbolism is as much so, for it reiterates the conceptions and principles of our creed and Church. If art is comforting and educational, as it elevates the senses, and administers to them its pleasurable stimuli, symbolism is as much so, for it is the poetry of religion, and attaches our affections to our creed by the magic touch of its recondite and beautiful allusions.

Thus, the thoughts presented in the general discussion of the use of art in service (Chap. I.), are adequate to recommend symbolism as well, and it is in connection with other lines of religious influence that we wish to define the utility of symbolic methods to the Christian in this place.

The destruction of the efficacy of the Christian cultus shall make headway when the mysteries of its sacraments, and the mysteries or miracles of its dispensation, its sacred history are disallowed and repudiated. When the office of baptism becomes a harmless, and somewhat trival ceremony or amusement, as the Rev. Henry Ward Beecher now regards it, when the Holy Communion is simply a commemorative act retaining *per se* no supernatural character, as with the Zwinglianism of the day, then shall surely follow the slow dethronement of Christ, the gradual lowering of the standard of spiritual grace, the resumption of an illicit and injurious paganism, and the atrophy and disappearance of our finer virtues. If this is so with the broad doctrines and general facts of Christian faith, it shall prove more dangerous to the structure of the Church. When the triumph of "common sense," united with the insidious plausibility of scientific inference, shall have made Holy Communion the prolonged practice of the Roman rites of sacrifice, and baptism *solely* a plagiarism from Buddha, then the outlines of the Church shall fade into an atmosphere of every-day notions, and commonplaces, and its functions and its holy places and its orders be relegated to a place alongside of the mummeries of Mormonism, or the dusty playthings of mediæval superstition. This leveling and process of dissolution will be a logical necessity—we think, indeed, an accomplished result—when, as we say, the mysteries of the Christian sacraments, or the mysteries of Christ's history, and the revelations from God to man through him shall be denied or explained away. We believe that the use of symbolism helps in the Catholic mind to maintain unimpaired man's appreciation of mystery, or more justly, his realization of mystery, and assists his mental receptivity for the presence of mysteries in Christianity, keeping him not only susceptible to their beauty and hallowing emanations, but in the way of analogy helping him to secure for himself, at least a hypothetical ground for a conviction of their necessity.

To afford some show of proof that this may be claimed for symbolism shall form in this chapter our chief aim, as it is our best apology for its use.

A symbol is a sign for something, and is taken as a suggestion of that thing, a convenient contraction of language or things or actions, to recall or prefigure or express a greater matter, and is chosen, if well chosen, for some accidental or fanciful or real connective association with the thing symbolized. Three things may be legitimately symbolized, facts, ideas, and mysteries— themselves only facts less comprehensible than common facts—and one symbol may compositely embrace the three. A throne, to the courtier, symbolizes the king as a fact, and royalty, government and dominion as an idea. The cross, to the Christian, is a symbol of the fact of Calvary, of the idea of redemption, of the mystery of the passion. To the Mason, the rough ashlar, or a stone in a rude and unpolished condition, is emblematic of man in his natural state—ignorant, uncultivated and vicious, and this stone, when polished, becoming the perfect ashlar, symbolizes his trained mind, chastened passions, and elevated hopes. Indeed, in Freemasonry, symbolism seems to form the nucleal principle of their organization, and the symbolism of the temple

"Is that which most emphatically gives it its religious character. Take from Freemasonry its dependence on the temple ; leave out of its ritual all reference to that sacred edifice, and to the legends and traditions connected with it, and the system itself would at once decay and die, or at best remain only as some fossilized bone, serving merely to show the nature of the once living body to which it had belonged."*

It is the perfect form of a symbol to graduate the

---

* *Encyclopædia of Freemasonry.* Albert G. Mackey, Article on Symbolism of the Temple. The Freemasons represent the interior and spiritual man by a material temple, and they are directed to build up this temple as a fitting receptacle for truth ; while the history of Solomon's temple, their ancestral type, is regarded as the epitome of human life, "now sinning and now repentant, now vigorous with health and strength, and anon a senseless and decaying corpse." The second temple, that of Zerubbabel, becomes a symbol of the second life, "where the last truth shall be found, where new incense shall arise from a new altar, and whose perpetuity the great Master had promised when, in the very spirit of symbolism, he exclaimed, 'Destroy this temple, and in three days I will raise it up.'"

recollection of an event or a fact into a general idea, which underlies or is born of or suggested by the fact, while there may be superadded to it the further signification or foreshadowing of an ethical or spiritual mystery. And in this is the origin, or if not the origin, the essential interest of symbolism and its cultivating influence. It is a method of concentrated expression, by which the mind is thrown into a revolution of thought, and is incited by the suggestiveness of the symbols to speculate over the idea symbolized. When a mystery, an inexplicable concatenation of phenomena and agents both equally removed from ordinary occurrences and experience, is thus indicated, the symbol becomes imbued with the character of the idea; it becomes the objective representation of the idea; it is involved in the mind with the beauty or the wonderfulness or the sanctity of the idea. If the figure of the symbol is intimately connected with the idea by *history* or *design*, or some *apposite kinship of meaning*, then it more completely embodies the idea, until it assumes a vicarious identity with the mystery, and, as long as it is used, fixes the attention upon the latter by the most effective of all appeals, its sensible presentation. The mental satisfaction gained by this is considerable, and the stability of a mental recognition of the idea symbolized greatly confirmed. A symbol in its highest form, and especially as connected with religious ideas, becomes to us a substitute for a verbal explanation or statement, which itself is inadequate to circumscribe or present with certainty the idea. The symbol stands for a mystery, but the use of the symbol which itself is sensibly apprehended, keeps alive the realization of the idea, and that very vividly, because of the reality of the symbol. The process of cerebration or mental coining, by which a symbol enters the currency of human expressions and objects, and becomes a counter for religious or moral or other convictions, has been well enough described by Prof. Kedney: *

" The idea itself is vague and fluctuating, and can only fix itself and clarify itself by finding some outward expression. That which exists as a waning and brightening, dissipating and combining object for thought must float into the sky of imagination in order to acquire shape. The vague idea must seek to express itself by symbol, and as the symbol itself cannot transcend the idea, it must, after a time, exhibit its own inadequacy, and start the mind on a new enterprize after a new solution."

We have in Christianity a number of, humanly speaking, incomprehensible dogmatic positions, which are accepted by faith, though not blindly nor foolishly, as they entirely harmonize with the transcendental needs of human life. Yet though apprehended metaphysically, as it were, they need concrete expression and availability for popular retention wherever these articles of faith are involved in the acts or functions of the Church. In every possible way, as long as the use is not abusive or misleading or meretricious, true ritualism employs symbols, and their use has the salutary, or, shall we say, politic effect, of keeping alive man's sense of the marvelousness of religious gifts, of their unique and pre-eminent character, of their mysterious origin in the Godhead, and their transcendental nature,

---

* *Hegel's Æsthetics.*  Rev. Jno. Steinfort Kedney.

as evidences of the supernatural, and the subtle system of predestinated means by which the human is
reconciled to and assimilated by the Divine life. In
Christian symbolism we possess an example of the
finest type, and it is the most rich and composite.
The religious nature, in many phases, encloses the poetic and a certain indefinable appreciation of the mysterious, the unknown, the unknowable, the unseen,
penetrates both. These persuasive types and symbols
feed and strengthen the whole religious body, and so
far nourish the mysticism of our nature as to enable us
to keep our convictions in the theological and necessary rudiments which, presented apart, unassociated
with poetic analogies and beautiful synonyms, viz.
symbols, would be rejected or accepted with that hard-
headed, often hard-hearted, tenacity which repels and
oppresses, and is often very likely to mutinously change
into unrestrained scepticism. It certainly must not be
inferred from these words that we would make symbolism a substitute for exact religious training, or that we
reverence a vague sentimentalism. Not at all. We
urge the use of symbolism for its culturing influence in
that direction, which enhances the value of theological tenets, and educates a spiritual insight, which once
gained makes our creed both more reasonable and more
beautiful. The Rev. E. Miller, has comprehensively
said : *

"Symbolism presents great charms for minds which are of a
poetical or dreamy cast ; and in some provinces of the religious

---

* *History and Doctrine of Irvingism.* Rev. E. Miller.

movement, in the earlier part of the present century, was pursued with eagerness and ingenuity. Indeed, as long as symbolism is kept within bounds, and is merely the interpretation, or the legitimate application, or even the expansion of doctrines otherwise ascertained, it is not open to objection. And if the tyranny of matter-of-fact minds, prone sometimes to condemn and scout all that they cannot themselves realize, prevailed so far as to ostracize all symbolism, not only the poetry of Christians would suffer inestimably, but a cold preciseness would repel many warmer hearts, and the free flow of the numerous springs of reverential and loving thought in the Catholic Church would be dangerously impeded."

Thus symbolism, as itself a formal expression of ideas dimly apprehended, or that defy explicit definition, or of mysteries involved indissolubly in the texture of Christianity, helps to maintain the supernatural aspect of worship. "Symbols are not proofs, nor can the meaning of any symbol be proved. They strengthen faith in facts proved from other sources, but by themselves they can prove nothing, because their meaning has to be discovered not in themselves but in other scriptures." * When symbols of beauty having a discoverable value in reference to the things symbolized are used, and their apposite combination forms a fabric of attractive as well as recondite allusion to the veiled things of Catholic faith; when their use " may also present a visible memorial of additional important truth, as for instance the light which is kept burning before the altar, when the Holy Sacrament is there, symbolizes to us the Lord's invisible presence, but is also, from its very nature, a memorial to us that he who is our life, is our light also, and not ours only,

---

* Quoted by the Rev. E. Miller from *Appeal to all Who Believe.*

12

but 'the light which lighteth every man that cometh into the world;'" * when further, involution of symbolism in the art material of worship elevates and spiritualizes that material, then symbols are directly auxiliary to faith; they deepen devotion, they arrest attention, they provoke contemplation, and they nurture that sense of the hidden and mystical in the economy of God's revelation to man which it is largely the purpose of religion to pioclaim.

Yet further, they establish within the Church a source of mystical teaching, by which is not signified, as the ignorant and thoughtless may imagine, a system of superstition, cajolery, and the odds and ends of fanatical delusions; they establish, we say, a source of mystical teaching, which reacts upon the whole body of the Church, preserving it from rude assault and perverse indifference in its laity, from theological dilettantism and offensive latitudinarianism in its clergy. And as they develop yet more to the eye of an illuminated faith the concealed lines of union between the things of heaven and their fleeting types on earth, they also fill the mind with the clairvoyance of spiritual insight, and it is realized or felt,

"That the Church is one and indivisible, singular in existence, the temple of the Holy Ghost, and the organ of his voice; indefectible in its life, immutable in its knowledge of the truths revealed, and infallible in its articulate enunciation of them; that the sacraments are channels of grace, each after its kind; that the operations of the Holy Ghost as the illuminator and sanctifier of the Church and of its members are perpetual." †

---

* Quoted by the Rev. E. Miller from *On Symbols used in Worship.*

† *Temporal Mission of the Holy Ghost.* Henry Edward Manning.

If the Catholic Church shall retain the fealty of her children, and if she shall enforce the principles of Catholic faith, the sense of mystery in her sacraments must be protected and strengthened. Then she shall be saved from the devastating effects of that Puritan temper whose deficiencies Green well indicates in his remarks on Milton's great epic. He says: *

"Throughout it we feel almost painfully a want of the finer and subtler sympathies of a large and genial humanity, of a sense of spiritual mystery. Dealing, as Milton does, with subjects the most awful and mysterious that poet ever chose, he is never troubled by the obstinate questionings of invisible things which haunted the imagination of Shakespeare. We look in vain for any Æschylean background of the vast unknown."

The desirability of keeping alive such feelings of reverent awe before the wonders of religion and the Christian dispensation may strike the shallow and presumptuous as singularly ridiculous, but to quote Dr. Strauss (*The Old Faith and the New*), "every mystery appears absurd, and yet nothing profound, whether in life, in the arts, or in the state, is devoid of mystery."

Now, it is true, not by accident, but by a philosophic sequence in thought, in consequence of the association of ideas with forms, that the ritualist who has carried into the church ceremonial the observances of symbolism, has also revived Catholic doctrine in the Church in the direction of the supernatural. He has insisted on the transcendental efficacy of sacraments, on the sacredness of the office of the ministry, on the spiritual body of the Church. He has suddenly lifted the plane of worship from that of a commonplace con-

sciousness of seriousness up to the higher levels of a
fervent devotion, an actual adoration before the *mysteries* of the Church's gifts. Symbolism has charged
the services of the Church with the subtle emanations
of poetic feeling, and has not lessened their dignity.
The church building has become a symbol itself, and
the Holy Communion addresses the loftiest hopes and
the deepest meditations of man's heart, while beauty in
suggestive imagery gathers around its celebration without changing its salutary and substantial benefits. In
reality it increases those benefits in exact proportion to
the increased reverence and sense of awe with which
they are received. Glimpses of various applications of
symbolism in the church service shall be given, but the
matter cannot here be treated in detail. Neither need
it be, for the strength of our defense. We are contending that symbolism in church architecture, in
church services, in decoration, in vestments, in action,
in language, is a necessity in the Catholic Church,
because this Church, holding to the sacramental system,
must preserve within itself the consciousness of the
sacramental mystery, and must cultivate the same in
its members. Symbolism offers the most effective, indeed the only objective instrumentality which can be
utilized in worship for doing that very thing.

It will be advantageous to call to mind some of the
examples of symbolic use which ritualism shows us.
The font, at the door of the church, teaches that baptism is the gate by which we enter the Church ; the
body of the church represents the Church Militant ;
the choir, the Church Triumphant ; the screen, the gate

of death; the altar, the presence of the Divine Spirit; the two lights at the celebration typify Christ's human and divine nature, and his relation to the world as *its* light; the cassock of the priest is emblematic of a spirit of recollection and devotion; the surplice, of innocency of life and purity of heart; and the vestments for celebration have various meanings (see Chap. I., p. 33). The mitre of the bishop is emblematic of his office, in allusion to the Pentecostal gift, whose visible expression was "tongues of fire;" incense, used at the altar, typifies the rising upward to God of the prayers of the faithful, while, as the altar is typical of the mercy-seat, it symbolizes the intercessions which surround the throne of God; and "the altar is censed in the midst first, because that is the place of honor, being the spot where the blessed sacrament is consecrated; afterwards on the epistle side first, because to the Jewish Church first the ministry of intercession was committed; then the gospel side, because it is now committed to the Christian Church; then, again, from the gospel to the epistle side, in token that Jew and Gentile are all one in Christ. The congregation are censed in acknowledgment that through the incarnation all are partakers of the Divine nature; and in order—first the clergy, next the choir, lastly the laity—to show that, though all one in Christ, all members have not the like honor." * At the litany the priest descends to the body of the church, to show the common ground of all, as requiring God's help. Processions are typical of the Church's

---

* *The Ritual Reason Why*, by Charles Walker, from which we have obtained nearly all our notes on this topic.

progression, and are sad or festal, and so are correspondingly treated in their accessories of cross and banners. The mingling of wine and water in the chalice "represents the mingled tide of blood and water which flowed from our Saviour's side ; and so reminds us of the two great sacraments of the Gospel, baptism and the eucharist, the latter of which cannot exist without the former."* Water is poured over the fingers of the priest before consecration, as a symbol of the purity with which he should approach the holy mysteries ; the priest recites the preface with disjoined hands, as that it is always meet and right to praise God ; with hands laid on the altar, as meaning that through and by Christ we should give thanks ; hands joined before the breast, as uniting heaven and earth, in the ascription of the Sanctus. At the elevation, writers see a ritual representation of the lifting up of the Lord on the cross, and a memorial of the saying, " I, if I be lifted up, will draw all men unto me." In the high celebration the procession of thurifers and taper-bearers with the deacon, before the singing of the gospel, signifies the *progress* of the Gospel of Christ. These fragmentary selections from the continuous stream of ceremonial detail in ritualistic services are taken to suggest how effectively they may be made to heighten the solemnity, the mystical character of the sacramental and other offices, forbearing to consider the ornamentation and interest the service derives from their use. †

---

* *The Ritual Reason Why.* Charles Walker.

† If any one is interested in this subject of symbolism as illustrated in church architecture, and wishes to study its minutiæ, we recommend to

But there is strong presumptive evidence besides, that it would be well to employ symbolism, because the system of God's prophetic presentation of the scheme of Christ's redemption of mankind has been something very near to, or quite like, symbolism.    This, at least, has been the teaching of the doctors of the Church, and we address, solely, churchmen whose acceptance of the Church's general position is complete, but whose attitude toward ritualistic or ceremonial practice is one of hostility and suspicion.    The system of types, critically distinguished, we believe, from a system of symbols, is yet closely allied to it, and would, we think, justify the latter absolutely.    God's method of types, embodied in the Old Testament, has proven an almost inexhaustible subject of study, and, if we are willing to admit that much ingenious extravagance of interpretation has been elicited by it, yet the residue of exact hermeneutics that remains, after a liberal deduction for such vagaries, is most ample for the support of our views.

The majestic retinue of figures which pass through the historic scenes of the Old Testament, with their varying and expressive experiences, are the types—a symbolic language—of that greater Figure, upon whom the hope of the world hangs; the numerous episodes and signs attendant on the alternations of progress and retreat of the Hebrew host, but a symbol of the Chris-

---

his attention the famous work of Bishop Durandus, entitled *The Symbolism of Churches and Church Ornaments,* translated by the Revs. John Mason Neale and Benjamin Webb.    J. G. F. and J. Rivington : London, 1843.

tian's pilgrimage ; the wonders and miracles, the whole
texture of the scriptural story, points, with a connected
movement in all its parts, to the advent of a Deliverer,
and illustrates, in its pictorial allusions, the intimate
facts of spiritual life.   The Bible, in its various books,
has been, and is, regarded by conservative authority as
a reflection of the phases of religious progress.   As the
Rev. A. Jukes has said : *

" I do not attempt here to enter on the reasons for this form; but
I notice one fact, namely, that the word is given to us in many
books, or sections, each of which, I am assured, is a divine chapter,
with one special end, illustrating something in God and man, or the
details of some relation between the Creator and the creature."

And the Rev. R. Payne Smith says,† that in the Old
Testament

" Were the types and shadows and figures of the law, and many
symbolical acts, both in the ritual and in the history of the nation,
and typical personages—of all of which we know that the Jews regarded them as intended to convey doctrinal truths."

This, perhaps, is not symbolism, but it justifies symbolism ; and certainly, in the worship described in the
Old Testament, symbolism is omnipresent, while in the
Revelation of St. John the whole vision is, as it were, a
kaleidoscope of symbols, shifting and combining in yet
stranger and more mysterious forms.

Again, we would mention some reflections provoked
by the different uses of the word symbolism, which
have, perhaps, only a fanciful, and yet to us interesting,

---

* *Types of Genesis* (Preface).   Andrew Jukes.
† *Bampton Lectures*.   Prophecy ; A Preparation for Christ.

value in this connection. " By symbolism," says Dr. Moehler,* " we understand the scientific exposition of the doctrinal differences among the various religious parties," etc. In other words, symbolism is, or pertains to, a creed or system of faith. Now, symbols express ideas, as we have seen, and in religion these ideas are virtually dogmas, and hence a properly constructed fabric of symbols in worship is, in a measure, an expression of faith, an illustrated creed. The conservative and protective influence of symbols, even in this way, it being understood that their meanings are known, must be considerable. This is not, of course, universally true, as many symbols are poetic simply; and yet, reflection upon any device used in symbolic worship is a religious exercise, and the inevitable translation of a symbol into religious thought is a valuable practice, and has a tendency to confirm religious convictions. This method of defense involves the reactional plea on the part of the worshiper, that he is not burdened either with too much or too obscure symbolism.

Lastly, the system of symbolism is inevitable in an expressive worship ; for worship, to adopt an expression of Emerson's, is the *externization* of the worshiping soul. The world is a concrete bundle of symbols to the introspective eye. Emerson, the prophet of Orphicism, says:† " We are symbols and inhabit symbols; workmen, work and tools, words and things, birth and death, all are emblems ; but we sympathize with the

* *Symbolism.* John Adam Moehler, D.D.
† Essay, The Poet.
12*

symbols and, being infatuated with the economical uses
of things, we do not know that they are thoughts."
We must not censure, rather approve, the solemn
pageantry of symbols. The Church must be subordinated to the methods of nature, must follow the lines
of the creative force without us, the visual manifestations of God, as we know a workman by his works. She
must veil her mysteries in symbol. The symbol expresses an idea without defining it, and by suggestion
leads the mind to speculative thought. All nature is a
symbol, and, in a certain comprehensive sense, Catholic
worship is a symbol also.

Ritualism has reinstated in its prominent position
the celebration of the sacrament, it opens the Lord's
Day with its solemnization of the Christian's life in
this great office, thus symbolizing the way of entrance
to those hallowed joys which Paradise promises hereafter, and as a type of that redeeming sacrifice which
makes our Sunday what it is. Ritualism has brought
into use the altar itself, adorned and beautified, as a
type of our sacrifice to God of "ourselves, our souls,
and bodies," offered in unison with the symbolic sacrifice of Christ, and offered with thanksgiving. Ritualism
has arrayed the altar and the priest in vestments
speaking to the eye of purity, of joy, of sadness, of
preparation, of waiting; it has placed upon the altar the
cross, the symbol of the Passion, which a wavering and
timid Protestantism ludicrously avoids; it has added
lights as emblems of spiritual radiance, and the illumi-
nating splendor of Christ's presence upon earth; it has
rehabilitated the priest, clothed him with the powers

the Church has always said it gave him, but seems ashamed to acknowledge when bestowed, and invested his life and his position with the august value of a *type* of Christ. Ritualism has filled our churches with the Christian emblems, and built temples whose form and arrangement minister to the faithful, by their wealth of symbolic meaning. Ritualism has summoned the imagination to furnish its contingent of devotional beauty to the service, and the embellishments of art are subordinated to the moral glory of which that art sensibly speaks.

"Le nom de symbolism embrasse assez completement les diverse voies par où l'homme reussit ou aspire soit à ennoblir le monde exterieur en se faisant dire les choses immaterielles par les objets sensibles, soit à transfigurer un simple fait en y puisant à la fois l'aliment du cœur et celui de l'esprit."*

### COMMEMORATION.

The commemoration of the great events of history, or the good deeds of great men, is generally considered apposite and praiseworthy, but the sluggish spirit of Protestant Episcopacy appears to fear the resumption of disused festivals or fasts in the Church, or the more correct and expressive observance of those we have already. If this unamiable spirit of carping censure and opposition comes from lazinesss, it is discreditable, if from ignorance it is inexcusable, if from timidity and

* Quoted by Louisa Twining in *Symbols and Emblems of Early and Mediæval Art.*

a fear of Romanizing tendencies, it is foolish. The current Church practice itself in this feature is essentially ritualistic, having always preserved the Christian year of seasons, and in varying degree the incidental days of saints and martyrs. But ritualism, in its truest sense, develops the spirit of commemorative practice far beyond this. It not only emphasizes the calendar as it should, but it reiterates the events of Christ's life, the significance of Christ's name, the importance of Christian sacraments, the royalty and beauty of Christian teaching. It recalls, as a friend recalls the tones, the thoughts, the words, the acts of his dead comrade, the presence of Christ; it insists upon perpetually celebrating the Eucharist, and celebrating it with arrangements and such impressiveness in music, in ceremonial, in acts of corporal worship as to make that presence a reality to those who witness it. This is a new spirit or phase of commemoration, and goes vastly more deeply into the principle and trueness of commemorative exercise than does the simple observance of days and seasons, noted on the Church's calendar, an observance often negligently made, with no accessories of poetic truthfulness, and no recognition of poetic suggestions.

The spirit of grateful commemoration breathes throughout the ministrations of the ritualistic Church. The seasons are emphatically distinguished by appropriate and significant colors, special days as Palm Sunday, Good Friday, Ash Wednesday, Christmas, Easter, Whitsunday, Ascension day, Epiphany and others, have their importance shown in the decorations, and in the service of the Church, and this unstintedly and with elaboration.  The cross, not only as an emblem, but as a memento of Christ's death, is constantly used.  This exhaustive and penetrative commemorative spirit, at times mingling with a parallel current of symbolic inference and suggestion, imbues the very actions and movements of those engaged in the service; as when the choristers and clergy turn at times to the east, as the place of Christ's birth, or to the altar as the throne of Christ in the Church, as in the progress of the priest from the epistle (south), to the gospel (north) side of the altar, back and forth, representing the passage through Christ, from the dispensation of the Old Testament to that of the New; as in the celebration of the Eucharist at the consecration of the elements, the gestures used are imitative of those our Lord made; as in the Introit to Communion representing our Lord's advent.  The whole service of the Communion is commemorative naturally, and can be studied with reference to this single principle with profit.  The spirit of commemorative practice is evinced in the vestments of the clergy, the ornaments of the church, its paintings, its frescoes, and stained windows.  The clothing of the priest is Syrian and apostolic, in type, recalling the habit of our Saviour; the amice represents the linen rag with which the Jews blindfolded our Saviour, and is a symbol of the helmet of salvation.  The alb and surplice, while emblematic of purity, are also regarded as representative of the white garment Herod put upon Christ.  Besides this symbolic meaning, the girdle, maniple, and stole also recall the cords and fetters with which Christ was bound, the chasuble represents the seamless vest of Christ, and the cross upon it, that which he carried up the hill of Calvary. Commemoration, understood in this sense, enters the service at many points, and finds in the ritualistic custom, its most complete expression.

Let us now pass to some considerations which may excuse this spirit and practice of commemoration in the eyes of churchmen, though it seems incongruous that they, of all men, should ask for a defense of such earnest and helpful and natural usages. Perhaps the most simple apology, obvious and important, for the extended use of such commemorative methods as we have instanced is its mnemonic value, and this of course, especially through the Church's year, its seasons and high days. It keeps alive our recollection of those things which it is desirable to remember, and which form the groundwork of facts upon which the superstructure of our creed rests. But there is another reason, less obvious, but of more importance for ceremonial commemoration. It is this, its realistic nature. We do not mean that such minute reference to Christ's life, the Christian life, and the events immediately connected with Christ's death, have any dramatic character, and so enact, as it were, a scenic rehearsal of the passion or other scenes of the Saviour's life, but that their influence is to make us feel the reality of those things we have accepted upon hearsay or the statements of a believer. While no ritualism shall or can ever establish any fact by itself in reference to Christ's life, yet these reminders, so interwoven with the texture of worship, with the to and fro movement of spiritual life in the Church, do anchor our faith insensibly by their reiteration, and make us, unconsciously, very retentive of the whole story of the redemption, as they do also increase our confidence in the truthfulness of that story. The dignity and detail of a service which incorporates in its texture and movement so many allusions, reminders and historic symbols, all harmonized by the dominant purpose of the whole, reflects a certain splendor to the indifferent mind, the forgetful or listless mind, as well as to the zealous and attentive, upon the subject matter of the religion itself ; and Christ, his death, his love, his effectual every-day intermediation is borne in upon the mind with a singular reality which the dull methods of ordinary practice never effect. These latter seem to remove and efface these same truths, or replace them with a skeletonized intellectual perception of an idea.

It is urged that the intricacies of commemoration are of no value—that they are not understood, are not followed intelligently—and the same objection is made to the use of symbolism. This objection arises from an ignorance of the necessary connection between the perfection of anything in art or nature, and the necessity for the exactness of its detail, the necessity for the complete reproduction of its parts. This rule in art is qualified by the limits of vision. The beautiful scene, the exquisite object are immediately appreciated by the eye of taste, but their multitudinous detail and minutiæ of component pieces is not. These latter are all there, and their sum total produces the resultant effect which we instantly admire. Remove the detail, strike out the underlying traceries of line and blending shades of color, and where has the beauty of the picture flown? The radiant butterfly is a marvel of loveliness, and that loveliness is largely or entirely due to the microscopic perfection of its parts. The aggregation of parts, their correct union and indissoluble sequence, forms a complete ceremonial whole in the ritualistic service; and whether or not the detail is all understood, its effect and its effectiveness are just so much strengthened by their use, and the practical result of memorizing Christ and publishing Christianity better secured. Again, such a service is intended for study, it is meant to stimulate and reward scrutiny; its general purpose is felt by the most superficial, though its subordinate beauties are unnoticed or ignored. The finer meanings are all there, however, to satisfy the desire of those who will search for them, and that they are there is the substantial cause of the popular impression made by the service. The ritualistic service is a fine tapestry, which arrests the eye and the mind of the casual spectator, telling him quickly the story on its breathing folds, while it repays the lover of beauty by the unflagging industry and skill shown in the composition and workmanship of its smallest parts. It is a piece of music where the whole effect, strong and exultant, or sad and plaintive, is produced by the masterly combination of lesser harmonies, from which, while the mind receives the impression of a single idea or a group of ideas, the studious and learned listener derives less communicable pleasure in recognizing its composite structure.

The commemorative spirit is one of love, of gratitude, of fidelity, and in the Church its gracious offices should be welcomed and cherished, not spurned nor derided. The principles of symbolism and commemoration coalesce, and their mingled meanings are embodied in single forms. They both nurture and refresh memory, stir the imagination, refine feeling and resuscitate faith. They attract the unthinking, the crude, the savage, turning thoughtlessness into attention, rudeness into breeding, and barbarity into love. To the poor they bring the emoluments of beauty, and breathe upon their devotions the sanctity of poetry; they summon the unseen to communicate with the actual; and they encourage the stammering lips in praise, and strengthen a faltering trust.

# CHAPTER III.

## CONCLUSION.

WE said in Part I., Chapter III., that we were engaged there in proving the universality of ritualistic methods, and claimed for ritualism a cosmopolitan recognition, as a humanly implanted instinct. We said we were not then concerned with defending it as beneficial or helpful, but were engaged in examining its origin, its extension, and claimed that the same laws governing its development were to be found in Christianity as they had been found in all other religions. In the last two chapters we have been busy in advocating ritualism as a needful and essential element in effective Catholic worship. Further, we said, in Chapter III., that we would not say anything "as to the kinds of rites, or choice in rites, consequences or tendencies." We have in later pages, indicated a number of ritual uses in the service which Catholic custom warrants. However, we have mentioned them in an illustrative way, to show what art, symbolism, and commemoration, the components of the ritualistic habit in worship, meant in the Christian Church, and have not attempted to justify them specifically. Such a task is quite outside of our purpose, as it is entirely beyond our knowledge. But while we have not trespassed upon such an extended field of learning as is included in the discussion of liturgical forms, we have felt convinced

that a rule must be laid down against excess of ritualism or super-ritualism, and that censure is deserved by
those whose practice is disfigured by affectation. This
duty belongs to the guardians of the Church, and it is
with the most moderate feelings of confidence that we
venture, in our own behalf, to allude to this topic.
The Church, in its Catholic tendencies, assumes many
forms which grade all the way from a slightly ornamented low church service to something very nearly
Roman. To a large number of earnest Christians who
heartily advocate Catholic doctrine, and who as firmly
resist papal aggression and Roman error, the equivocal
and misleading inferences established by some ritualistic methods are very mortifying. What lines should
be drawn between Catholic and Roman practice, can,
we suggest, be drawn plainly enough on the grounds
of doctrinal and liturgical differences—as the nega-
tion of papal supremacy and all it implies, the nega-
tion of mariolatry, of the worship of relics, of the
adoration of the species, of the use of holy water, of
the use of shrines, of compulsory confession, of transubstantiation. The ritualism appearing in the high or
low celebration of Holy Communion, and the proper
saying of morning and evening prayer will win its way
with certainty, if it is given no dubious expression, by
extra-limital practices. The awakened interest taken
by Christian thinkers in Catholic teaching will be encouraged and educated by a just and lawful restraint,
and the apologists of this unique revival will not be
confounded by inexplicable and disloyal customs. It
is certainly necessary to guard against this super-ritual-

ism, which has formed in some places a dangerous alliance, logically and actually, with Romanism. Whatever clearness can be given to the distinction between the ritualism of the Catholic Church and the methods of Romanism is most desirable, so that enlightened Protestantism, in its alarm, may not fall foul of a scarecrow, but may be permitted to inform itself exactly as to the fundamental ideas involved in Church worship. One other word, by way of remonstrance and caution, and we have finished. Affectations in service must cease, the unintelligible gibberish of celebrants, who seem to wish to speak Latin in English, who mimic Roman manner, and have a sort of emasculate bearing, repellant and unwise, detracts from the service because it is conspicuous, and injures because it is ridiculed.

Have we made our case clear, and does the *fact* of ritualism lose any of its terror, and wear a more reasonable aspect by what we have said? In the first place, we defined ritualism in service of any kind, religious or civil, as animated by three ideas—first, that of art; second, that of symbolism; third, that of commemoration. We showed that three bodies of Christendom, two representative, which were ritualistic, embodied these ideas. We showed that ritualism in a religion arose under the influence of—first, the presence of the object worshiped, either actually or vicariously in its sacraments; secondly, its possession of an historical record of itself; thirdly, upon the art ability of the people professing it; and, fourthly, the responsive nature of the same people to art, the last two incentives having a qualitative character simply. From the action of the first influence, we described the rise of the priestly function, and indicated its strong predetermining tendency to ritualistic practice. We showed that these influences all operated in the Christian Church, and that ritualism, as an organic necessity, must appear as it had appeared, in that body; and that, furthermore, its essential propagation, so to speak, began in the work and through the commands of Christ, as that work and those commands implanted the ritualistic generative principle in the Christian faith, which, whether or no it was at first clearly apprehended or elaborately displayed, was, by the law of development, which acted unquestionably under divine guidance, in later years consummately realized. This was a demonstration of the ethnic side of ritualistic life. In the second part, we defended the art of ritualism on the grounds of primordial union with religion, on the ground of its expediency, and on the ground of its educational influence; we also there insisted that we were entitled to regard art as including not only the representative arts, music, sculpture, and painting, but also the dramatization, as it were, of service, in vestments, processions, lights, etc. We defended the use of symbolism principally as assisting the worshiper in realizing the mystical character of sacraments, and the use of commemoration as a system of iterative preaching, by which our memories were unflaggingly stimulated; and throughout both paragraphs we indicated by suggestion how much might be claimed for both, on the grounds of their refining and elevating influence.

Ritualism, or the Catholic revival, has done a great work for the Church, and the measure of its power is less correctly defined by a chronicle of the cathedrals built and the moneys expended, remarkable as that has been, than by the story of such lives as those of Charles Lowder, Skinner, and others, and' by the fact that "the poor have the gospel preached to them."

Once before has the Church received a spiritual shock, which awoke it from sleep and turpitude, when, through the defection of the Methodists, and by their example of earnest and resolute sympathy with the sinner and the poor, "the 'evangelical' movement, which found representatives like Newton and Cecil within the pale of the establishment, made the fox-hunting parson and the absentee rector at last impossible."

But the Catholic revival has been far more striking and wide-spreading in its results, while its actual renovation and re-equipment of the Church service has been incalculable. It has revived the Church, without starting any dangerous schism; it has strengthened her within her originally defined limits. It has expanded her life, increased her resources, dignified her mission, and given her self-confidence. To how many has it brought a renewed delight in Church service, and put the doctrine and customs of the Church on a higher and more attractive plane! What a wide influence it has had—touching the human sympathies of the sects, infusing a new reverence and ardor in the uses of low churchmen, and teaching the important fact, that ceremonial and liturgy are not necessarily Roman, but are the prerogatives of the Church, and can never be alienated nor ignored.

And yet further, more comprehensively, we may, in conclusion, claim for ritualism, when penetrating and illustrating Catholic truth, a semi-psychological power over the human soul, as if it transformed and blessed it. It not only recommends and adorns Catholic doctrine, but it sweetens the spirit of the devout, and refreshes and enlarges that spirit, amplifies vision, transfigures life, and as it were anastomoses the varied threads of human interest with the lines of spiritual force into a golden and silken cord, that carries the darting thought to and fro, from heaven to earth and back again, dispelling the fear of death, and healing sorrow, and carrying into every corner of life the blessed visitors of heaven, pure thoughts and gentle words and brave hopes. Pater * has beautifully spoken of "the æsthetic charm of the Catholic Church, her evocative power over all that is eloquent and expressive in the better soul of man, her outward comeliness, her dignified convictions about human nature," of the " marvelous liturgic spirit of the Church, her wholly unparalleled genius for worship," but he has also not failed to stamp in words the *necessary* character of her ritual. He writes: †

" The ritual system of the Church, which must rank, as we see it in historic retrospect, like the Gothic architecture, for instance, as

---

* *Marius the Epicurean*, Vol. II., p. 139.
† *Ibid.*, Vol. II., p. 140.

one of the great, conjoint and, so to term them, *necessary* products of human mind, and which has ever since directed with so deep a fascination men's religious instincts, was then growing together, as a recognizable new treasure in the sum of things."

The ritualistic movement has a directly remedial or sanitary influence in the modern world of religious thought. We have alluded to its mystical tendencies, which, brought under the more severe discipline of dogmatic assertion, give to religion a keen relishableness for spiritual natures, without repelling intellectual men by wanton and chimerical fantasies. The world has lost its faith, in a measure, or where it has retained it, holds it simply as a valuable safeguard against chaos, and derives no vivid satisfaction, no deep saturating bliss from its profession. Ritualism, by arousing the half killed sense of the supernatural, has awakened the numbed religious instinct of humanity. It confronts the ultramaterialism of the age, which destroys religious feeling, by a superb and lofty insistence upon the omnipresence of spirit acting on the world through agencies that can neither be weighed nor formulated. This confident realization of "angels and ministers of grace," of holy sanctions and spiritual prerogatives, has rejuvenated the sense of the beautiful in worship. It has warranted the introduction of form, which gives to its creed an objective basis and a physical reality. When the reality of the idea is felt, then the finest art forms appear; an affirmative faith—not abstractions and wavering say-sos and verbal strategy—brings to the surface of the times, in all departments of thought, the vivid image, the excellent art, the breathing, intense ritual. Professor Weir says* that such a time is at hand, when "it will again be made manifest that an affirmative faith, *realizing the unseen*, is at the root of all art that is most moving in thought, as it is the inspiration of all that is most beautiful in art, for," he continues, "a faith that has become altogether abstract loses its fervor and its creative power; it is rendered incapable of bodying forth its formless ideals, from sheer lack of substance."

If we have striven to prove in these chapters the immanence of ritualism as a tendency in man's nature, and its entire desirability in his worship, we might naturally ask for some external evidence as to its success in the recent and still continuing Catholic revival, for such success would be a distinct corroboration of our claims. Now it is patent to all students and readers, and to even the casual observer, that the Catholic revival has no parallel in modern times as a religious movement. Its effects might be called almost revolutionary, and its power has proven to be irresistible.

"The great idea of the Church in its visibility and authority—in its notes of succession, dogma, and sacrament—sums up its meaning. Many will dispute the very possibility of any such Church or embodiment of spiritual power ; but there are few who will not acknowledge that the Oxford movement has done more than all other movements in our time to revive 'the grandeur and force of historical communion and church life,' and no less 'the true place of beauty and art in worship.' It is much to have brought home to the hearts of Christian people the reality of a great spiritual society extending through all Christian ages, living by its own truth and

---

* *Church Review*, Vol. XLVII., p. 116, Art in Worship.

13

life, having its own laws and rights and usages. In a time when the 'dissidence of dissent,' and the canker of sectarianism have spread to the very heart of our national existence, with so many unhappy results, the idea of the Church as a great unity—and no less the idea of Christian art—of the necessity of order and beauty in Christian worship—are ideas to be thankful for." *

* *Movements of Religious Thought in Britain during the Nineteenth Century.* St. Giles' Lectures. John Tulloch.

www.ingramcontent.com/pod-product-compliance
Lightning Source LLC
Chambersburg PA
CBHW031407270326
41929CB00010BA/1355